Holistic Special Education

D0874859

Holistic Special Education

Edited by Robin Jackson

Education Resource Center
University of Delaware
Newark, DE 19716-2940
T75133

Floris Books

P-SP
H 717
2006

First published in 2006 by Floris Books
© 2006 Robin Jackson

All rights reserved. No part of this publication may
be reproduced without the prior permission
of Floris Books, 15 Harrison Gardens, Edinburgh.
www.florisbooks.co.uk

British Library CIP Data available

ISBN-10 0-86315-547-2
ISBN-13 978-086315-547-5

Printed in Great Britain
By Biddles, King's Lynn

Contents

Acknowledgments

The writing of this book has been an unusual, indeed unique undertaking, given that most of the contributors have been drawn from a single source — the Camphill Rudolf Steiner School in Aberdeen. I am greatly indebted to the co-workers for agreeing enthusiastically to take part in this ambitious project, despite their heavy professional workloads and other commitments; the parents for providing moving testimonies of their family experiences; Anni D'Agostino for the magical pen and ink illustrations, which introduce each section of the book; Nancy Jackson for the photographs of the School's beautiful buildings and grounds; Denis Chanarin for his elegant architectural sketches; the editor of the *Scottish Journal of Residential Child Care* for granting permission to reprint the article 'Residential special schools: the inclusive option'; and the School's Council of Management for their wholehearted, sustained and generous support for the project. I am particularly grateful to Christian Maclean, Gale Winskill, Katy Lockwood-Holmes and Ulrike Fischer of Floris Books for their infinite patience, sound advice and ongoing encouragement. It is my hope that this book will be seen as a worthy and timely successor to Henning Hansmann's *Education for Special Needs,* which was first published by Floris Books fourteen years ago.

Robin Jackson

Foreword

Following thirty years as a director of the Camphill Rudolf Steiner School's Company and close on twenty years as its Chairman, it is an honour, as well as a humbling experience, to present this book on the holistic special education, as practised in the Camphill Rudolf Steiner School, in Aberdeen, Scotland.

From the 1940s to the present day, many books have been published on a wide range of topics as they relate to Camphill, the Camphill Movement, Camphill Schools, Camphill Villages and Camphill Training Centres, both in the United Kingdom and throughout the world. One might be excused for asking why we need another, when as recently as 1992, we had Henning Hansmann's book on *Education for Special Needs,* which describes practice in Camphill Schools. There are two answers. Firstly, this last decade has been an extremely challenging time in the field of education for children with special needs, where 'inclusion' has dominated the political agenda; and secondly, this book is unique since most chapters have been written by individuals actively engaged at a 'hands on' level within the School.

Whilst the School has been a pioneer in providing education for children with special needs, it has also led the way in educating and training specialist teachers and practitioners in the field of curative education. This is reflected in the partnership between Camphill School and Aberdeen University in the development of the Bachelor of Arts course in Curative Education. The national professional and academic recognition of this curative education course is already reaping benefits for the School's pupils.

It is particularly refreshing and rewarding to read parents' evaluations of the impact of holistic special education on their lives and the lives of their children. They are to be commended for allowing us to share with them not only the many challenges that children with special needs present to a family but also the many joyous and rewarding moments.

What of the future? We have progressed successfully over the past sixty-five years and are currently in good heart. I feel excited for the future, particularly when reflecting on Mahatma Gandhi's observation that: 'The future depends on what we do in the present.'

George R. Morgan
Former Chairman, Camphill Schools and Camphill Scotland

Introduction

ROBIN JACKSON

This book has two principal aims; firstly, to give the reader an insight into Camphill philosophy and practice as they are exemplified in the life and work of the Camphill Rudolf Steiner School in Aberdeen; and secondly, to make the case for residential special schools at a time when the purpose, value and future of residential special education is being called into question. The book is also addressed to those professional workers who have a responsibility for placing children and young people in care settings, and to parents who are looking for a suitable school for their child with special needs. What makes this book different is that most of the contributions have been written by co-workers actively involved in the day-to-day life and work of the Camphill Rudolf Steiner School in Scotland. In a true sense, the writing of the book has been a community undertaking.

The Camphill Rudolf Steiner School is part of the global Camphill Movement that currently extends to over twenty countries. Of the one hundred Camphill communities throughout the world, most are village communities making provision for adults with special needs. Around ten percent of Camphill communities are schools for pupils with special needs. By virtue of its size and the range of services that it offers, the Camphill Rudolf Steiner School in Aberdeen is exceptional. This book focuses on the curative education principles and practice, which underpin the holistic special education provided by the School.

What I hope this book will demonstrate is that, since their foundation over sixty years ago, Camphill Schools have frequently been at the forefront, not only of educational thinking but also of professional practice (Chapter 1). They have anticipated many of the trends, which today are regarded as progressive, imaginative and ground-breaking. It is not difficult to cite examples. At no time have Camphill Schools ever subscribed to the deficit model of disability, which highlights the deficiencies of children at the expense of their positive attributes. Each child with complex needs is seen as a unique individual with a potential that it is the Camphill Schools' responsibility to identify and nurture. In order to develop that potential a holistic approach is taken which embraces care (Chapter 2), education (Chapters 3–4), therapy (Chapters 5–10), crafts (Chapter 11) and medical activities (Chapter 12). A strong emphasis is also placed on the provision of a balanced and coherent curriculum, in which the role of the creative arts (music, art, drama, dance) is accorded comparable weight to the more instrumental aspects of the curriculum (language and mathematics).

The present heavy and narrow emphasis on the instrumental aspects of the school curriculum, which is evident in the wider educational system in the UK, would have greatly appealed to Thomas Gradgrind, the schoolteacher, described by Charles Dickens in his novel *Hard Times*. 'Fact not Fancy' were his watchwords. There was no place in his curriculum for imagination, creativity and spontaneity. He would no doubt have relished the opportunity to teach in a system governed by performance criteria, targets, and league tables, and in which the creative arts played little or no part. The educational philosophy of Thomas Gradgrind is the very antithesis of what Camphill Schools seek to do, for it is recognized that without opportunities for 'Fancy,' any education offered will be desiccated, joyless and alienating.

An essential feature of the relationship between the child and the co-worker in the Schools is its reciprocity, which dispenses with all notions of those giving and receiving care. It is a relationship based on mutuality in which each learns from the other. Acceptance of this model presents a challenge to conventional professional relationships. Camphill Schools recognize that human services will only flourish where they are imbued with humanity, and that this can only be done when professional practice is structured in such a way that the primacy of relationships is re-established. If a socially-responsive, responsible and genuinely inclusive society is to be created, it is necessary to promote, respect and cherish the humanity, which resides in every child.

Another relationship to which the greatest importance is attached is that between the Schools and the parents (Chapter 18). It is recognized that parents are not simply the recipients of a service but are equal and active partners, and have the right to participate in all the relevant decision-making concerning their child. Co-workers accept that parents know a great deal about their children and that their insight and experience are essential in arriving at appropriate decisions concerning their child's future. While co-workers rest their professional authority on the technical expertise they possess, the parents are seen as the experts on their child.

Since their foundation Camphill Schools have accepted that they have a responsibility to attend to the spiritual growth of the child, an area in residential childcare that has been consistently neglected, despite the fact that the right to spiritual well-being is firmly embedded in the 1989 UN Convention on the Rights of the Child. The Schools strive to ensure that a child's spiritual well-being is nurtured in the same manner as his or her physical and intellectual well-being. Curative education seeks to link the conventional natural sciences and spiritual science, thus necessitating a holistic approach embracing body, soul and spirit.

There is growing professional awareness that the social pedagogic model found in other European countries, which is not simply concerned with a child's schooling but relates to the whole child, is a model which deserves wider attention in the UK (Chapter 19). It has been argued that those residential special schools, which adopt such a model, provide a more inclusive and normal setting; one in which the individual needs of the child are more likely to be met. A particularly important facet of this model is the radical transformation in the nature of the relationship between care worker and child from clientship to friendship.

The importance of mutuality in relationships is also reflected in the concern shown by Camphill communities for the lands on which they are situated. Camphill Schools recognize that they have a duty, as stewards of these lands, to tend them with diligence, care and respect. Long before organic farming was accorded the high profile it enjoys today, Camphill communities were farming their lands biodynamically (Chapter 14).

A frequent misconception about Camphill communities is that they are in some way detached from the real world. Such a view merits a robust challenge. Camphill Scotland, of which the Camphill Rudolf Steiner School is a part, along with a handful of other voluntary organizations in Scotland, vigorously and tirelessly lobbied MSPs to have a statement of general principles included within the Regulation of Care Act, including the key principles of diversity and choice. That sustained pressure bore fruit for these principles are now set out in the Regulation of Care (Scotland) Act 2001.

In March 2003, a significant landmark was reached when the Scottish Social Services Council recognized the BA in Curative Education Programme as an appropriate qualification for those working in the residential child care sector in Scotland (Chapter 15). This Programme is offered in a unique partnership between the Camphill School in

Aberdeen and the University of Aberdeen, and is the first time that a qualification in curative education/social pedagogy has been professionally recognized in the UK. It is also the only instance in Scotland of a care qualification that is offered in partnership between a Higher Education Institution and a service provider.

An innovative and distinctive feature of the Programme is its life-sharing character where the students live in a residential childcare setting for twenty-four hours a day. This provides students with the opportunity for the concurrent acquisition of theoretical insights, practical skills and personal growth. The transdisciplinarity of the Programme not only challenges traditional professional philosophy and practice, but also equips students with the knowledge, understanding and skills to work in a range of different disciplines. One of the aims of the Programme is to produce critical, reflective and intuitive practitioners who are capable of acting in a creative, innovative and ethical manner. For many of the students, who are drawn from all around the world, participation in the Programme can be a life-changing experience (Chapter 17).

It is generally accepted that only those organizations that are flexible and able to adapt to rapid change are likely to survive. The unique combination of living and working in the same community setting helps to build, maintain and strengthen the capacity of the Camphill Schools to respond to external challenges. There is a sense in which the Schools constitute a genuine *community of learning* in which reflection on practice is strongly encouraged, and where organizational needs are regularly assessed and reviewed (Chapter 16).

One feature, which almost all visitors to the Scottish Camphill Schools are struck by, is the beauty and tranquillity of the physical settings in which they are situated. This is not an incidental extra, but a crucial element that contributes significantly to the quality of life experienced by both children and co-workers. The buildings in which the children and co-workers live are carefully designed to achieve a harmonious balance of visual appeal, simplicity and utility (Chapter 13). To the observer the unconventional appearance of some of the buildings may come as a surprise, until one realizes that their organic shape often subtly mirrors the character of the physical environment in which they are set. There is now a growing acceptance of the fact that both natural and built environments impact upon the physical, mental and spiritual health of the individual — a fact that has been known intuitively in Camphill communities for many years.

Living in an environment, which is free from the all-pervasive, disruptive and polluting effects of noise, is essential because of the importance of having moments of stillness each day. These moments of stillness are essential both for the children and the co-workers to allow time for reflection and physical, mental and spiritual refreshment. They form part of the Camphill Schools' daily rhythm. Rhythm is crucially important for it provides an impulse and framework that enables often bewildered and disoriented children to experience a measure of stability, security and predictability for the first time. There are few chapters in this book which do not stress the importance of rhythm — whether it is the rhythm involved in different kinds of therapy or craftwork, or the rhythmical nature of human relationships, rhythm is the living pulse that sustains the work of the Camphill Schools.

It would be wrong to convey the impression that the Scottish Camphill Schools have effortlessly and painlessly arrived at the position they have reached today. The greatest challenge has come from external pressures, which have required fundamental changes in outlook and practice. However, one of the most important discoveries made by the Schools is that through engagement with 'the outside world' sensible accommodations can be arrived at, which meet external requirements and which do not threaten or undermine Camphill philosophy and practice (Chapter 20).

Over forty years ago Karl König, the founder of the Camphill Movement, recognized that if the Movement was to have a future it needed to evolve. The vision that König presented does not involve the pursuit of grandiose, extravagant and unattainable goals, but encourages a willingness to respond to the needs of the time in an open but judicious manner:

> The Camphill Movement is young enough to expect many years of work to come. I can foresee tasks in many fields of human endeavour: in education and medicine, in agriculture and industry, in arts and music. Our hopes should not reach too high, but they should not confine themselves to fields that are too narrow. (König 1993)

1. History and Philosophy

ANGELIKA MONTEUX

To light a candle is better than to curse the darkness.

— Ancient Buddhist saying

Founded in 1940, the Camphill Rudolf Steiner School is for children with special needs, and is situated on the banks of the river Dee on the western outskirts of Aberdeen. The name 'Camphill' derives from the fact that Camphill Estate is thought to be located on part of an old Roman expeditionary camp, and in the 1970s a gardener on the Estate was lucky enough to find a Roman coin in the soil. It has been suggested that Camphill was a place of execution as one of the roads leading to the Estate is called Pittengullies Brae, and *Pittengullies* is believed to be a corrupted form of 'pit and gallows'! There are many stories from the early Camphill days which tell of ghostly activities — flickering lights moving around old, partly-ruined buildings and footsteps heard at night — which stopped when prayers were said for lost souls.

The location of Camphill in the Dee Valley has a particular significance, as it was one of the main routes for Irish missionaries. Many of the monks who initially came to the north-east of Scotland were linked with the seminary in Bangor, County Down, which was one of the world-renowned centres of Celtic Christianity, and from where missionaries travelled to Switzerland, Burgundy and Lombardy to set up monasteries. Celtic Christianity absorbed pre-Christian religious faiths and traditions (e.g., pagan festivals), was firmly grounded in the life of the local community, placed particular emphasis on the importance of a reflective and meditative approach to religious observance and practice, valued the intrinsic and extrinsic qualities of the natural environment, and was opposed to the centralized and secularized character of organized religion.

Directly across the River Dee from Camphill lies Maryculter, which was the location for one of the two major Preceptories of the Order of the Knights Templar in Scotland; a devout medieval military religious order that combined the roles of knight and monk in a way the western medieval world had never seen before. The Order was suppressed by Pope Clement V in 1312 but was never completely dissolved in Scotland. It is interesting to note that eight hundred years before the creation of Camphill a well-ordered, disciplined, international Christian community existed on the south bank of the Dee, which was driven by a strong religious impulse to serve others and to husband the lands in its ownership with diligence and care.

The philosophy and ethos of Camphill draw together a wide range of cultural, spiritual and religious traditions such as ancient Buddhist and Hindu wisdom, Judaism, Christianity, Quakerism and other faiths, all of which are united in curative education. This is perceived and respected by professionals, families whose members are pupils or residents in Camphill communities, and by those individuals with special needs who are educated and supported in their quest for a meaningful life. Such recognition is not universal. Even after sixty-five years, there is still a curious mix of ignorance and misunderstanding as to the purpose of Camphill. This is often expressed by likening Camphill to an island: an institution separated from its wider environment. It is hoped that this chapter will lay to rest some of these misconceptions and misunderstandings through describing and explaining the historical background, and the philosophy on which the practice of curative education are built.

Beginnings in Vienna

Before the Second World War, a group of young people, mostly from Jewish middle-class families, gathered around the paediatrician, Karl König, in Vienna. Some were originally his patients. Others, especially those who were medical students, met him through his lectures and then told their friends about him. Regular study meetings and lively participation in Vienna's social and cultural life led to the formation of a close-knit group of friends, united by the ideal of making the world a better place.

> New worlds opened for us. Sometimes I would tell my friends of Dr König ... Three of the friends were studying medicine and as a result of their growing interest in anthroposophy two of them took part in a conference for medical students in Arlesheim. It was there that they got to know Dr König. The ring began to form ... We asked Dr König to meet our whole group and it was from that time onwards that we had meetings together whenever he came to Vienna ... There was one man who could listen. (Lipsker in Bock 2004, 70)

Karl König was born in Vienna on September 25, 1902, an only child of Jewish parents, who owned a shoe shop in the Jewish quarter of the city. His school years were not easy as he was intellectually precocious. In his childhood he was often overwhelmed by his experiences of the poverty and suffering around him. He would refuse to eat the food prepared for him at home, aware of those starving. On one occasion he gave his coat to a beggar, unconcerned about his parents' likely anger. Although small of stature and with a deformed foot, he had a powerful personality (Pietzner 1990). When he was eleven, his parents found a picture of Christ in his cupboard; an early sign of his later commitment to Christian ideals. During his medical studies he came across the anthroposophical work of Rudolf Steiner, which he soon embraced as the source of knowledge and inspiration for his work as physician, researcher, scientist and teacher.

The pioneering phase

In the years following his graduation from medical school in 1927 König built up a successful medical practice, whilst at the same time continuing his study of anthroposophy. Dr Ita Wegman, the leader of the Medical Section at the Goetheanum, in Switzerland, invited König to work at the anthroposophical clinic in Arlesheim, and it is at this time that he had his first encounter with curative education at the Sonnenhof, one of the first curative homes for children with special needs in Germany. It was here that he watched the 'Advent Garden,' an Advent celebration, during which children with severe disabilities, each holding an unlit candle walked to a burning candle at the centre of a spiral of moss, lit their candle and on returning placed the candle on the spiral, thus creating a spiral of bright lights. This celebration is still enacted in many Steiner Schools and curative homes, including the Camphill Rudolf Steiner Schools in Scotland. König was so moved by this experience, that he decided on the spot to:

> ... dedicate my life to the care and education of these children. It was a promise I made to myself: to build a hill upon which a big candle was to burn so that many infirm and handicapped children would be able to find their way to this beacon of hope. (König in Bock 2004, 47)

The seed for the Camphill Movement had been planted. Together with his wife, Tilla, he built up and worked for seven years in

Pilgrimshain, a curative home in Silesia. Threatened by the political climate under the Nazis, he decided to return to Vienna, and began to make plans to structure their lives around the needs of children with special needs.

When the Nazis annexed Austria in 1938, König, and those around him, realized that because of their Jewish background they would have to leave and find new homes. After unsuccessful applications to several European countries, they were invited to Scotland. In 1939 they began to arrive at Kirkton House, located near Insch, in Aberdeenshire, which had been offered to them by Theodore Haughton, the laird of the Williamston Estate. Theodore's wife, Emily, had received treatment for breast cancer at the Arlesheim — an anthroposophical medical centre — in Switzerland. The Director of the Clinic, Dr Ita Wegman, knew Dr König and suggested that he and his family seek refuge in Scotland with the Haughtons (Jackson 2005, 2006).

It is at Kirkton House that the adventure to establish the Camphill Schools and curative education in Scotland began in earnest. It was an unlikely group of individuals. Most of the new arrivals had never done any practical work or encountered poverty, and had left behind a comfortable life and diverse careers in medicine, photography, dancing, chemistry and art. Only one of them had trained as a curative educator. Finding themselves in a cold, dark house without electricity or running water, they had to learn to light fires, cook and grow vegetables, in a country whose language they barely understood. In all of these endeavours Karl and Tilla König guided them. Tilla had come from a Moravian Brotherhood family and brought with her the traditions of discipline, devotion and care for the environment, as well as a sense of order that penetrated to the smallest detail, and so made an essential and lasting contribution to Camphill by emphasizing the importance of creating and maintaining a beautiful and harmonious home environment.

Karl König was a more strict and demanding leader who asked each person to exert all of their strength in the venture of building a community. Anke Weihs has explained how they all had to learn three tasks which were entirely new to them — hard work, learning to live together and the study of anthroposophy (Weihs 1975). This subsequently developed into the economic, social and spiritual aspects of the Camphill Schools' organization and the framework for curative education in Camphill.

At this time Karl König was frequently absent from Kirkton House, either studying for a British medical degree at St Andrew's University or travelling to London to apply for entry permits for more of their friends. In spite of many hardships they were held together by a common ideal and vision to create a community that would bring healing and help to those in need, and protect their value and dignity wherever, and whenever, this was threatened. They also wanted to offer a counterbalance, however modest, to the events in Hitler's Germany. In essence, they were seeking to light a candle that would bring new hope to a dark time:

> Only the help from man to man — the encounter of Ego with Ego — the becoming aware of the other person's individuality without enquiring into his creed, world conception or political affiliations, but simply the meeting, eye to eye, of two persons creates the curative education which counters in a healing way, the threat to our innermost humanity. (König in Pietzner 1990, 25f)

When Britain entered the war in 1939 life changed and overnight they became 'enemy aliens.' As they had no radios, they had little access to local or national news and thus were sometimes unaware of regulations. On one occasion failure to comply with blackout regulations not only led to a reprimand from the local police but may have raised neighbourhood suspicions (Weihs 1975).

Karl König's four children now joined the little group at Kirkton House, and a few children with special needs began to arrive. It soon became obvious that Kirkton House was too small. The publisher W.F. Macmillan provided the loan that permitted the Community to purchase the Camphill Estate on June 1, 1940. Macmillan's son, Alistair, was one of the first pupils at the Camphill Schools.

However, before this could happen, all the men were arrested on Whitsunday 1940 and interned — the married men in the Isle of Man and the single men in Canada. The women were left to fend for themselves, and decided bravely to go ahead with the move, which had been planned for June 1. Karl König had earlier made contact with George MacLeod, the founder of the Iona Community who had promised the help of twelve young Church of Scotland ministers with the moving of their belongings, but they never turned up, so the women were left to do all the hard work themselves.

Whilst Karl König usually gets the credit for founding the Camphill Movement, it needs to be said that without the courage and determination of the women, Camphill would never have happened. The women were actively supported by the Church of Scotland, which made a donation of £600 that was administered by Mr Downie Campbell, who later became the first Chairman of the Management Council and a good friend of the Camphill Schools for many years. Whilst the women were having to cope with the practical matter of running the Camphill Estate during a war, the men made the best of their internment by conducting a daily 'University,' deepening their knowledge of Steiner's work and developing ideas for the spiritual and therapeutic life and work in Camphill. Meanwhile Tilla König was corresponding with George MacLeod to see if he could assist in securing the early release of her husband and the others who had been interned (Jackson 2004).

Anke Weihs described the men's homecoming as a mixed blessing. They returned to their friends and families full of ideas and inspired by a time of intense spiritual activity, but they were not returning to Camphill, as the women had created Camphill while they had been away. It was the women that 'had stoked boilers, washed laundry, tended children, worked the garden' (Weihs 1975). As a result the men and women had to find one another anew. By striving together they overcame the inevitable tensions and went on to establish the Camphill community, which subsequently became the home for curative education. Karl König is quoted in the *Aberdeen Press & Journal* on October 21, 1940 as saying:

> I have several English and refugee children here at present, but I hope to do something for Scottish children especially. I was told by the Board of Control in Edinburgh that this is the first private institution for such children in this country. ...
>
> The children become part of the community under our system — and it is of course, a Christian Community. (Pietzner 1990, 39)

Although members of the pioneering group were mostly either Jewish or atheist, it was the Christian element that was gradually developed. Thomas Weihs (1980) described the celebration of the Christian festivals as the 'most effective therapeutic factor in our life.' (Private Notes)

Community ideals and ethos of curative education in the Schools: 1940–45

Community ideals and structures were now developed under the practical and spiritual guidance of Tilla and Karl König, who were revered as mother and father figures, but feared by some because of their high expectations. Karl König was by no means an easy man to live with. Like many great personalities with a mission, he was described as having a fiery temperament and quick temper whenever he perceived inadequacies. However, he also had a deep and loving interest in each co-worker. Co-workers felt that even in a brief encounter with him he had the ability to reach and understand their innermost being (Pietzner 1990). Not everyone, however, agreed with his particular leadership style, and some left to set up anthroposophical organizations elsewhere. Hans Schauder and his wife, for example, left to establish the Garvald School near Edinburgh.

Based on the three labours to which reference has already been made, a threefold structure arose: (1) spiritual/cultural, (2) social, and (3) economic. The quality of each sphere was profoundly influenced by the work of three individuals who were identified by Karl König as the 'Three Stars of Camphill' (König 1960b): Amos Comenius (1592–1670), a Bohemian philosopher and educator with his vision of a universal college; Count Ludwig Zinzendorf (1700–1760) with his ideals of a Christian social order as practised by the Moravian Brotherhood; and Robert Owen (1771–1858) with his attempts at establishing a new economic order. What is not widely appreciated is that the religious thinking of Zinzendorf and the other two stars identified by König, Comenius and Robert Owen were strongly influenced by the English reformer, John Wyclif (1328–84).

The ideals of these three stars were influential in helping to create what König described as the 'Three Pillars of Camphill' (König 1960).

(1) *The College Meeting* (Comenius) This comprised activities involving study, learning, research and professional development. It found its focus in formal meetings, designed to deepen the understanding of individual pupils, and in collaboration with all professionals concerned with

finding appropriate therapeutic responses to their particular needs.

If such a College Meeting succeeds, it is the result of the common effort of everyone who takes part in it. It then turns into a true symposium. To recognize the child's individual nature at once means to realize the necessary curative and educational treatment ... The whole Community of co-workers participates in it and achieves in a common spiritual effort the fundamental approach to each individual child. (König 1960, 36)

(2) *The Bible Evening* (Zinzendorf). This was a contemplative gathering in which participants turned to the Gospels and/or community related topics in an atmosphere free from everyday practical concerns. König saw these regular weekly gatherings creating a strong and intimate bond among the co-workers (König 1960). Those participating met in a sublime realm as brothers and sisters. This practice was extended into such activities as celebrating seasonal festivals, religious observance and pastoral care.

(3) *The Fundamental Social Law* (Owen) was formulated by Steiner (1919, 50) in the following terms:

In a community of people working together, the well being of the community is greater the less the individual worker claims for himself the proceeds of the work he has done and the more he makes these over to his fellow workers. Similarly he allows his own needs to be met out of the work done by others.

This means that the motivation for work should lie in the love for, and need of, the other person and not in the level of wages. König expressed the Law in this way:

None of us regards the money which goes through our hands as a personal possession. We do not earn money; we administer it ... it is never a question of 'sharing the cake' in the most equal fashion. We can only share the work, not the proceeds. (König 1960, 43)

This explains why to this day many co-workers agree not to receive regular wages but use financial resources creatively to support each other out of mutual trust.

Finally, reference should be made to what König defined as 'The Three Essentials' (König 1960):

(1) the conviction that the spiritual individuality of each person is unaffected by outer disabilities;
(2) the importance of the ongoing personal development and meditative work of the curative educator; and
(3) the development of a Threefold Social Order.

Steiner had suggested a new ·structure for society giving it three main areas or spheres: free spiritual life — education, culture, and religion or *spiritual sphere;* the sphere of rights or *legal sphere* — law, social questions and capital; and, the *economic sphere* — work, industry and individual needs (Steiner 1919). He related these to the ideals of the French Revolution: *liberty:* the choice of a free spiritual life; *equality:* fairness in the legal sphere, and *fraternity:* brotherliness in the economic sphere. This intricate interrelationship of ideals and principles, which forms the spiritual-social background to the aims of the curative education offered in the School is best summed up in the Mission Statement contained in the School's brochure:

> The Camphill Movement, which was founded in 1940, works to create communities in which vulnerable children and adults, many with learning disabilities, can live, learn and work with others in healthy social relationships based on mutual care and respect. Camphill is inspired by Christian ideals as articulated by Rudolf Steiner and is based on the acceptance of the spiritual uniqueness of each human being, regardless of disability or religious or racial background. (Camphill Rudolf Steiner School: Annual Report 2003–2004)

A phase of consolidation and expansion: 1944–64

The work at the School soon expanded with the acquisition of parts of Murtle Estate in 1944 and Newton Dee Farm in 1945. Newton Dee was first used to house 'delinquent youngsters' who, under the guidance of

Thomas Weihs, worked on the land and in the craft workshops. Weihs later became Medical Officer and Superintendent of the School. Newton Dee took on its present task as a community for adults with learning disabilities in the early 1960s, and 1950 saw the acquisition of Cairnlee Estate as a home for adolescent girls.

True to the ideals of the Second Essential, König started a training course for co-workers in 1949 — the Camphill Seminar in Curative Education — which was entitled *Community as a Path of Learning*. The Course was affiliated to the Council of Curative Education and Social Therapy of the Medical Section at the Goetheanum, in Dornach, and in 1980 the Course achieved recognition by the British Accreditation Council. In more recent years the Course was developed into the BA in Curative Education Programme, which is now offered by the School in a unique teaching partnership with the University of Aberdeen (see Chapter 15).

An essential step in the development of the School was the opening of St John's School in Murtle in 1948. It was originally intended for the education of five co-worker children but they were soon joined by pupils with special needs. This shows that the School was at the forefront in recognizing the right of all children to an education, irrespective of ability. At the same time the School was putting the principles of integration and inclusion into practice. In 1955 the School catered for 257 children most of whom were drawn from English and Welsh local education authorities. In his Superintendent's Report for 1952 König outlined the following terms of admission which reflect the Fundamental Social Law:

> The usual fees are six guineas per week, inclusive of full board, education and medical treatment. The fees are not fixed, however, but can be adjusted according to the means of parents or guardians. By this arrangement we try to make our Schools open for all classes of children. There is no distinction made between lower and the higher fee-paying pupils in the provision of food, education, treatment, or other amenities. (König 1952, 24)

Around this time the work expanded beyond the Dee Valley to England, Ireland, Germany, USA and South Africa. In 1954 Botton Village was established in Yorkshire, which was the first community for adults with special needs, and was set up at the request of parents whose children had reached school-leaving age. Whilst consolidating the teaching in St John's School, innovative approaches were introduced in the form of intensive work with deaf and blind children in classes using specialized therapies. For the first years, education for all pupils was initially centralized in Murtle then a change took place when pupils were moved to the other Estates, so that the young children (seven to eleven) had their classes (Lower School) in a new Schoolhouse on Camphill Estate, where education was arranged according to their needs.

In 1957, serious illness forced König to pass on the role of Superintendent to Dr Thomas Weihs and his wife, Anke. They continued to broaden the participation and responsibilities of co-workers in the running of the Camphill Schools. In 1972, Weihs no longer considered the position of Superintendent as a true expression of Community ideals and asked the Camphill Meeting — the decision and policy-making body of all committed co-workers — to nominate five people to jointly take on administrative and managerial tasks (Weihs, T. 1972). The proposal of creating five Principals was then endorsed by the Company Council in 1972.

In 1989, the Principals handed over their task to a group of 'Co-ordinators,' some of whom were Registered Managers. The Co-ordinators, who are accountable to the School's Council as well as to the Camphill Meeting, delegate many tasks to, and closely collaborate with, other task groups within the Schools. In this way the principle of shared responsibility is practised in the form of group management rather than the more traditional hierarchical model of line management.

Another important moment in the history of the School was the opening of the Camphill Hall in Murtle in 1962. It was the first Hall to be built in the wider Camphill Movement and was designed for cultural and social events, and to hold international Camphill Conferences. The first Camphill Conference was held in 1963 and one of the outcomes was the creation of the Therapy and Child Guidance Colleges to complement the work of the already existing Teachers College (Weihs, T. 1972). Stimulated by insights coming from the Child Guidance College, it was decided to abandon the age differentiation of pupils on the different estates for the sake of better integration and flexibility.

> Older and younger children, boys and girls, severely retarded
> children and young offenders can be helped to a relation-
> ship to one another by means of which they can experience
> mutual needs and mutual help, which, of course, presupposes
> basic respect and love for the person in the environment in
> which this integration is to take place, if it is to be of a more
> profound healing value. (Weihs, T. 1972, 7)

In 1964 König moved to a Camphill community, Brachenreuthe near
Überlingen, on Lake Constance, in Germany, where he died two years
later. For many this was a tragic loss and the end of an important and glo-
rious phase in the history of the Camphill Schools. At a Schools festival
in 1964 he addressed pupils and adults for the last time, speaking words
of comfort and support by creating the image of a rainbow, saying:

> It is the image which tells us: 'behind and within us there
> is the sun of joy and love for everything that exists; but the
> rainbow will only appear when in front of us there are the
> millions of drops of pain and tears, of sweat and labour ...
> Then the rainbow of hope for the future shines up and we
> see the beauty and wonder in all our life and existence.
> (Unpublished notes)

The vision of the founding group to create communities 'with' and not
'for' people with special needs — what today are called 'life spaces' — had
become a reality. Karl König's words had been put into practice:

> These children must feel that the earthly world has room for
> them as well as for others; that their way of living is appreci-
> ated ... then curative education can start; and this must be an
> education not only developing the intellectual forces but the
> whole being. Every aspect of life in the community plays an
> important part in this ... The teacher must live with the child,
> eat and sleep near the child, share the daily work and the daily
> joys. The warmth of the family and contact with the world are
> both necessary for these children. (König 1952, 21)

Now a new era could begin.

Further developments and new challenges: 1964–90

For over two decades no major changes occurred in the Camphill Schools but several new initiatives took root elsewhere, which built on the Schools' experience and success. The following Camphill communities were established: *Templehill* (Auchenblae), *Beannachar* (Banchory-Devenick), *Blair Drummond* (near Stirling) and *Corbenic* (near Dunkeld), which were all centres of Further Education and Training for young adults with special needs. *Ochil Tower School* (Auchterarder), a residential school for pupils with special needs, and *Tigh a'Chomainn* (Peterculter), a half-way house, were also set up. The task of Cairnlee Estate also changed with the transfer of pupils to the other Estates, and a therapeutic programme of Further Education and Training for Young Adults was introduced in Cairnlee House, while two other houses on the Cairnlee Estate were given over to a further new initiative: *Simeon Care for the Elderly.*

In many respects Thomas Weihs took over Karl König's role, sharing his medical work with a couple of other doctors; travelling across Britain lecturing; interviewing prospective pupils, as well as conducting research and writing (e.g., *Children in Need of Special Care*). After his death in 1983 his surgery in Murtle became the home of the Camphill Medical Practice. It was during this phase that new buildings were constructed and many of the original buildings were renovated and improved.

In the early eighties over 200 pupils were living on the three Estates along with about 170 co-workers and their families. The waiting list had no fewer than 400 applications (Weihs 1983)! The majority of pupils came from England and their journeys to and from home were a major undertaking. A specially organized sleeper train with four to five carriages, which was announced as 'The Rudolf Steiner Special,' took excited pupils and their escorts on the overnight journey to London stopping at many stations on the way. These journeys could be eventful with children locking themselves in the toilets, pulling the emergency chains and generally giving the escorts sleepless nights. But the trains were always staffed by kind and helpful guards — often the same ones — who provided a steady stream of hot tea and biscuits and tools to open locked doors. The guards were so dedicated that even during national rail strikes when all other trains had stopped, 'The Rudolf Steiner Special' was the only one moving in Britain!

During this phase many new training courses were created, mainly through the initiative of the School's co-workers. Apart from the Seminar in Curative Education and the Camphill Nurses Training, both established by König, courses were established addressing the professional development of co-workers focusing on Youth Guidance, Biodynamic Farming, Mental Health, Home Making and Creating Adult Communities.

In 1990, the School, as well as the worldwide Camphill Movement, celebrated its fiftieth anniversary. There was a justified sense of joy and pride in the achievements that had grown out of the dedication and struggles of that small group of homeless refugees. This satisfaction did not last long however, and the last decade of the twentieth century brought with it many trials, challenges and even crises.

A time of crisis and renewed pioneering: 1990–2006

New laws, policies, guidelines and regulations in the UK brought with them new requirements and a different style of inspections. All had significant effects on the work and lifestyle of the School. Initially these processes seemed to be a threat to the ethos and special quality of life and work of the School, whose unique approach did not appear to fit with the many new requirements. Fear, uncertainty and tensions arose among the co-workers. Co-workers began to ask if they would have to give up their Camphill ideals. Would they have to comply and become just another special school? Or would the School have to close down if it failed to comply? These concerns were further aggravated by the introduction of the policy of inclusion, which ignored the special brand of integration and inclusive practice offered by the School.

The impact of new regulations and the adoption of the inclusion policy caused great insecurity and many began to question not only the ongoing need for curative education, but also the relevance of the traditional Camphill ideals, values and practices. Were they still adequate and meaningful in the modern age? Looking back now it is clear that this crisis of confidence opened the way to a phase of renewed pioneering. The perceived attacks on fundamental Camphill values and principles led to a process of re-appraisal and re-evaluation of Camphill traditions. This gave new insights into the essential character of curative education and the confidence to start a dialogue and positive exchange with professional and government bodies. It was important to open doors to the wider professional environment and to make the wealth of knowledge and experience gained in the School available to others, whilst at the same time gaining new insights through that exchange.

An important contributory factor to the ongoing change has been the requirement for those working in curative education to be appropriately qualified. Most co-workers had been internally qualified through the Camphill Seminar but possessed no officially recognized external qualification. So a new wave of training and study began. A major triumph was the transformation of the old Camphill Seminar into the present BA in Curative Education Programme. In March 2003 it was recognized by the Scottish Social Services Council as an appropriate professional qualification for residential childcare workers in Scotland — the first anthroposophically-oriented training to gain national recognition.

Other more subtle changes were also taking place. One example was a changed attitude in the Economic Sphere. It was increasingly recognized that many people, owing to their life circumstances, needed to be employed and receive wages, and that they were in no way less dedicated to their task than the traditional Camphill co-worker. The Schools now employ a significant number of people to support work in the classroom, household, workshop, administration and the training of co-workers.

Arising in part from the difficult times that were experienced in the 1990s, a new and positive spirit has arisen. It will be our ongoing task to maintain constructive dialogue and collaboration with professionals and with local authorities and regulatory bodies so that negative or uninformed attitudes can be changed and positive and mutual relationships established.

Finally, there is currently an initiative to explore the material held in the Karl König Archives in Camphill House, where his study has been preserved containing his writings, notes for lectures and articles and research papers. It has been proposed to make this material available to students and professionals for ongoing research in medicine and curative education through the creation of a Karl König Institute.

Underlying Philosophy of Camphill

The underlying philosophy of Camphill is founded on Rudolf Steiner's anthroposophy. Rudolf Steiner (1861–1925) developed a method of spiritual research to balance and enhance the materialistic approach of the natural sciences of his time — a science of the spirit, or anthroposophy; a holistic world view.

> Anthroposophy is a path of knowledge connecting the spiritual in the human being to the spiritual in the universe. (Steiner in Heymann 2003, 5)

This approach finds expression in many fields: medicine, biodynamic farming, pharmacy, art, education, curative education and social work. The centre for all these activities was, and remains, the Goetheanum in Dornach, Switzerland, the home of the Anthroposophical Society and The School for Spiritual Science. It is here that professionals from different disciplines come together to work in the fields of research, teaching and practice, all of which inform the work of the Camphill Schools.

Each person is seen as a union of three actively interrelated elements: *the body* — physical, genetic and hereditary aspects; *the soul* — emotions, feelings, intellectual faculties and consciousness; and *the spirit* — self-determination, dignity, self-awareness and personal values. Whereas the body and soul only have a temporary existence, the spiritual aspect is understood to be of an eternal, universal and divine nature, which transcends time and space as well as the boundaries of race, nationality or religion. These three elements are the vessel for a fourth one — *the individual human spirit.* Even before birth it is argued that *the individual human spirit* begins a process of gradual integration with these three other elements. This continues throughout life, giving to the individual a unique personality, and a meaning and purpose to life.

All anthroposophical activities are based on the conviction of the eternal nature of the human spirit and on a modern understanding of karma, which has evolved from Hindu and Buddhist teachings. Unfortunately, karma has been interpreted in the past as being a form of a punishment for misdeeds in former lives, but Steiner took a different view, which was influenced by Christian ideals. He indicated that repeated earth lives have the purpose of giving individuals the chance to gradually develop the full potential of their human qualities of wisdom, compassion and love. Illness, accidents or disability can, therefore, be seen as opportunities for development, as learning situations in which skills and qualities can be acquired not only for one's own personal benefit but also for the benefit of humanity. This calls for mutual understanding, support and love rather than judgment and punishment. Attitudes, which spring from this understanding, have a powerful and distinctive influence on the ethos of Camphill communities and on practice in medicine, care and curative education.

Anthroposophical curative education

Anthroposophical curative education is a literal translation from the German *Heilpädagogik* (Healing Education), which was already in use in Germany towards the end of the nineteenth century, in the sense of 'Special Education' (König 1960). Steiner developed this definition further in 1924 when he gave a course of twelve lectures on the subject (Steiner 1924). The recognition of, and respect for, the value and dignity of each individual, and the conviction that every life has a purpose, helps explain the positive approach of curative education. This approach does not work with a deficit model, which usually highlights an individual's disability, but strives to reach out and support the spiritual essence of the child which may be hidden by outer appearances.

Steiner was not alone in his concern for the care and education of special needs children. Other early pioneers included: Edouard Séguin (1812–80), who helped mentally-disturbed children in Paris; Hans Jacob Guggenbuehl (1816–63), a Swiss doctor, who developed special educational methods, therapies and residential care for people with special needs; Heinrich Pestalozzi (1746–1827), who argued that children should pursue their own interests and learn through activity, and Thomas John Barnardo (1845–1905), who established schools and orphanages for homeless children in London (Luxford 2006).

The realization that everyone — helpers, teachers and therapists, as well as those who need care and support — is on the same developmental path and seeking their own individual balance of body, soul and spirit led to a recognition that the roles of *teacher* and *pupil* are often reversed, and the above mentioned mutuality of support becomes a reality. This is because 'health' should not be understood in terms of the absence or the presence of illness but rather as a constant balancing act between extremes. An example of this is our body temperature. It is necessary to find and maintain the healthy balance between extreme cold and heat for us to be well. This can vary from person to person as it is an individual characteristic. In general terms this means that all of us are trying to find our own individual position on the scale between the extremes of hot and cold, lively and dull, sensitive and insensitive, factual and imaginative. The balance we establish is expressed in our unique personality or constitution.

We all meet obstacles in the process of development and to that extent one could say that everyone is disabled or imperfect. Yet on the other hand, the obstacles and imbalances can be seen as offering points for growth. In other words, our individual constitution with all its limitations is the perfect tool for further learning so that it could equally be said that no-one is disabled or imperfect. Learning to understand and support this highly complex and often vulnerable human situation calls upon the creativity, empathy and the deep inner commitment of the curative educator. Steiner's call to those he instructed was 'to become dancers' and to develop an active interest in the other person and an attitude of enquiry to gain insights.

> ... that is what you need — enthusiasm in the experience of truth ... Can't you become dancers — why, you should be leading lives of joy — deep inner joy in the truth! There is nothing in the world more delightful, nothing more fascinating, than the experience of truth. (Steiner 1924, 180f)

Based on the threefold understanding of the human being, curative education is a multidisciplinary and holistic approach which brings together education, home life and therapies to address the needs of the whole child. Crafts, artistic activities and meaningful work are also integral parts of curative education. The professional roles involved are those of teacher, carer, doctor, therapist, craft instructor, artist and work master. Their particular roles are described in later chapters.

Active and ongoing collaboration between these different professionals is essential to support children with special needs so that they may harmonize their threefold constitution, develop to their full potential and find the unique meaning and purpose of their life.

Conclusion

Camphill has itself become the centre of a now worldwide Camphill Movement with over one hundred life-sharing, integrated therapeutic communities for children, young people and adults with special needs, ten of which are located in Scotland. This expansion has had remarkable results and today, the carers, teachers, therapists, doctors, artists, gardeners, farmers and craft instructors, who make up the Camphill communities, are drawn from many countries and diverse ethnic and cultural backgrounds.

The main task and challenge which remains is to continue the pioneering spirit of the founders — the last of whom has recently died — and to be open to change and the needs of the twent-first century, whilst at the same time maintaining the central values of curative education. We need to continue to respond to the call made by Thomas Weihs in the last year of his life:

> And my plea and hope for the future is, as I have already said, to stress that we must not lose this potential of tolerance and love, and that we must also be aware that we must resist the increasing trend to feel that we have to control, to manipulate, to show up the consequences — this will only have momentary success. It will always and inevitably undermine human values, human potentials. It is the integrity and divinity of human existence which we must uphold, acknowledge and further. (Weihs 1983, 24)

2. Care: The Art of Living

MANUELA COSTA & CHRISTOPHER WALTER

One of the best ways to try and convey what goes on in a house community in Camphill is by using pictures and images, which not only free the reader's imagination but also are truer to the art of living. When creative human beings — children, adolescents and adults, both young and old — come together and participate in each other's life, then the drama of creation begins. The intention is to create a painting, a piece of music, a tapestry, whereby each individual's colour, tone, can find its expression. The red can be strong and fiery; the blue calmer and quieter; the yellow springy and quick. It is here that the art begins, the art of allowing each colour to find its expression, in order to paint a picture that is beautiful and harmonious. Each house community in Camphill is individual and has its own tone and range of colours: the general impulse is expressed individually depending on the way these colours mix and mingle.

On entering the large, colourful entrance hall to one of our houses, you will find a well decorated home with fresh flowers on the table and attractive pictures on the walls. Various activities may be happening in the different rooms: baking with a pupil in the kitchen; pupils coming in from a long autumn walk; teenagers gathering to play music in the sitting room. Stay for longer and you will experience moments of happiness when children and co-workers share a joke, and less happy moments when a co-worker is having to comfort a distressed child: moments when the whole house community comes together for some lively social activity and moments when pupils spend time alone in their room, or engage quietly in an activity with a co-worker. There will be times of rush and bustle when washing up, getting ready for school or cleaning bedrooms, and times of peace when the children wind down after a long day and prepare for sleep.

Attending to small details

The house provides a space that is non-threatening, safe, secure and welcoming. Thus much attention, thought and care is given to creating and maintaining a well cared for environment. The impact of light, warmth, forms, shapes and sounds is thought about before decorating any room — whether it is a common room or a room for a child who is about to join the house community. This 'attention to detail' is a major aspect of curative education in the home. It is often the case that a room can both affect and reflect how a child is feeling. An environment that is ordered can help counter the effect of possibly chaotic thoughts and emotions. Anything broken in the house is quickly repaired, not simply because it may be dangerous or unpleasant to look at, but because in repairing broken things we convey the message that confusions in life, too, can be mended.

JASMINE

When Jasmine came to our house, she looked grey, pale, tired, thin, and frightened. She had not slept properly from the moment she had been born. Her parents also looked totally exhausted, for the family had experienced acute sleep deprivation for at least eleven years. The longest Jasmine had ever slept at any one time had been two to three hours and that was with either her mother or father being present. From conversations with Jasmine's parents, it became clear that if she was going to sleep someone else needed to be present in the room with her. Now Mary, who was roughly the same age as Jasmine, had a large room, she loved company, chatting and socializing and was delighted at the prospect of sharing her room with Jasmine. When Jasmine came to see her room, she looked around it and then curled up in a corner. That corner was obviously the place where she felt most comfortable. It was a warm and slightly shady corner. We subsequently discovered that Jasmine enjoyed warmth and not too much light: she also liked to curl up and hide — often concealing her face under covers or a hood. The co-workers came together with the purpose of planning and building a bed for Jasmine. The brief was to construct a bed that looked like a 'hiding place.' The walls of the 'bed house' were to be padded to provide warmth and a canopy was to be hung to prevent too much light from entering. Jasmine was delighted with her bed house. She crawled in, touched it, giggled and then curled up in it. Eventually Jasmine began to sleep for longer and longer periods. Then the point was reached when she did not like her bedhouse any more. As Mary and Jasmine grew older, they decided not to share the room any longer; however they remained good friends. Jasmine's sleep problems had been cured for good.

Diet

Food affects how we feel as much as our environment does. We want the best for our children and young people and provide a varied and wholesome diet based on biodynamic and organic produce. New tastes, smells and textures are also part of acquiring and broadening experiences. One of the keys to tasty food in Camphill is that magic spice called 'love.' If when cooking, one thinks of each person one is cooking for — their likes, dislikes and peculiarities — and then cooks a meal that will satisfy everyone, we will succeed despite a lack of the 'right' ingredients!

JOSEPH

When Joseph first came to Camphill, the only things he enjoyed eating were crisps, sausages, mashed peas, mashed potatoes, baked beans, fish fingers and orange juice. Joseph suffered from acute and painful digestive and bowel problems that caused him to be irritable and prone to losses of temper. In order to help his poor digestion we saw it as our responsibility to widen his diet so that it included drinking more water and eating more vegetables and fruit. After a year Joseph began to eat different kinds of food. How did that happen? Every day Joseph was given the things he enjoyed eating. However, as he was sitting at the table with other children and co-workers, he started noticing that the others were eating different things. The co-worker sitting next to him made a special point of saying how delicious a cucumber or orange tasted or how wonderful the stew or pudding smelled. Added to these comments was a gentle question: 'Would you like a taste, Joseph?' This led Joseph to taste a little piece of carrot and then a lettuce leaf. And so it went on. Although Joseph still has his favourite potatoes and sausages, he now eats from a wide range of vegetables and fruit. This is not only benefiting his digestive system but Joseph now feels much more comfortable with himself, which has led to less irritability, agitation and fewer temper tantrums.

Daily rhythm

House life is all about creating a healthy rhythm. The daily rhythm gives a structure, purpose and dynamic to each day. Pupils are often woken up with music and then helped to prepare for breakfast. Some wake up quickly, some slowly. Each individual has his or her own rhythm. For some facing the world every morning is a pleasure, for others it is a hardship. Some need to be awakened with a little knock; others will need many knocks. After breakfast the children help with the washing up and then go to school. Returning for lunch, they enjoy a leisure break until afternoon classes that start at 3.00 pm. The evening meal is at 5.30 pm after which daily tasks are shared out and pupils go to their evening activities. Some may go swimming or play basketball with their peers: others may simply stay at home or go for a short walk and then ring family and friends. By 8.00 pm the younger pupils are preparing for bed, whilst the older ones chat quietly before going to bed a little later. Towards the latter part of the evening the lights are dimmed and each child will have their individual time with their carers. We also pay attention to the way the pupils go to sleep. This may take the form of a story before bedtime or a private conversation during what we term 'settling time.'

ROSIE

Rosie's most exciting time was the evening. Throughout the day, she was usually lively but when evening came she became hyperactive. She would jump up and down, fall into giggling sessions, clap and talk incessantly. Rosie was also scared of the night. She often thought that once asleep she would never wake up as sleeping was like dying. In order for Rosie to relax and go to sleep her carer would spend at least two to three hours with her. First of all they would go for a walk. The carer would listen to all of Rosie's stories. This meant listening to them again and again, as Rosie did not have an extensive repertoire. After a walk lasting around three quarters of an hour Rosie would begin to slow down and be ready to go inside. She would have a relaxing lavender bath followed by a biscuit and warm drink — not coffee or tea as this increased her agitation. Rosie became progressively calmer. After putting on her pyjamas, her carer would gently massage Rosie's hands and feet, as they were usually very cold. She was now finally ready to lie down in her bed. The carer would read Rosie's favourite story, sing a lullaby and say a prayer. The prayer spoke about hope and the fact that just as morning followed night so Rosie would be back the next morning after her sleep.

Rhythm and routine

The daily rhythm in the house is like breathing — from early morning peace to lively activity during the day and back to a calm in the evening. There is variety within this rhythm, for flexibility is a key quality of curative education. Some children, to the dismay of adults, may ask repeatedly for the same story, evening after evening. Whilst this provides the child with a sense of security, certainty and predictability, if one is not careful one can become stuck in the daily routines. Then what once was life-giving becomes life-stealing. To keep a measure of flexibility one needs to break routines, habits and patterns; for example, taking a different path to school, or going for a meal in another house. With some children and young people one may have to work at 'loosening' routines, with others one may need to establish them. Whatever the individual's situation may call for, one does have to look at the totality of a child and young person's day so as to discover this harmonious balance.

JEROME

Jerome loved routines, tidiness and orderliness. His favourite companion, and his guide through life was his watch. His books were meticulously ordered, by height and thickness. At the table anything with handles and labels had to be turned either to the right or left. The kitchen was his grand stage where pots, pans, kettles, knives and forks performed a majestic symphony of orderliness. In the sitting room there were often disagreements as he had to align the sofas with the square carpet and so everyone had to move position. If people refused he would go into a storm of spitting, cursing and swearing. In order to help him we devised a number of games that we could laugh about together. Laughter broke rigidity and brought back the balance we all needed. For instance, we played a kind of chess game at the table with the salt, pepper and other condiments. Jerome particularly liked this game as we would 'mess up' and he would tidy it up after waiting his turn!

Our holistic approach is intended to support the child in developing an inner balance that is neither too outgoing nor too solitary; too active or too passive. Balance is interpreted here as an active, rather than a passive, state and is different for each child. It is important that we support children to find a balance that is individually healthy and that enables them to be who they want to be in the world.

The week, too, has its pulse. In one week this might mean a parent visiting and taking their child out for the day, a social worker coming for a review or other significant people dropping in for an hour or two. The active school week alternates with the weekends when pupils may go on outings or just follow their own individual interests. Sunday has more of a reflective and festive quality to it, and some pupils attend a non-denominational service at Camphill. Over the school year pupils and co-workers celebrate different festivals together. These provide opportunities for joining together to prepare for the festival, whether cooking, getting the house ready or making decorations etc. In this way we come together in a different fashion than during our daily activities and routines. These moments live on in the pupils' memories and give them a sense of time and process in their life.

The school year begins with the autumn festival of Michaelmas when we harvest vegetables with the children. During the harvest meal we express thankfulness for the earth's gifts and for each other's strengths. During Advent we gradually prepare for Christmas with plays, celebrations and evening gatherings in our houses. Coming together in this way, we can share warmth and caring at this dark time of the year. Pupils also take part in plays and many shine and reveal unexpected talents. As Spring approaches we celebrate Easter together, and feel the new life that comes from the warming sun as we paint eggs and plant new flowers in the earth on Good Friday. And during the long days of Summer we celebrate St John's Day on June 24 with a huge fire around which we can all gather, letting the flames carry upwards our hopes and wishes for our future.

Rhythms and rituals

The importance of rhythmic interactions that foster group cohesion has been highlighted by Maier. In his view rhythmicity is a potent force not only for linking people together but also in fostering a sense of internal togetherness. Life comprises a wide range of natural rhythms from the regularity of the heartbeat to the change from day to night. Maier has argued that rhythmicity is an essential ingredient in human communication and development. In attempting to communicate effectively with a child the carer has to fall into step with the child so that they dance to the same tune. The child and the caregiver then search for ways to establish and maintain that joint rhythm in a mutually inclusive way. An awareness of this engagement can help carers pace their interactions and further their capacity to interact and to speak with, rather than to, a child. There are many ways that house life can help to promote this. For instance, playing individual and group games such as throwing a frisbee, catching and throwing a ball, running together or joining in with folk dancing. Then there are all the things we do together: caring for the animals, making an aeroplane model or building an igloo on snowy days.

If we are to understand the impact of rhythmicity upon personal relationships we need to progress from mere sensitivity to purposeful engagement with the children served. We need to be aware not just of what is said, or the kind of activity in which children are engaged, but of the importance of this 'give and take,' which involves a clear cycle of approach and withdrawal. And if meaningful relationships are to be created, it is necessary to maintain each other's rhythm. It is, therefore, important for us to learn to listen, look and explore the pulse of groups with which we are working in a new way.

Rituals represent an institutionalized form of rhythmicity that culturally confirm a repeated and valued practice and bring a sense of togetherness to the participants (Maier 2004). Rituals have a particular significance in group care so long as they are the rituals of the child rather than routines imposed by adults. Joining in the same song at the beginning of every meal can be a unifying experience or a chore, depending on whether this activity has been spontaneously internalized or merely serves an adult's need for order.

Spiritual dimension

At Camphill Schools our fundamental ethos is based on the recognition of the importance of a spiritual dimension within daily life. Those working in the childcare sector have a responsibility to attend to the spiritual needs of children just as much as their physical, emotional, intellectual and social needs (Jackson 2003). If we are to take a truly holistic view of the child, the spiritual dimension cannot be excluded. In broad terms, spiritual well-being can be defined as a sense of good health about one-self as a human being and as a unique individual. A clear duty is placed on those providing care to ensure that a child's spiritual well-being is nurtured in the same manner as his or her physical and intellectual well-being. Thus, all carers have an ethical responsibility to recognize and respond to spirituality as it is presented within all human beings, and they must be equipped to recognize, understand and deal with this dimension (Jackson & Monteux 2003). Placing vulnerable, often emotionally-deprived, children in care settings where staff are either discouraged or not permitted to offer affection, reassurance and comfort is to expose children to yet another insidious form of abuse. In such a situation no kind of meaningful relationship is possible and without that relationship the chances of the child experiencing spiritual growth are seriously impaired.

It has been argued that permission to discuss spiritual matters with children could lead to situations where children are coerced into adopting the religious beliefs of particular staff members. But it has been pointed out that responding spontaneously to children's questions on spirituality is quite different from care staff imposing their religious beliefs on the children, or initiating conversation about such matters before the children ask for it (Friesen 2000). It would be unfortunate if co-workers felt afraid to speak with children about spiritual matters because they were fearful of reprisal or of being told that it was wrong to engage in such discussion. When a relationship of trust and mutuality develops between co-workers and a child, it is natural for them to share parts of their life story with each other and to share what they think is valuable and important in their life. In Friesen's opinion, this is the essence of spiritual care. Spiritual care and support do not result from the acquisition and application of a series of techniques and skills, it comes through sharing and learning from one another. It comes by addressing questions that relate to the value and meaning of life (Swinton 2001).

Building relationships

The interconnectedness and mutuality of relationships are the foundation of curative education. Through our responsiveness to the whole child and the deeper layers of their being, we seek to foster a developmental and healing process. The house community is the space within which these efforts take place, to appreciate and foster a child's positive qualities. Every day we attempt to draw out each child's potential so that they can make their individual contribution to house life. This is not easy as many of our children come to us with emotional and behavioural difficulties. Co-workers in a house community face the daily challenge of thinking through issues facing children and finding ways together of supporting and encouraging their growing independence. For an anxious child this may mean supporting her in her attempts to manage her difficult feelings throughout the day. For others, it may mean helping them to learn how to put their coats on, or to go peacefully into sleep. In this way we aim to provide a coherent and meaningful experience for everyone. As we do not just work with individual children it is essential that we catch the tone and 'pulse' of the whole group within the house. We need to know where the tensions lie, which child sparks other children off, and which child has beneficial effects on others. It is also important that we find the right way of valuing a child's privacy within the life of the group. We try to deal with all personal issues as sensitively as they would be managed in the child's own family.

It is important to stress the mutual character of the relationship between co-workers and children. We are travelling together on a journey. While we may set out with many valid aims and objectives for a pupil and include these in care plans, unless we are open to learning from the child, we will not be practising curative education. Only by reflecting on our daily practice — whether individually or in the weekly house evening — can we become aware of our own prejudices and assumptions. Through focusing on a child's strengths and by identifying their interests, skills and talents, as well as their difficulties, we learn to meet them as a whole person. Our aim is to support people in moving towards wholeness and balance, a balance that includes disability as part of the reality of their existence.

When we are experiencing difficulties with children, it helps if we make a conscious effort to search and rediscover together what it is that they uniquely bring to the world. We may spend a whole week on that task and then share our thoughts and images. It is often the case that if one takes the child or young person 'into one's sleep' at night by thinking about them, picturing them playing, resting, interacting, a 'solution' to what had seemed an apparently impossible problem appears as if by magic. Inwardly, this can be a 'eureka' moment!

ROGER

Roger came to us as the last stop before a possible referral to a secure unit. His story is not atypical of many of the other young people that come to Camphill. He had moved from foster home to foster home and from one school to another. He was used to being restrained: he was permitted no hugs, cuddles or even pats on the shoulder because of his past history. He was well acquainted with reward and punishment systems, star charts and different supervisory regimes. What this had taught him was quite simple. In order to be loved, one needed to behave. This proved a pointless strategy as one needs to be loved first. Our task in the home was to love Roger despite his behaviour. He tested our approach to the extremes. However, we persevered and slowly started to build bridges and gain his trust. Roger began to smile back, to look us in the eye and allow us to get nearer to him as a person.

It is the task of those working in the homes to create 'a space' between themselves and the individual child where they can meet. Our focus is on understanding and truth rather than explanation and prediction. As human beings are creative and are constantly changing, we need to learn how to meet each other afresh each day.

Working with parents

The house community exists within a wider environment that includes the families and friends of the children. A critical moment in the life of the child and his family arrives once the decision has been taken by the Schools to accept a child. We collaborate closely with parents to ensure that the move is as smooth as possible for we recognize that this step will make a huge difference in the family's life and also mark a major transition for the child. We arrange for the family and child to see around the house, the child's bedroom and to meet the other children who will be living with them. Children need to be reminded of how it felt for them when they first came and they are encouraged to help the newcomer settle in. The family visit provides an opportunity for the parents to ask all sorts of questions; for example, when can they phone in the evenings?

What happens at weekends? It is also an opportunity for parents to pass on vital health information, or just the fact that their child always has a bath in the morning. The children often have many questions too. Whilst we try to answer these questions we recognize that many children are more at ease in raising these later with their parents. When a child does not live with their natural parents it may be the social worker or foster parents who visit.

It is particularly important for us to understand, and be responsive to, the individual needs of families, when living and working with their children. It is the child's family that usually provides the ultimate sense of security in the life of a child and this has always to be remembered. It is the family that often knows the child best and can sometimes provide helpful clues to explain a child's behaviour when we are at a loss. Children keep in touch with their parents with regular phone calls and parents are encouraged to visit as often as they wish. As an increasing number of our children are day pupils or live near Aberdeen, many go home every other weekend. Parents regularly come to collect them and this provides us with many opportunities for communication and working collaboratively.

Caring for the carers

Anyone caring for individuals is going to need support since caring on a daily basis requires commitment, love, constancy, patience and authenticity. It is important that we learn to know the difference between our own needs and those of the children. It is too easy to become fixed and inflexible in our views about children. Whenever we find ourselves saying: 'Of course she's got to come for supper' or 'He's going to help with the washing up and that's the end of the story!' we need to realize that we are in danger of reacting emotionally rather than responding to an individually perceived need. At such moments our emotions can prevent a clear and unprejudiced perception of a particular situation. Children then suffer from our unreflective exercise of authority, which does not respect their autonomy and personal freedom. To see another person clearly one needs to work hard at knowing oneself. Only by clearly knowing and understanding one's own beliefs, feelings, thoughts, motivations and dreams will we be able to help the children and young people with whom we live and work. If I do not know myself, it will always be my unreflective self that stands in the way of any encounter.

It is often who we are rather than what we do that makes the difference in other people's lives.

Whilst each co-worker finds his own approach to developing emotional balance and reflective practice, it is recognized that consistent and thorough supervision has an extremely important part to play. Through this process a mirror is held up to our actions and feelings and from that reflection we can learn more about ourselves. In addition to this essential, regular formal feedback and support, community life provides us with many opportunities for receiving informal advice and constructive criticism. This may be in the corridor, around the kitchen table or when we meet a colleague on the road. Helping each other in this way assists us in realizing our true potential.

The journey continues ...

Many children and young people come to share part of their biography with us, part of their life. Some come for short periods of time, some stay longer. Some move on to other Camphill places, others to different schools, others create their own homes in town or countryside. A few, like Roger, may move on from Camphill to a secure unit for a time. However, after five years, Roger paid us a visit with his girlfriend. He was happy, had found a job and was studying. He came to say thank you for his years at Camphill and to acknowledge that he had sometimes been 'a silly kid.' Many move on but keep coming back to visit year after year. Others do not visit but ring up periodically to ask for advice. We have always tried to develop free relationships with those we have cared for and this continues after they leave. Wherever they go, we let them know that we are still there if they want to contact us. But they also need to move on into the wider world. That is why they came — to gain the strength to be themselves in the world and now we must trust them as they continue with their journey.

3. Education

PAULA MORAINE, BIRGIT HANSEN & TERRI HARRISON

———•———

Every educational approach places the child's learning needs at the centre of its focus. In Camphill Rudolf Steiner School the particular educational approach used stems from the philosophy of education originally formulated by Rudolf Steiner in 1919 for the first Waldorf School in Stuttgart, Germany. The School quickly expanded to include classes that were organized specifically to meet the special needs of children with learning difficulties. This marked the beginning of anthroposophical curative education.

In Camphill Schools the curative educational approach offered has always been based on the theories, principles and practices of Waldorf education. The philosophy of curative education is founded on the ideals and beliefs about learning articulated by Rudolf Steiner in his many books on education. Rudolf Steiner indicated that the human being can be expressed in the threefold sense of body, soul and spirit comprising thinking, feeling and will. Waldorf education expresses this threefoldness by an approach to education which involves hands, heart and head. In every classroom we strive for a balance of thinking, feeling and will in all our teaching and learning activities.

Both curative education and Waldorf education recognize that important developmental milestones take place in seven-year cycles. In the first seven years we allow children to learn through activity and imitation — to learn by *doing* (birth to seven years) All young children tend to be imitative by nature and given the vast amount they learn in these years, we can conclude that their powers of imitation are considerable! In the next seven-year cycle, the child learns through lively imagination and loving authority (seven to fourteen years). In this phase it is important to establish a new trusting relationship with the teacher. Wherever possible, the teacher stays with the same class for a number of years, developing and deepening the teacher/child relationship as a secure base for learning. Only later does the more independent, factual/scientific approach to individual knowledge become essential (fourteen to 21 years). These years prepare the child for approaching adulthood through a carefully constructed series of experiences that are defined by the individual's needs and capacities. The years between fourteen and twenty-one are supported by a steady increase in practical approaches to learning. We help them build skills and abilities that can be applied in the working life of an adult.

How the principles of curative education are implemented is an essential consideration. The whole school maintains a strong daily, weekly, monthly and yearly rhythm. Strong rhythms provide continuity, predictability and security to school life. Routines are useful in certain settings and provide structure to a particular part of the day, such as the sequence of events that occur during the course of a school morning. Rhythms are revealed in a series of main lesson blocks that are delivered throughout the school year. The yearly curricular topics are delivered first in main lesson, which takes place in the two hours at the beginning of each school day. The main lessons, which have their own structure and rhythm, draw on the content of the Waldorf curriculum. The class always stays together as a group for main lesson, only later splitting into special skills-building classes.

At the beginning of the school year, an Individual Educational Plan (IEP) is written which draws on the Record of Needs. The IEP identifies and formulates long-term targets from which short-term learning goals are drawn up. Appropriate therapies are identified for the child and incorporated into their school day. The therapies can occur at any time throughout the day.

The Waldorf curriculum is adapted in such a way to provide content that is appropriate for the major developmental needs of each child, despite any learning or communication difficulty the child may have. The teaching is also informed by the national standards of the particular country. A careful blend and balance needs to be achieved in order to facilitate maximum benefit for the children. Responding to the individualized learning needs of each child is part of the strong educational ethos practised in Camphill Schools.

Early years

The Early Years Programme is embedded in the world of nature, play, music and stories. We recognize that both education and care form part of a totality within an early years setting and that the curriculum should reflect this by being developmentally appropriate for children younger than seven. Play strengthens the imagination, allowing young children to develop and deepen their concentration, consolidate their understanding of the world and become creative, sociable, adaptable and inwardly flexible. To meet the learning needs of a young child opportunities are provided for communication, imitation, imagination and joyful experience. During a walk in the forest, while singing a song, or while playing make-believe, these serious learning aims are being met. The child is learning to participate in a social setting, to communicate, to follow instructions and to imitate worthy activities. This process is supported and enhanced by activities using language, movement, craft, puppetry, seasonal celebrations, music and meaningful daily tasks. We believe that young children can benefit from such a non-invasive early intervention programme and that all of these learning goals gradually prepare the child for entry into the more formal educational years.

The difference between the Early Years experience and entering Class 1 is possibly less pronounced than in other types of school provision. The children are still encouraged to learn through play and movement, while a more organized approach to the day is introduced as the beginning of formal learning. In every school day there will be activities that stimulate the learning centres in the brain and nervous system. Movement involving full body actions and rhythms is essential for stimulating balance, equilibrium, laterality and dominance. All the senses — sight, smell, taste, warmth, hearing and touch — are gently stimulated. Each pupil is able to experience the full range of spatial orientation (above/below, in front/ behind, right/left): it may be hidden in a poem or song, which accompanies the movement involved in a game. Although there is a 'rhythmic' time during each main lesson in which these exercises and activities are formally introduced, they can take place in a variety of ways throughout the school day. In addition, there will be music, poetry, arts and crafts each day, chosen as a support to the regular curricular lessons that occur in main lesson. All of these activities in the early school years provide opportunities for sensory integration and practising communication skills in a wide variety of situations.

As the class remains together for all of main lesson, this is the time to offer curricular content and activities that are appropriate for every child of a certain age, regardless of their individual ability. In second lesson, the class is separated into ability groups where either individual or small group teaching can take place.

CLASS 1

In each school year of the Waldorf curriculum there is a main theme guiding the story content. In Class 1 the stories in main lesson are fairy tales and nature stories. These are either the archetypal and imaginative fairy tales from such sources as the Brothers Grimm, or they might be stories the teacher has created from experiences in nature. The stories, which can be told over several days, can involve pupils in enthusiastically acting out parts of the story.

Mathematics begins with the introduction of the quality of numbers, counting, sequencing and differentiation of the four mathematical processes of addition, subtraction, multiplication and division. Counting and moving in rhythm is a good approach to learning and remembering new mathematical concepts that are introduced in Class 1.

Literacy lessons in Class 1 begin with the rather unexpected topic of the straight line and curve! First of all, the children are taught to draw straight lines and curves, then to draw a letter and from the letter to draw a word. The final stage is learning to read what they have drawn or written. Any reading accomplished in the first school years arises out of reading what they have written, for writing arises out of drawing. Or put another way, first we do things and then we understand them. The organization of this basic introduction to life-long academic skills is one that can be repeated irrespective of the age of the child.

CLASS 2

Class 2 continues many of the learning goals of Class 1, deepening and intensifying mathematics and literacy aims. Word games, word families and phonetics all lead towards more literacy skills. The four mathematical processes continue, including value placement, vertical positioning of the numbers and memorization of the multiplication tables. This is a year of intense work on communication and simple processing activities. Gradually the pupils are able to sit together for longer periods, listening to a story or engaging in small projects and activities.

The Class 2 curriculum speaks to the polarity between the human being and the animal kingdom in nature. The children hear stories and legends of saints as well as Aesop's animal fables, and this is a curricular expression of the developing social skills that are emerging in Class 2. Teachers often notice a change in friendship patterns in the class, which are accompanied by an increased interest in peer dynamics. The children may act like 'saints' one day, and the next day be at odds with each other and fight like 'cats and dogs.' All of these social polarities are guided by the imaginative content of the stories told in main lesson.

CLASS 3

Class 3 is a large step socially, practically and academically. Everything in the Class 3 curriculum is based on practical work. In mathematics, the 'Measure of All Things' curriculum includes learning about time, weight and volume. Along with this are the Old Testament stories of the Hebrew people, presenting in story form imaginative pictures of how human beings gradually changed their relationship to authority figures and took on more personal responsibility for their own lives. The main lesson blocks, related to housing, clothing and farming, guide the Class 3 child toward becoming familiar and comfortable with living on earth and learning to use nature to help. The practical activities are structured to include a good deal of experience outside, working on the farm with animals or in the garden growing food. In the classroom, there is suddenly a more formal learning arrangement with the introduction of desks and tables. The academic part of the school day is much more individualized and structured around the learning needs and capabilities of each pupil.

CLASS 4

In Class 4 pupils begin to develop social independence and personal friendships. Pupils now need some individualized projects that they can take responsibility for and share with the class. Such projects can be tailored to highlight the specific strengths and interests of each pupil, and are related to the curricular content of the main lesson. The curriculum includes stories from Norse mythology that highlight the duality between the highest ideals of the gods and the wishes of the individual. Zoology is introduced and covers the kingdoms of nature and the families of animals. Geography begins with a local survey of where the pupils live and go to school and then spreads out to the broader neighbourhood. Reading progresses to the point where for some pupils, they move from learning to read to reading to learn. Opportunities for oral expression are encouraged with pupils re-telling in their own words the stories from main lesson. In mathematics, fractions are introduced, which offers an opportunity for the child to understand the concept of being part of a greater whole.

Middle School

The Classes 5 to 8 form part of what is called Middle School which covers the ages ten/eleven to thirteen/fourteen years. The pre-teen years are usually an active and vibrant time for the children. During these years they often express great curiosity and longing to 'explore' and 'find out for themselves:' new faculties of reasoning now become available to them. New pupils are often admitted around the age of ten or eleven. These are children who have somehow managed to cope in a mainstream school up until now. Sadly many have already attended four or five mainstream schools before their needs are properly recognized. It is only then that they are referred to the Camphill School, either as day pupils or full boarders. Wherever possible the teachers continue to stay with their class but as class sizes increase there is often a process of adjusting classes to accommodate new pupils. This can be both a challenging and healthy experience since this is the age when social peer groups become more important.

Throughout the Middle School, music, art and practical activities play an integral part in all the lessons. This provides an opportunity to work in a truly inclusive manner. As all the pupils are of a similar age but with different levels of ability, there is the possibility for the pupils to interact with their peers and learn to appreciate each other and their own strengths. This social aspect can be a great challenge for many pupils, especially for those within the autistic spectrum. The social 'nest' of the class provides a safe space where pupils can grow and learn.

It is important to recognize that the quality of the social fabric does not depend on the amount of time spent in the classroom. At Camphill, the external environment provides a fantastic resource for learning outwith the classroom walls. Many pupils benefit from a restful walk, others from more structured outdoor lessons.

The routine and structure of each school day — in fact each school year — aims to create breadth, balance, coherence, continuity and progression in a rhythmical manner. This is one of the important principles of Steiner-Waldorf education. The day begins with the main lesson during which the class works with a specific topic for three to four weeks at a time such as history, sciences, literature or geography. By concentrating on one theme for several weeks time and space can be given to each subject in an artistic and practical manner. It allows the pupils to deepen their understanding of each subject and learn to apply what they are learning to themselves and to the world at large. All the pupils, irrespective of their ability, are allowed to experience a subject on equal terms during the main lesson hours.

The activity-time devoted to each subject allows for different teaching approaches. For example, during a geography lesson some pupils may write an essay about the Cairngorms. Others may build a model, others may paint a picture of the hills, and others may climb a hill in order to experience at firsthand the concepts that have been discussed. Thus everyone works with the same theme but according to their ability.

CLASS 5

In most European countries this would be the first year of secondary school, a time of transition and a new beginning. We often find that eleven-year-olds seem to change inwardly even though they may not change their class or teacher. It is a lively, active age when great curiosity and interest is shown in their surroundings. The children at this stage are usually healthy and agile, enjoying movement and physical activity.

The curriculum channels this interest by introducing the geography of their home country but in a more structured and formal manner. There is an examination of the structure of the land in relation to the plant and animal life, as well as lifestyles within the population. This topic leads to visits to different local industries and significant geographical sites. Botany is another important subject, which is offered in several block periods throughout the year. Class 5 pupils love to learn from 'real life' and often express a need to 'see for themselves.' The visits and outings are therefore very important in internalizing such subjects as geography and botany. The history lessons look at human evolution through the ancient civilizations of India, Babylonia, Egypt and Greece.

Many parents question how their children with special needs can learn and benefit from ancient history. This is a valid question, as ancient history may appear to be quite distant from most of us, let alone a child who has difficulties in connecting with the modern world. The activities relating to history lessons are practical and engaging. One class, for example, used the story of the Trojan Horse in their mathematics lesson. They built a horse large enough to hide two children inside! This involved a whole range of practical activities — designing, measuring, cutting, hammering, and painting. At the same time the project provided a wealth of sensory experiences.

CLASS 6

If we move down the corridor and look into Class 6, we might wonder how all of these 'sturdy' twelve year olds were once the graceful, agile eleven-year-olds from yesteryear. In this class, we sense a great hunger for facts and a need by the pupils to find out things for themselves. The teacher's word is no longer accepted without question! Many of these twelve-year-olds have suddenly developed a great love for loud music and huge, colourful posters. They are not only 'hungry for facts' but also for strong sensory impressions. The curriculum responds to this need by introducing relevant science subjects: the science of sound, light, and colour (acoustics and optics). Now accurate observation needs practice because the subjects taught require observing the phenomena in order to formulate rules.

The need for exactitude and clarity of thought is emphasized in other subjects, for example, geometry. There may be some pupils whose co-ordination and motor skills do not allow them to make exact drawings with ruler and compass; however, they may be able to experience the geometrical patterns through movement. The teacher can, in fact, create dances, which include the different shapes which appear in the geometry lessons.

The history lessons in Class 6 turn to the Roman and Medieval times. History becomes part of the children's own lives and experiences. Rudolf Steiner advised teachers to teach history to this age group as it might be seen through the eyes of a participant of the time rather than as a specta-tor. The newfound skills of observation, as well as the need for precision and clear rules, reflect a stage of consciousness similar to that evidenced by the Romans and their society. Furthermore, there are many features in our own culture which can be traced back to the Roman era.

CLASS 7

Further down the corridor we hear the hustle and bustle of Class 7. They are preparing their class play about Christopher Columbus. The thirteen-year-old is at an emotional and lively age: a time of inner exploration and greater depths of feeling balanced by an outgoing and inquisitive nature. At this age the youngsters seem ready to identify with the longings and aspirations, as well as the struggles, of the great Renaissance explorers and scientists. Accompanying the pupils through Class 7 is rather like spending a year on the *Santa Maria*. The 'ship' is constructed in the woodwork lessons, the planks, winches and pulleys having been tested in the physics lessons when discussing mechanics. The barrels have been 'packed' with nutritious food with the appropriate balance of carbohydrate, protein and vitamins to prevent scurvy. Knowledge of what is required results from the fact that the class has just completed a main lesson block on nutrition, health and hygiene.

The use of the compass, sextant and other sailor's instruments was discussed during the lessons on astronomy. Thus, preparing for this play involved all the subjects studied in Class 7. It also meant that the sensitive child who was only able to stay in the class for a short time each day made his contribution through his own individual school programme. He may have designed the leaflets or painted the scenery or baked the ship's biscuits. The new desire for self-exploration is made possible through drama sessions, where a deepening understanding of the pupils' own, as well as other people's, emotions and feelings can be explored.

Class 8

The last year in the Middle School is often an important turning point for now the 'bubbles' of puberty turn into the turmoil of adolescence. The youngsters experience great inner changes, which they may not understand and find difficulty in expressing. The history lessons respond by turning to times of change — the American and French Revolutions. At this age youngsters readily identify with the call for freedom and equality and over the next few years, they will hopefully discover the responsibility, which follows in the wake of such changes.

The physics lessons focus on the mechanics of air and water. The pupils learn about and help to make different types of pumps and steam engines. They are introduced to the first inventors of these machines, their personal struggles, and what these innovations have brought to society. The science lessons reflect the theme of inner and outer change. Anatomy is studied in the natural science lessons with particular focus on the structure of the skeleton and muscles. In the geography lessons, they learn about the whole world and the industrial, trade and cultural connections between nations.

At a time when many youngsters feel self-conscious, sensitive and possibly more introverted, geography can have an almost therapeutic effect by helping the youngster connect to the world at large through opening up an awareness of the predicament of others. We can start by looking at what is on the dinner table. How many products are we using from other countries? Where are these countries? What is the climate like? What do we know about the people's lifestyle? What conditions do they work under? The possibilities for explanation and learning are endless.

The youngsters usually turn fourteen during Class 8. It can be a dark time for some: for others it can be like a roller coaster ride. At this point the art lessons become increasingly important. Throughout their schooling, the pupils have learned to draw, paint and model. This has often been done together with other lessons as a way of deepening and enhancing that subject. In Class 8 pupils learn to draw with black charcoal and create 'light-filled' pictures using only black. This can have a strong therapeutic effect when adolescence hits and the outside world seems dark and unfair. Thus the curriculum can be used in a therapeutic manner. However, education can only become truly therapeutic if the head, heart and hand come into a healthy balance, and the pupils learn to experience themselves as individuals seeking to realize their own potential.

The pupils begin their school day, everyday from Class 5 till Class 12 with these words:

> I look into the world
> Wherein there shines the sun
> Wherein there gleam the stars
> Wherein there lie the stones
> The plants they live and grow
> The beasts they feel and live
> And Man to Spirit gives
> A dwelling in his soul.

I look into the soul
That living dwells in me
God's spirit lives and weaves
In light of Sun and Soul
In heights of world without
In depth of soul within

To Thee, O Spirit of God
I seeking turn myself
That strength and grace and skill
For learning and for work
In me may live and grow.

This verse refers to an outer world and an inner soul world and the fact that the child has to fulfil his potential between these two polarities.

Upper School

The healing potential of the Waldorf curriculum continues into the Upper School. Young people enter their final stage of school at fourteen years of age and bid farewell to their class teacher from the Lower / Middle School. The relationship to their new teacher derives less from the 'loving authority' of the Lower and Middle School class teacher and is based more on the authority of each subject presented through the curriculum. The overriding principle of 'goodness' warmed the early years of school; the principle of 'beauty' provided a backdrop to the work in the middle years; now in the Upper School the guiding principle becomes 'truth.' The Upper School teacher needs to encourage enthusiasm for the underlying truths that form natural laws, evolutionary and cultural development and the human being's complex interrelationship with the world around him. An enthusiasm for discovering these truths also helps forge the young persons' ideals and personal values as they progress through the Upper School. An education warmed with enthusiasm raises the young person's awareness from self and the 'pain' of adolescence to the awe inspiring qualities of the world around them.

The class teacher now becomes more of a 'class guardian' who supports the young person's development by helping them reflect on their behaviour, concerns, achievements, hopes and fears. The Upper School teacher's task is to facilitate independence in thinking, feeling and will, through active interest and involvement in all aspects of the young person's life.

The fruits of educating head, heart and hands become apparent in the Upper School. From approximately fourteen to eighteen years of age young people develop new ways of thinking as a result of engaging in the fertile ground of experiential learning. The young person is now ready to develop an understanding of the world. The seeds of moral judgment have been sown through the curriculum, as well as the imitative and imaginative approaches of the earlier years. A loving interest in the world is fostered through creativity, experiential learning and the imaginative, artistic approach to teaching. Sound moral judgment, strong personal values and individual ideals are therefore the fruits that can be harvested in the Upper School through the cultivation of thinking, feeling and will that takes place in the younger classes. The Upper School aims to help the young person discover themselves through an active engagement with the world around them, and through the development of compassion and empathy with their fellow human beings. Young people are encouraged to think creatively, develop balance and depth in their feeling, and to apply their ideals, creativity and loving attitude for the world around them to their practical skills.

As the young person with special educational needs enters the years of adolescence and begins to experience his individuality more strongly, there can be a realization of personal limitations, of barriers to learning and of the obstacles that lie in the path of developing an individual's potential. This can become a time of personal crisis. The upper school curriculum, together with curative education, works as a healing response to these questions, fears and self-doubts. Young people can emerge through these difficult years as strong, self-confident young people who value themselves and the contribution they can make in the world.

CLASS 9

The pupils in Class 9 are aged fourteen to fifteen years. Whilst their transition into Upper School marks a clear step in their school career, there is a smooth progression of the subjects covered in the lower classes.

The subjects of Class 9 aim to engage the young person's awakening powers of reasoning and judgment. The pupils begin to synthesize their knowledge of the world as an interrelated whole and see human history as a progression. In history of art the pupils study the development of art over the ages. The pupils experience not only changes of style but also changes in the purpose of art as humanity has developed. The pupils learn to observe, practically engage with, discuss and understand the subject through a balance of collaborative and individual activity and study. At the end of the course the pupils have their first experience of surveying the whole of human history. Many of our young people learn to recognize and express personal taste and opinion through this main lesson. They can experience the power of art as a tool of communication, as an outer expression of inner experience, and as a means to give form to imagination.

The rich art lessons are balanced by the many science topics studied in Class 9. The skills of observation, reasoning and hypothesising taught in Classes 6, 7 and 8 are developed further through physics, chemistry and human biology in Class 9. Two physics blocks link with the history curriculum by studying the invention of the steam engine and telephone. Through working on an understanding of the physical processes involved, and by building models and performing experiments that reveal scientific laws, the pupils come to understand the impact of these inventions on society. Through studying the biographies of the great inventors, the pupils come to appreciate the ideals, visions and the necessary enthusiasm to bring about change. They also begin to understand the responsibilities that such human beings have to the world through their power to change and harness the environment. For all the pupils these lessons provide an opportunity to ask 'how does it work?' and to grasp how machines are elaborate tools, which are created according to physical laws and result from human ingenuity.

Science and art are woven throughout the Class 9 curriculum and the humanities provide a background to this work. In geography pupils look at the mineral structure of the earth, the forces of the earth and the process of mountain building and the movement of tectonic plates. Again force and change are taken up as themes. The pupils also start to form a clear 'world picture' by studying the earth as a whole. Thus the pupils of Class 9 practise using their senses to make careful observations of the world around them, learning to harness their new powers of thinking to make judgments and reach understanding. They learn about the human potential both to create and destroy. This raises moral and ethical issues that may be reflected in the artwork that focuses on black and white techniques to explore balance and contrast.

Pupils in the Upper School continue their work on literacy, numeracy, language, communication, movement and sensory integration. Although the pupils are fourteen years and older, the national guidelines in English and mathematics continue to provide a helpful developmental approach to teaching basic skills and provide a useful benchmark for assessment and evaluation of learning. Homework and independent study are important aspects of the Upper School. Some pupils research topics of personal interest or relevance to main lesson themes. These are presented as written and/or verbally presented projects. Pupils are now challenged to engage in problem solving activities where they need either to think for themselves or to engage collaboratively with others.

Information and Communication Technology (ICT) has an important place in the Upper School curriculum. ICT provides support for learning and helps many pupils access areas of the curriculum through use of specialized software and access devices. The internet creates opportunities for research and communication. Language and communication lessons are integrated as much as possible into other lessons and practical daily life, in order to provide meaningful and relevant contexts for social skills development and the use of speech, signs and symbols. Likewise, movement and sensory work tends to become increasingly related to work skills training and craft lessons.

Class 10

The young person of fifteen to sixteen years of age continues to develop thinking skills and becomes more balanced in the emotional turmoil that accompanies early adolescence. The aims for Class 10 are to bring this balance more to the fore through helping the young person discover an inner equilibrium and self-control in themselves. Many areas of the curriculum now call on precision and accuracy as the young person begins to harness his new skills and gradually becomes master of his physical body, feelings and thinking. In human biology the pupils turn to the major organs of the human body paying particular attention to the processes of respiration and circulation. The pupils learn to recognize the rhythmic qualities of the human being and how balance and rhythm are vital aspects of all human processes. They explore the qualities of their emotional life through the physiological study of the heart and respiration, and also discover important aspects relating to health and illness. Most importantly, they learn to respect the human being through the beauty and wonder of form, function and process in the miracle of life itself.

Respect and responsibility for the world around the young person is also explored in geography. In Class 10 the whole world is considered. The themes of rhythm, interdependent cycles and systems again come to the fore as the pupils discover the qualities and movements of atmosphere and hydrosphere. Ocean currents, the water cycle, the circulation of air and the layers of the earth's atmosphere are key themes for the main lesson. Once again pupils learn about the impact human beings can have on their environment, and about our responsibilities to the world upon which we depend. chemistry lessons allow the pupils to explore the polarities in nature through studying the properties of acids and alkalis, as well as the polarities in their own inner life.

Through the curriculum of Class 10 the pupils learn to apply their thinking and make choices and decisions based on insight. Practical class projects are begun in Class 10 which require pupils to apply their thinking and problem-solving skills, whilst at the same time learn the social challenges of working in a team. Craft work in the school's workshops also provides essential opportunities for the development of practical, personal and social skills (see Chapter 11, 'Crafts'). Many of our pupils learn to value themselves as well as appreciate others through the practical work they undertake in Class 10.

CLASS 11

As young people approach school leaving age at sixteen, they are supported to make a conscious and informed decision about whether to stay on at Camphill and continue with their schooling or whether to leave. Parents, social workers, educational psychologists, as well as the staff of Camphill, help the young person explore their options and reach a decision. If the young person chooses to stay on at

Camphill, his final two years of formal schooling gradually lead to more work-oriented experiences. The process of making decisions, which have an important impact on their lives, can be daunting but also empowering. Young people often make a step towards seeking independence and become more mature and personally responsible after reaching this point. As a consequence the mood of Class 11 is very different from Class 10; maturity and self-confidence begin to be apparent.

During this year many of the young people formulate questions about their identity and purpose in life. This searching is supported through the themes of main lessons during the year. *Parzival,* a medieval text written by Wolfram von Eschenbach, is one of the central themes of Class 11. It tells the story of a young knight's search for his identity and destiny, whilst he struggles to overcome personal weakness and face the consequences of wrong choices and decisions. As the story unfolds Parzival is able to put right his own mistakes and heal the suffering of others, by finding empathy and compassion. This story is studied as literature, as well as through artwork and drama; it also provides a backdrop for the pupils' study of medieval times in Class 11's history block.

Embryology is introduced in Class 11 and culminates in the study of human biology. Through this subject the young person explores questions about identity and destiny. In physics the class turns to wireless technology, from the invention of the radio to a study of satellite technology and its use in mobile phones, computer technology and television. Through science the pupils discover the microcosm and macrocosm, from the form and function of a single cell to man's attempt to know and understand the universe.

Apart from continuing in the craft workshops, the young people also start to take on work experience placements during this year. Work placements may be within the School, such as working in a kitchen, laundry or maintenance workshop, or at another local Camphill community, working with older people at the village shop, farm or bakery. Towards the end of Class 11, some pupils are ready to take up work placements in the local community and may have the opportunity to work for a local business or service. (Some pupils also decide to attend Aberdeen College on one of the part time courses.)

All pupils in Class 11 have the opportunity to develop their independence skills through work placements, projects and practical lessons. Basic skills in literacy, numeracy, communication and movement continue throughout and are offered as small group or individual lessons. Whilst some pupils need these basic skills to help them develop life skills and independent living skills, others choose to work towards national qualifications.

Class 12

The transition between school education and the adult world of work and learning can be exciting or daunting for any young person, particularly those with learning difficulties. The twelve years of education using the Waldorf approach have been preparing the young person for this point, equipping him with the resilience, independence, self-confidence and sense of purpose to find his place in the world. Class 12 continues, as Class 11, with one hour of whole class teaching in the main lesson and then the rest of the day being devoted to work experience, college placements, basic skills and life skills lessons. The young people tend to work more individually in Class 12, and the main lesson becomes a point of reuniting with the rest of the class to take stock and share experiences.

The main lesson themes of Class 12 focus on drawing together the learning of the whole curriculum, integrating understanding of the world and its phenomena, and development of humanity through world history. The pupils study the whole history of mankind through key themes that highlight human, social and cultural development through the ages. History of art in this final year focuses on the development of architecture. The zoology main lesson brings together all the work in animal and human biology giving an overview of the animal kingdom and man's place in nature. Social responsibility is a theme taken up in the study of social and economic world geography, as well as technology and its impact on society and the environment.

Graduation day is a very important point in the life of every pupil in the Camphill Rudolf Steiner School. The class spends a significant part of the final school year preparing for this event, inviting family, friends, previous teachers, house co-ordinators and others who have worked with them through the years. The pupils often prepare a play or some other artistic presentation for the graduation and this provides an opportunity to work together on a class project for the last time.

It also allows for artistic expression of self-confidence, social awareness, initiative and creativity that each one has gained during their
school years. To mark their graduation each pupil receives a book
of collected thoughts, pictures, poetry or personal memories drawn
together from everyone in the school who has known the pupil; a gift
that is often cherished for years to come. The graduation is a festival
of past achievement and future promise; it is a celebration of individual
accomplishment and the opportunity for everyone to send a young person off into their adult life with their love and warmest wishes. Whilst
the graduation marks the end of an important phase in the young person's life, it is also the beginning of a new phase. On leaving Camphill
Rudolf Steiner School, it is our hope that these young people will
show not only a loving respect for humanity but, above all, a belief in
themselves as human beings, who have an important contribution to
make to our world.

4. School Leavers' Programme

LAURENCE ALFRED

As the time nears for any child to leave school there is often a certain trepidation felt by the parents as a future approaches which will be different from the known present. Children are often told that 'School days are the happiest days of your life,' and parents could say much the same. As the time for leaving school approaches uncertainty for all parents comes along in its wake. What for many years has been a clear routine from one day to the next is broken.

Now take a step back and imagine having a child with special needs. School-leaving is rarely a straightforward smooth transition from nursery, to primary, to secondary, to graduation. The uncertainty of school leaving has been with parents since their child was very young. In fact it often starts from the point at which they are told or realize for themselves that their child has 'special educational needs.' They then hear from other parents with similar 'problems' that they face a life of fighting the system in order for their child to receive an education which meets their special needs.

By the time many pupils are referred to the Schools they have often been school leavers on more than one occasion. They are sometimes described as 'casualties of the system;' children who have been 'included' in their local schools in order to satisfy certain political and financial considerations.

Aims of the school leavers' programme

It is the aim of the Camphill Schools to work with all the relevant parties to make the transition between Camphill and the next placement as smooth as possible, while at the same time providing a curative educational programme that supports the pupils through this transition. Our educational approach aims to prepare our pupils to become 'citizens of the world' by helping them to achieve their potential as human beings. We do this in the belief that what we offer them will strengthen their inner being so that they can meet their future with resilience and confidence. Although we are aware as co-workers that it is never too early to begin to think about the next placement, many parents need time to consider the issue. Nevertheless the School finds itself in a difficult position, as it is not its responsibility to determine when, or to where, a pupil should move. The key people here are the pupils themselves, their parents and the local social services departments.

In our experience this process is a difficult one. There are a number of reasons for this:

— pupils often do not have the maturity at sixteen or eighteen
  to make decisions regarding their future;
— parents often have difficulty accepting that their child has
  grown up and needs to move away from the 'safe' setting offered by Camphill to an often 'alien' environment;
— parents are also often tired with official processes remembering
  the long battles to get their child into Camphill in the first place;
— pupils who have been placed are often given a low priority
  by their social worker whose main task seems to be 'crisis
  management';
— there are too few quality post-school forms of provision
  available to meet the variety of needs our pupils possess;
— the policy of social inclusion works against any genuinely
  open discussion because the political dice are loaded towards
  placement in some form of supported living in the local
  community; and
— decisions are often finance, rather than needs, led.

For these reasons we often feel we have to take the lead in the process.

The early leaver

TRANSFER

For a number of years we have had discussions with our local authorities about taking pupils for a short time and then transferring them back into the state or independent sector. The impetus for this development was the School's belief that the younger children are placed in Camphill the more we are able to offer, as the children are less 'formed' in their behaviours.

The idea here is that children can come to Camphill and for an agreed period of time receive an appropriate therapeutic programme before returning to mainstream schooling. At the same time a support package can be built up around the family at home so that when the child returns, there is a safe and well-supported environment in which the child can flourish. Within the last six months we have admitted two very young pupils aged five and six with such a plan in mind and it will be interesting to see how successful the process of reintegration into mainstream will be.

When we look at individual needs, it may be that the step directly from Camphill to mainstream is too great and that a gradual transition would be more helpful. Such a move might go via the Aberdeen Waldorf School which offers the same curriculum as Camphill, although one which is not designed for children with special needs.

DISMISSAL

Unfortunately there are occasionally situations when the Schools are unable to meet a particular pupil's needs. In such circumstances the situation around a pupil is generally well known and understood by professional workers. The decision to dismiss a pupil may follow a number of reviews and possibly suspensions. To support this process the Schools have a Discharge Policy and an Exclusion Policy, which all parties work with, even though it can be stressful for all involved. The Discharge Policy states:

> When a pupil's placement becomes unmanageable or suddenly breaks down, an emergency review will be held within three working days in order to determine the best way forward. This will only happen in extreme circumstances, for example when a pupil is a danger to himself or others.

THE STATUTORY PROCESS FOR PREPARING LEAVERS

All pupils attending Camphill should be in possession of a Record of Needs which is a document which summarizes assessments which have been undertaken and outline the services that need to be put in place to meet any special educational needs that have been identified. Around the age of fourteen a Future Needs Assessment is carried out. This is a formal review of the Record of Needs that considers the range of options available upon leaving School. It is the first formal step towards preparing for the transition from Camphill to the next form of provision. At this point, even if there has been no previous involvement with the social work department, a social worker from the local authority is invited to participate in the process as she needs to get to know the young person in order to judge whether the pupil is a 'disabled person' under the terms of the Disabled Persons Act 1986. Also involved, often for the first time, is the Careers Officer who will assess the pupil's suitability for a supported work placement or College placement.

Following this meeting a plan should be formulated with regard to the pupil's future. This plan should be reviewed at least once a year. It is important to remember that at this stage the pupil has the right to have their views as to their future heard and noted. This may well be at odds with those who believe they know the pupil best. In Camphill we have sometimes fallen into the trap of not taking the pupil's view seriously enough with the result that the pupil has resorted to some kind of challenging behaviour to ensure that his views are heard.

It is believed that if all concerned with a pupil begin the planning process early enough then the transition will be a smooth one and the correct support and provision will be in place once the pupil leaves.

As the school leaving age is sixteen, pupils can leave School at the end of the term prior to their birthday. Once sixteen is reached no pupil needs to stay at School any longer and the local authority cannot insist that a pupil attend if that is against their wishes. The pupil must want to continue attending School and as we have noted, problems can arise if their views are not taken into account.

Education Departments will financially support a pupil to continue at school up until the age of eighteen and sometimes nineteen. However, should a pupil wish to leave school then social work funding is required. There is then a change from children's to adult services with the result that the pupil may not be as well known and a different political and financial climate may prevail in the adult services division. Care management then becomes the main player for the young person and his family. The whole area of entitlement to benefits, family pressures, inadequate post-school provision, lack of effective planning and support services all conspire to put unbelievable pressure on the young person and his family to agree to a future that may not necessarily be in the young person's best interests but rather happens to fill a vacant space in a local authority's provision. The result is that many of our pupils end up at home with their parents in tense family situations, or end up in sheltered accommodation.

Preparing pupils for transition

The end of Class 10 — when the pupils are sixteen — is the end of compulsory education for most of our pupils, although some might have reached their school-leaving age earlier in the year. Together with parents, local authority representatives and co-workers from Camphill, the young person is helped to realize that his general schooling has now ceased and that he must have a say in his own future. This process will have already formally begun at the Future Needs Assessment review and informally with teachers, parents and friends.

If the pupil stays on into Class 11 this is often marked by a change in living situation. After having lived in a house-group made up of children of different ages, the young person joining the senior programme, moves into a group with his peers. At the same time the role of the group parent or key-worker changes, wherever possible to that of a friend. The young person is encouraged to take more responsibility for himself and to find a co-worker with whom he wishes to relate. Within the peer group the young person is encouraged to develop poise and maturity in his human relationships. Guidance is given in the domestic responsibilities of running a household. Emphasis is placed on helping the young person come to terms with, and accept, his difficulties in a positive manner, thus enabling the young adult at eighteen to have a more realistic approach to his or her future.

The young people continue to be grouped in classes according to their age in Classes 11 and 12, although during these two years, formal schooling within the classroom gradually decreases and training in vocational, social and independent living skills receives greater emphasis. During this period an increasing amount of time is spent in the craft workshops. The aim of the workshop placement, apart from gaining experience in various materials, tools and work processes, is to develop motivation, discipline and thoroughness necessary to produce worthwhile and practical objects for the Community.

Learning to work in a team is of equal importance. The young people are involved in different outdoor projects, which help to foster a co-operative and creative attitude. They are both directed to take on specific projects in gardening, landscaping, general estate work and maintenance, as well as being involved in the researching, planning and construction of specific items, such as playground or barbecue equipment. It is hoped that the pupil will experience many different types of work and that he will begin to think not only about what he would like to do once he leaves school but more importantly what he is able to do.

In Class 12, formal schooling is offered on a day-release basis once a week. The Class 12 curriculum includes artistic and physical activities and individual tuition in life-skills. Less emphasis is put on group activities and a large proportion of the day is spent on individual work placements. The young person is also helped to become increasingly independent. Young people are placed in work situations according to their individual ability. Opportunities are available in the Tools for Self-Reliance Workshop, the laundries, gardens, kitchens, weaving shop and joiners' maintenance workshop. When it is felt appropriate, individual youngsters are placed with local firms and craftsmen for a prolonged period of work experience. This helps give them a realistic awareness of their abilities and limitations: it also encourages them socially to find a place in working life. At the end of Class 12 a formal graduation ceremony takes place to which parents, friends, past teachers, therapists and house parents are invited.

At the annual review held during each year of the Programme discussions take place concerning the young person's future placement. All possibilities are examined and a plan of action agreed, which is then monitored over an agreed time scale. While it may be appropriate for the young person to continue to live and work in a Camphill community, there is no automatic right of transfer and an application would need to be made to each Community that might be able to meet the needs of the youngster. At this planning stage it is important to listen to the views of the young person, as it may be that at eighteen the time has come for the young person to have some time away from a Camphill setting in order to experience other ways of living and working.

For some it may be decided that a further year in the Schools would be beneficial. However, a formal application needs to be made for a place on that transition year. This is a carefully designed course structured to meet the specific needs of the individual: it may include life skills training, craft work or work experience. The course offers the opportunity for young people to deepen their skills while awaiting a move to their next placement. By offering this extension pupils can be helped to complete their education at the end of Class 12 without the worry of a further move during the course, as such a move can be a difficult experience both for those who leave early and those who remain behind. The introduction of such a transition year has proved beneficial for many youngsters.

The following case study faithfully and sadly reflects the experience of many of our school-leavers.

STEWART

I left in July 2004. At least six times in my reviews we talked about where I was going to live once I left Camphill and what I wanted to do. I never really wanted to talk about it because I didn't want to think about it because it used to worry me. It still worries me even though I left the Camphill Rudolf Steiner School six months ago. However I did decide I wanted to live and work in Aberdeen.

I had a look at Beannachar but did not like the idea because I couldn't go to Aberdeen to work. I also looked at Tigh a'Chomainn and even had a trial there, but decided I didn't want to go there either because I wasn't sure about whether I wanted to live there. I thought I would rather live in Aberdeen. My social worker found me a social worker in Aberdeen to find a flat for me but she only visited me twice at my reviews and once at my work placement at Newton Dee. Since I left I have not seen or heard from her.

I left Camphill in July and went back to the Wexford Care Centre where I used to go for my holidays. I thought I would only be there a short time before getting my flat in Aberdeen. This hasn't happened. What did happen was that I went to Wexford House and at first had a couple of holidays. I was then in the middle of August put into my own flat in Wexford House. Somebody stayed with me for the first night and then I was left alone. Since then I have been by myself. The beginning was quite scary and I did not want to do anything wrong. Although I have got used to it now, I know I am only safe once I lock the door. I sometimes manage to cook something like a bacon sandwich, sausages or French toast. Sometimes I also make pasta. I had someone help me cook it. For breakfast I often eat the same as what I had the night before, or some biscuits, crisps, coffee or cereal — whatever happens to be in the house. I am allowed to choose things for the kitchen at the Unit. I usually eat lunch at the Unit and sometimes supper. Otherwise I eat in my flat. The Unit is only seven minutes away.

During the day in the beginning I needed to have loads of interviews for a National Insurance number so I could get some money. It took ages — they needed to find out absolutely everything about me. I do not know why. I looked at jobs in the Job Centre once or twice. Otherwise I haven't done a lot except watch telly.

I do have a job on Saturdays helping in a local shop polishing the windows. I get some pocket money for that. In the shop I also count the money. Everybody knows me because it is such a small village. I also work there on Sundays. I usually sit around because you cannot make a shop busy. We just have to wait until a customer comes in. I get £15 on a Saturday and £12 on a Sunday.

I couldn't get a place at College. Most of the time I am bored — but I will keep trying. I have been in trouble since I left. On Friday and Saturday nights there is a disco at a pub where I have been banned. I got to know some boys through one of the staff members at the Unit. They are all young and asked me to buy them alcohol and cigarettes, but I didn't do it. One night they were in a shed behind the pub and then came back to my flat. They gave me a joint to smoke. Then they made me another one and then came back with some vodka. I smoked the joint and drank some vodka. It made me feel terrible. They were laughing and I was very dizzy and then sick. There were about ten of them.

I'd like to build up my independent living skills so I can gain a bit of trust, if I go eventually to Newton Dee Village. I am not planning to be there my whole life — I want to enjoy it.

I used to work in the Store at Newton Dee. It was a good beginning. I learned to do the order, to listen to what people told me to do, weigh things and to learn to work. I was also cleaning and filling the shelves. It was a good place to work and gain some experience. I also had work experience at a local supermarket but stole some things so was fired. They had to do it. They had no choice. I hope I have learned my lesson now. I have learned it, although I also stole from Newton Dee, and from the house I was living in in Camphill. I've really learned it now though. I don't want to be in trouble with the police and be arrested and put in prison. I would be very sad.

Conclusion

While it is the case that some pupils make the transition from Camphill to their next placement with relative ease, the majority do not. Even when the planning seems to have gone well, both parents and former pupils experience a sense of bereavement resulting from moving away from a place where care had been the key consideration and where the achievement of adult independence had been seen as the principal goal.

Professional workers often make the following kind of observation to grieving parents who are concerned that their children are no longer receiving the same quality of care.

> He's an adult now and he is free to decide whether he wants to wash, or eat breakfast. He can decide for himself whether or not he wants to join any evening activity or whether he wants to sit in his room by himself.

The question of inner preparation for pupils and their parents needs to be addressed by the School, but it may well be argued that all young people and their families have to face these realities when their children leave school. For those former pupils who move into a 'care in the community' setting, it seems to me that they are moving from a secure community setting in which they are able to exercise a certain amount of independence to a situation where they become increasingly dependent and insecure. Of course, there are examples where all has gone well but these are, in my experience, few in number and when they do occur, they are usually the result of increased parental support and involvement. What I have described is an indictment of the society in which we live. It reveals the true value we have for those with special needs who seek to live amongst us. They continue to remain near or at the bottom of political and financial priority lists and the quality of life many subsequently experience is eloquent testimony to that fact.

A few years ago at a conference for professionals, academics and policy makers, involved in the field of learning disability, the following question was posed to the audience by one of the speakers:

> You are the people who support inclusion and the care in the community agenda. How many of you have anything to do with people with special needs in your non-professional life?

Very few participants raised their hands. 'That,' the speaker said, 'says it all.'

5. Play Therapy

KAHREN EHLEN

Play therapy as practised within the School is an important aspect of our therapeutic work with children and young people with a range of learning disabilities and emotional and social problems. Play is a creative process that restores health to the whole organism and especially to the soul life of the human being. It fosters resilience and well-being and is essential at all stages of the life cycle from childhood, through youth to adulthood and into old age. This creative spark within the human being represents the eternal childhood forces within us. It provides a necessary metaphor for real life situations; an 'as if' quality to a child's experience, so that the re-enactment of events in their life becomes possible.

Play is a child's natural medium for making sense of, and digesting, their experiences. Play offers the opportunity to explore ways of being, of establishing identity and building self-esteem. It provides children with the opportunity to develop their own skills and take charge of their body and practise the social skills required throughout life. Through play and the world of imagination and symbols, children become 'little play directors' organizing actors on the stage to re-enact the epics of their life. Many people still believe that play is of secondary importance to study and work. However, it is well documented that it has a major influence on a child's healthy development and is of continuing importance for well-being through adolescence and adult life. The School sees play as a necessity for the development and well-being of people of all ages.

The use of play within the house and classroom setting is generally recognized and encouraged in the daily life within Camphill. Play is an essential aspect of the therapeutic work to help children build meaningful relationships, learn to communicate and develop their use of language and their motor skills. Within classes aspects of play may be incorporated into the teaching style offered to specific pupils in order to meet their individual needs. For others, play may lead to more formal artistic elements involved in presenting class plays or dramas, or through the house environment to the promotion of hobbies and leisure pursuits, or other creative craft activities. Preparation for seasonal activities may also fall within this framework.

By fully engaging in playful activity, using the whole body during the day, a therapeutic antidote to sleeping, eating and mobility problems is created, which promotes an overall balance in well-being and general health. Many children with learning disabilities find it hard to take charge of their body, develop a body image and achieve full control of their body movements. Through play, in which practice and repetition of physical co-ordination skills occur, children are able to learn and achieve independence in the best manner.

The importance of play for a child's well-being has been recognized in the 1999 UN Convention on the Rights of the Child (UN Charter 1999):

> Section V: All children have a right to rest, play, and have a chance to join a wide range of activities.

The National Care Standards with respect to early education and childcare up to the age of sixteen states:

> Standard 5.3: You know that the activities that are provided by staff will allow the children and young people to enjoy both organized and free play and leisure and recreation, including quiet times.

And within care homes for children and young people:

> Standard 15.1 (Daily Life): You are encouraged and supported to take part in activities which develop individual talents, interests and hobbies. The activities reflect the needs, abilities and interests of yourself or other young people, as individuals or in groups.

A variety of play therapy approaches are offered in the formal individual therapy sessions for children and young people. Some of these approaches are therapist-led and others child-led. Individual therapy plans are based on an assessment of the child's needs by a multidisciplinary team comprising the school's medical officer and co-workers involved with the pupil in the house, class and therapy settings. Following referral to the Play Therapy Department further specific assessments are made and a specialized therapy plan is devised, identifying the most suitable approach for each individual. The therapists from the Department also support co-workers to create and maintain therapeutic activities for individual children in other settings. A threefold approach is on offer.

Child-centred play therapy

Within Camphill Schools, play therapy is offered to those children who can communicate verbally, or can demonstrate through their play that they have a basic understanding of language. Play therapy is child-centred with play the primary medium and speech the secondary one. It is a dynamic process between the child and therapist in which the child can explore at his own pace, can follow his own agenda and use issues from past or current experience, whether consciously or not. A confidential and safe setting is provided within which the child is enabled to form a therapeutic alliance with the therapist. This relationship enhances and fosters inner growth and change, and can help the child to develop a greater sense of identity and self-esteem. The play therapy process helps to reduce inner confusion and shifts the child's perspective on a particular event, whether it is abuse, loss or some other problem, so that they are less likely to internalize blame. This process can result in an improved self-image and a sense of empowerment, which allows them to face the current demands in their daily life.

Whilst West (1996) has expressed some reservations as to the value of child-centred therapy with children with certain disabilities, our experience has shown it to be beneficial, even though it may take longer for the benefits to become apparent. It could be argued that children with learning disabilities need play therapy more than other children, since many have suffered various types of neglect or emotional, physical or sexual abuse, or have experienced several major losses during their lives due to the impact of their disabilities. Many children with learning disabilities who have severe emotional and social problems, have undergone repeated rejection, discontinuity and inconsistency while growing up because of a loss of a cohesive family experience, or have been placed in temporary care settings with a variety of carers. All this is added to the normal challenges of growing up.

Within play therapy, the child grows by participating in a trusting relationship in which acceptance, unconditional positive regard, empathy and the opportunity for reflection are provided. This promotes greater self-awareness and the realization of the child's own potential. Though the therapist is accepting and non-judgmental, this does not mean she is totally permissive. Clear boundaries are negotiated, which help the child to move from set, inflexible and defensive habits towards new ways of expressing their thoughts, feelings and moods. The therapist is aware of the potential for aggression or destructiveness in play, but through the application of their skills children are enabled to express these, and other strong emotions, creatively and in an imaginative way. This gives the child the experience of having control over their emotions that are often impulsive and overwhelming in daily life.

Our experience is that both children and adolescents benefit from play therapy, although for adolescents a greater range of craft type materials, board games, or clothing for drama and role play, may be needed, in addition to the usual toys. Many adolescents are not ready for the direct involvement offered by counselling when facing some of their complex problems. Play offers the adolescent an opportunity for the expression of things which cannot yet be formulated in words. The play therapy setting also offers them the choices they need to find an acceptable form of communication.

The therapist needs to work consciously so that an inner space is created for the child that is consistently open, non-judgmental and accepting. The therapist is also required to develop a high level of empathetic understanding of the child, and to communicate this understanding to the child through reflective comments. To be able to provide this consistently the therapist needs to engage in continual training. Anthroposophy can help the therapist in such training by encouraging receptivity and tranquillity, openness of mind and clear thinking, active involvement and positive objectivity. It is essential that the therapist creates the inner space for working within themselves as part of an ongoing commitment to their work. Equally, the therapist's skills in observation and reflection are vital for their work.

The curative educator and especially the therapist must be aware that their own habits and attitudes influence the 'life space' of the child with whom they are working. Within the therapy room, the therapist seeks to create 'a nest,' which may work directly on the physical organism of the child and influence that child's well-being. By working on the child's emotions and actions, the therapist can help to harmonize the child's breathing and rhythm of sleeping and waking. Through this process the therapist enables the child to develop new habits of living and being, which are no longer driven by bizarre and restless behaviours. The therapist's role is like that of a mirror. Reflection helps to bring more peace and harmony to the inner life of the child. Through the 'genius of language' and 'tuning in,' true, deep and empathetic communication begins to flow and 'the right word' said at 'the right time' helps to create order, where formerly there was chaos and confusion.

In the endeavour to perceive the wholeness of the child, the therapist is guided by the image of the human being, which can facilitate a healing process within the child. This 'image' of the human being is best understood by seeing it as consisting of body, soul, and spirit, and by being aware that the spirit essence of the person is eternal and carrying a unique divine spark within it. The body and soul, however, may be affected by illness or disability as they are bound to the emotional and physical processes within the body.

Play therapy may be short or long term. With our pupils some may initially require a period of more directed play to develop their play and communication skills before embarking on more formal sessions of play therapy. Play therapy is most effective when carried out in regular weekly sessions of fifty minutes' duration, and where family or main carers and other important adults in the children's lives have given their positive support. For some children who are acutely ill more intensive work may be required involving two or more sessions a week. In extreme cases, daily sessions over a period of six to eight weeks may be needed to transform their ill health or pathological behaviour. Most pupils receive one session per week during the course of an academic year and following a review of their needs long-term therapy may be prescribed.

Play sessions are recorded with the child's knowledge. Drawings and other creations are kept for the child by the therapist. Confidentiality is maintained and any need to disclose content from the sessions because of the therapist's concern for the child's well-being or safety is discussed with the child, where that is possible. Similarly, any information that is required for a therapy progress report is discussed with the child, and by so doing not only is trust in the relationship sustained but the therapist's professional, ethical and legal obligations are also met.

Intensive interaction

The intensive interaction approach developed by Hewett and Nind has been incorporated into our therapeutic play work (Hewett & Nind 2000). This approach complements and closely matches the School's own approach to working with children and young people who are pre-verbal, and have not reached the stage of using or fully understanding symbolic communication. Our previously developed therapeutic play work with pre-verbal children followed traditional methods of child-centred interaction, in that they were based on the therapist and individual becoming jointly focused on each other, sharing some mutuality and wishing to repeat an enjoyable experience. This intensive interaction approach makes use of a range of interactive games that normally occur between an infant and main caregiver. There is no particular task that has to be achieved but rather a process of sharing, being together and communicating, by using the languages the individual child has created for him/herself.

The attitude of the therapist is one of respect and value for the pupil and for the process of communication the pupil may have evolved. This approach is about accepting the child as he is while offering him new opportunities and making interactions understandable and achievable. Intensive interaction is process based and not target based, and requires a high degree of intuition and an ability to 'tune in' to the individual with whom the therapist is working. It is possible for this mutual relationship and style of communication to develop into a social and fun-filled experience for the child, which leads the child to wishing to repeat the experience. It may also lead into a more playful, turn-taking interaction. This particular approach has been used successfully with children with severe learning disabilities, particularly those in the autistic spectrum who do not appreciate a directive approach, but who can respond and actively engage in their own way and at their own pace to a person-centred and non-directive focus.

DEVELOPMENTAL PLAY (THERAPEUTIC/FOCUSED PLAY)

In developmental play the therapist provides a calm and harmonious environment with reduced sensory stimuli so the initial emphasis is on establishing a therapeutic relationship of shared focus and turn-taking with the child. Once the child has achieved this and it can be sustained, the therapist introduces a restricted range of play equipment suited to the developmental stage and skill level, which the pupil has achieved within their play functioning.

A developmental area is chosen, based on an assessment of the pupil's ability and their preferred sensory experiences. The relevant materials are then chosen and games prepared. Posture and gross co-ordination, vision and fine co-ordination, hearing and speech, social behaviour and play are focused on and progressed in small steps through repetition and playful games. Maintaining the child's interest and building on their ability to concentrate for longer periods requires a patient, enthusiastic, open and accepting approach. The therapist is required to remain creative and flexible, making each session feel as if it were the first time that the pupil had enjoyed the experience. Through the therapist's enthusiasm and perseverance, the children are led at their own pace through the individual activities making up the therapy session. This experience is intended to stimulate the child to wish for, and initiate, more shared activity.

In this manner a process of focused and directed play activities may be introduced by the therapist to lead the child's play through a developmental process in which more complex skills are built on following upon the successful achievement of the previous level of skill and ability. A range of play sequences are worked through, from exploratory and sensory play, to body awareness and orientation games, shared play, turn-taking, imitative play and symbolic play, where the child possesses the requisite abilities.

Each stage can take some time, and repetition is essential in order to establish both the skills and meaningfulness of the activity for the child. The children benefiting from this particular approach are usually more severely delayed in certain aspects of their physical, emotional and social development, and require a therapeutic programme, which emphasizes sensory integration and other curative exercises.

Therapeutic play and curative exercises are a part of every curative educator's tool kit. Knowledge of child development underpins all the curative work and it is essential that all co-workers in houses and classes understand these exercises, and build on them by using creativity and play to make the therapeutic activities enjoyable for the children. The Play Therapy Department offers consultation and advice to co-workers in the houses, in particular, and also to co-workers in classes, so that the therapeutic play programme can be extended into a child's daily programme. The sessions with the therapist are focused on monitoring and assessing progression, and advising when and how the next step should be introduced. Using therapeutic play on a daily basis:

— enables children to experience their bodies in time and
    space;
— helps them develop body awareness and self- image;
— facilitates their fuller engagement in their actions;

— makes them more conscious of their sense of their own well-
being;

— increases their social awareness of others in relation to themselves;

— stimulates their active interest and participation in the world;

— empowers them to master skills and actions necessary for
personal care, independence and interactive play with others.

Conclusion

Having worked in the School as a therapist for over twenty-five years
and having used a child-centred approach, I have had the privilege
of accompanying and witnessing the resilience and determination of
individual children, who have striven to achieve their potential. This
process of 'actualization' is vital as children identify with, and accept,
their destiny, resolve their inner questions and become empowered to
realize their unique identity. The core conditions of child-centred or
person-centred therapy, as developed by Rogers (1994), are attuned to
the anthroposophical aspects of curative education and social therapy.
The recognition of the 'image of the human being' lies in both. The
importance of the therapist or adult seeking to transform themselves as
a first step to helping others is central to both approaches. By providing
the optimum conditions for the individual to develop, and by working at
their own pace with the therapist and curative educator supporting and
recognizing their needs, the individual can become who they truly are,
not just conform to what others may wish them to be.

6. Music Therapy

COLIN TANSER

If you walked down the corridor through the heart of a Camphill School, you might hear the sound of several lyres playing together. As you came closer, you would see a group of players, perhaps being watched by young people walking past and pausing to sit down and listen. The department study sessions always start like this — a practical working together, which can lead to confidence and sensitivity when playing for the children. The team have a fundamental knowledge of the principles of curative education, and give the feeling of individually 'pulling in the same direction.' Equally, they can relate to a wider multi-disciplinary group, both in the sharing of knowledge and in a practical working together. The therapy comes from an approach which has grown out of the actuality of its unique circumstances and general philosophy, rather than making a direct copy of existing therapy schools, training or methods.

Many Camphill Schools benefit from beautiful and peaceful surroundings, where children and adults share their lives in a friendly, family setting. There is a rich rhythmic cultural life, good healthy food and excellent living conditions. Exposure to powerful sensory distractions — for example, TV or overloud recorded music — is limited to help minimize stress and promote peace. Against this background, music therapy is practised with both individual children and groups. The environment gives a surrounding warmth. Here, we are not battling with abrasive noises or an oppressive and dominating popular culture. Instead, the child's listening can incorporate a sensitivity to softness and a caring for quietness — which then can allow a building outwards towards more forceful sounds, if needed. In such a place, one can facilitate the growth of healing.

Working within a Camphill community, it is easy to set up a structure of formal meetings around the children, but in addition, informal meetings happen all the time. Keeping in touch in this way is extremely useful. Some children might attend the School for a limited time and this experience could have a profound effect on their lives. Others will be there for longer, perhaps even ten years or more. This gives a unique opportunity to observe and review the effects of music on the child's life.

Music as therapy is a specialized use of this medium for those with special needs. The child's day might start with their own individually composed 'Wake up!' music, sung or played on a recorder:

Or, more gently:

Of course, more general waking music may be used for a group of children.

A musical day will then follow: morning songs, assembly, grace before meals, seasonal songs, classroom music, social songs and dance and special occasions. At the end of the day, moving towards sleep, the child might hear the peaceful lilt of the lyre:

Colin Tanser

It can be seen that music as therapy must therefore exist within a wide area, taking into account the whole musical life in the School. The lyre players in the corridor are part of this.

However, a distinction can be made between 'music as therapy' and 'music therapy,' which is prescribed specifically for an individual child by the school doctor, to address a particular disturbance or imbalance with instruments and voice. Here the dynamics of music — melody, pitch, intervals, rhythm, beat, harmony and tonal quality — combine to work in particular ways; the task of the music practitioner being to compose, design and improvise with, and for the child, in order to meet his or her perceived needs.

It can be seen that 'music in the corridor' has many benefits. The music practitioners go to great lengths and infinite pains to perform well and to be conscious of what and how they are playing, because if music is to show a path of help for a child, the therapist must be there to support and show the way. Ongoing practice is needed to bring order to a child's dis-order (or even chaos). The students must be confident and secure within themselves. Emotions are expressed musically, but in a controlled and contained manner that brings order. They learn to initiate but also to hold back with patience, being sensitive to the other person, supporting and trusting, where needed.

As we go on to describe instruments, facilities, examples and strategies, it must be remembered that any situation will depend on who is working at that time, and on the different and individual natures of the children.

Lyre therapy: the search for peace

CASE STUDY

Into the Music Room comes a small, disturbed boy. He is cross; half crying and half shouting. It is his first visit and he does not know why he is there. He makes as much noise as he can. Suddenly, into the tonal arena, come three slow dignified chords from the lyre. The boy abruptly stops and listens before continuing in a much more subdued manner. The lyre music changes and becomes a predictable, lilting melody, which continues and expands for some minutes. He is now completely quiet and absorbed within the music. He sits listening intently, waiting for what will happen next ...

In an age of sound beams, electronic keyboards and increasing sophistication of all things musical, the central therapeutic position is held by a contemporary form of an instrument, more associated with mythology and ancient history, rather than present-day reality.

Yet, throughout the Camphill Movement, the lyre is frequently heard and recognized. A typical instrument might carry forty or more steel strings, closely strung across a large slender sound box. The strings are placed on separate levels and are played with a special technique using an upright position of the fingers of both hands.

There are many reasons for the lyre's use and popularity. When properly played, the sound quality of the lyre provides a healthy image

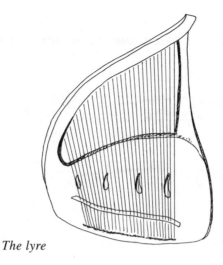

The lyre

of life. There is the instant birth of the sound — not accompanied by a 'knock' or 'click' as can happen with the piano or harp. This is followed by a growth to a swelling tone, which can best be described as a combination of clarity and warmth. This tone is sustained towards a gradual fading, which draws in the attention of the listener. In addition, the lyre has a mercurial ability to adapt to a changing response. It does not intrude but leaves the listener free. This makes it an ideal instrument for improvisation and musical conversation when working with children. They find they can move towards the lyre without fear of being suppressed or dominated.

It is a well-known curative educational principle that in the case of an obsessional child repetition of simple instructions given a little more quietly each time can help them to 'let go' and make changes. The lyre is one of the few instruments that allow the player the possibility of a 'diminuendo' towards near silence. In a similar manner, where this behaviour becomes manifest as a musical fixation; for example, the repetition by the child of a tight pattern of notes or rhythm, the lyre player, ever more quietly, can loosen and make fluid the child's response.

How does the music practitioner prepare for a day's work? One answer lies in what otherwise might be seen as a fundamental difficulty with the instrument — tuning! Every day and throughout the day, the lyre must be kept 'fine tuned.' This is achieved without rushing, before a session has begun. This in turn nurtures receptive listening and concentration, an inner peace which lights up the session. The musician must prepare by being outwardly, then inwardly in tune.

Looking through the window: facilities and instruments

What shall we sing a-bout to - day, Pe-ter?

What shall we sing a - bout to - day?

CASE STUDY

Looking out through the large bay window of the Therapy Room, Peter can see a wide expanse of sky and tall trees surrounding a meadow with grazing cattle. He slides his finger across the strings of a small chordally-tuned hand lyre as he chooses the next subject of our song.

Look ... look at that bird!

There's a bird in the tree and he's look-ing at me.

Younger children, looking at the same view, can sometimes launch into their song with even greater ease, showing refreshing individuality.

This is a shortened transcript of a spontaneous song from a seven-year-old girl. She had extreme atopic eczema — the room had to be kept cool, and she was aware of the ever-changing weather:

> We don't care if it's raining
> We have our own umbrellas
> We can go out in the puddles
> Splash, splash, splash, splash
> Go in the puddles
> We are the ones today

Now the sun shines bright
And the birds and the butterflies
Are out in the air
It's a little bit windy
But we really don't care
Because we've got a coat
And are covered in
Our ... clothes.

The room is friendly. It is well carpeted and quiet. Curtains at the window end, give a sense of being held even though the area itself is fairly large. It does not have the appearance of a music shop display because instruments are brought in (and removed) as needed. This pleasant environment reflects the School's policy of providing the healthiest surroundings for the growth of body, mind, soul and spirit.

'Home is where the heart is' — but the heart of music can create its own home — wherever that might be. The corridors have already been mentioned and many large or small rooms might be appropriate for different children or circumstances.

CASE STUDY

At one time in her life, a girl of school leaving age was finding it extremely difficult to stay in any schoolroom. She needed space to be by herself for a time, and had a special retreat outside in the grounds where she could sit down. The corridor group then played outside and were gradually able to approach her. Not only did she tentatively join in the therapeutic activities (formerly performed in the music room), but some hours after the session — and in calmer mood — she made a special point of thanking everyone. Musically 'dissonant,' the girl sitting alone outside had moved towards an acceptable 'harmony.' The music triad of melody — harmony — rhythm places this movement and relationship between tones, which strongly affect and reflect our feelings, right in the centre.

Stringed instruments work well in the area of moods and feelings, comfort and security. For example, just as Beethoven in the second movement of his *Seventh Symphony,* or Chopin in his *E minor Prelude,*

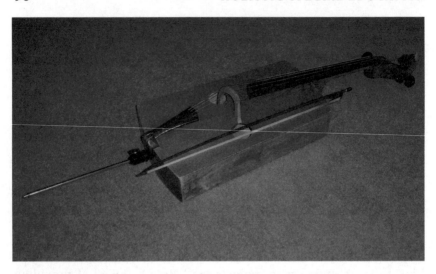

The tenor chrotta

achieve their effect by holding very static melodies against strong moving harmonies, so Tony, a boy with a noticeable tremor in his right hand, was able to sustain the bowing of an open string on a tenor chrotta. Not only was he able to improve the intentional control of his right arm, but his breathing became steady and he felt relaxed. Here, the motivation was the drawing in of the moving harmonies, played by the accompanying lyre.

The melodic aspect of the music triad is well served by wind instruments. Working therapeutically — flutes, pipes, trumpets, recorders, etc — are all awakening, memorable and conscious sound producers. Our youngest children respond particularly well to the music of pentatonic pipes. They can confidently follow the quiet, simple tones with their own movements, and later, sing easily-remembered melodies. Hand-made bamboo pipes with adjusted windways can produce the right tone and volume for children who are sensitive to sound. For those needing something more immediate and approachable, individually-tuned reed horns are easily played by the children themselves, and can facilitate a musical conversation. Most children who have difficulties in concentration, and who are easily distracted by sense impressions, can benefit from music with a strong melodic content. Melody helps to bring order into their chaotic thought life.

Nowadays, the rhythmic aspect of the music triad can so easily move towards mechanical beat and pulse. Consequently, our percussion instruments tend to be lightweight and not too loud. Both large and small glockenspiels are ideal for improvisation and musical conversation. Chime bars are highly manoeuvrable and special mention should be made of 'Choroi hand chimes,' where the way the instrument is held and moved affects the tone to the extreme that it is even possible to increase the sound after it has been initially played.

Percussion instruments work with the will. The child can be helped to be less 'wilful' and more able to engage in meaningful activity. Imagine a group of lively seven-year-olds first thing in the morning. They are running and playing in a small hall to the sound of a trilling triangle. Suddenly, it stops — and so do they. A circle is formed and a gong or large bell signals one step to be taken backwards. This is followed by more triangle running — shorter this time and two gongs. The instruments alternate until the stepping backwards overrides the running. The children can then sit down quietly. They now experience harmony from the strings of the lyre. Finally, the pentatonic pipe plays. The children are now able to concentrate. They follow the pitch of the melody with meaningful hand movements.

To conclude this section, mention will be made of the use of the piano and electronics in therapy. The strength of the piano is that melody, harmony and rhythm are integrated, giving a picture of the whole human being in one instrument:

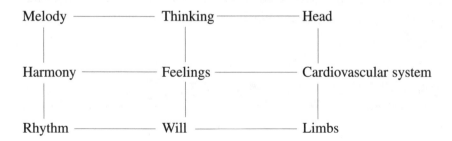

The volume of sound (for therapy sessions the piano is muted with strips of felt) and the initial knock of the action make it a difficult instrument to use with some sensitive children. However, some older pupils enjoy the feeling of power and dexterity and are able to manage the abstract layout of the keyboard. Electronic instruments and amplification are not helpful in therapy sessions because they move away from real, living sounds produced by human beings and acoustic instruments and can bring a false sense of intimacy. Instead the therapeutic aim is to increase the quality of listening, just like looking through a window into a darkened room, it takes a little while to adjust fully.

Examples and strategies — therapies in harmony

CASE STUDY

Jane was a nervous, tense seven-year-old who was not yet settled into school life. Where could she run to? Musical sounds, if she could find them. She needed to be close to music. In her house she had been described as 'A baby bird fallen from its nest.' The Child Study Group hoped that music might provide security for future development. The first stage was to build a new nest. Screens and cushions were brought into one corner of the music room. This soon became her space for listening. The next stage was to encourage Jane's participation in a more active manner. She seemed to want to touch and play various small instruments but could not quite manage to do so. So, after a break, her new nest became a chair in the centre of the room, and her bird song was a tune played on what ultimately proved to be her favourite instrument — the pentatonic pipe. Meanwhile, she would enter the room, walk around the periphery and gradually spiral in to her chair.

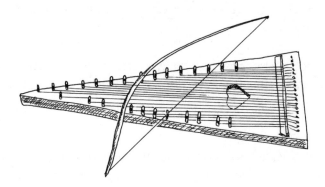

The psaltery

The clear thin tone of a bowed psaltery was then used to keep her attention fixed on short rhythmic variations:

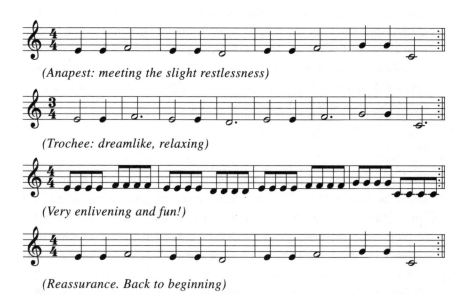

(Anapest: meeting the slight restlessness)

(Trochee: dreamlike, relaxing)

(Very enlivening and fun!)

(Reassurance. Back to beginning)

These were accompanied by the guitar, which carefully led to her 'Magic Bag' song (see next page).

At the conclusion, Jane would reach into the bag and draw out a small hand-held instrument. As the sessions progressed, she gained in confidence. There was always a song or activity ready for whatever came out of the bag.

Jane did not speak but was able to produce a beautiful, almost operatic vocalizing vibrato — seemingly at random. It was interesting to observe that she could create a similar sound quality by means of rapidly tapping the strings of a chordally-tuned hand lyre. The culmination of this block of sessions, however, was when after many, many attempts she managed to blow a note on her favourite instrument — the pentatonic pipe. She was so pleased! As a teenager, some of these activities lost their appeal. She would still run towards musical sounds. She loved to stand next to the accordion in Folk Dancing sessions or move right into the midst of a Pipe Band on Open Day. Jane enjoyed classical piano music and could contribute a bass note dialogue with simple melodies. Her vocalizing came more into tune with surrounding sounds and she was now able to share her musicality with those around her.

CASE STUDY

One of her fellow pupils was Neil. He also listened out for the sound of music but unlike Jane would not move towards it. His eyesight seemed very limited and his movement was slow and lacking in intent, his posture being loose and heavy. When he was seated however he tended towards restlessness. The school doctor and Child Study Group felt it was important that he should come into himself and gain an upright posture. Musically, there was the idea of him reaching up to the top of a tower to ring a bell (the tower being a human bell-holder). His stick was specially padded to suit his grip. Even though his bell was shiny and polished, the 'tower' had to meet the stick rather than the other way round. But things improved! A song was sung to help with the timing:

Bell Song

    As Neil progressed, the tower grew taller, eventually having to stand on a chair. Neil's sense of humour sometimes caused him to play bells in many unusual directions but he managed very well. When he walked around the school, he co-ordinated his voice and each step to a 'short-long-short rhythm.' Musically close to this is the Sarabande and this dance played at his side could certainly improve his mobility:

Sarabande

Once in the therapy room, Neil was fitted out with Morris Dancer's bells and encouraged to step on to a hollow platform holding light percussion instruments. As his feet knocked against the wood, improvised music would follow with Neil feeling a real part of the process.

At this time, working to improve his impaired vision, the art therapist had made use of the colour red. She now wanted to move him towards a peaceful blue. She suggested that we should stop banging things!

Musically we were able to follow and reinforce this move. All percussion was stopped and Neil was shown how to draw a bow across the strings of a tenor chrotta in a slow breathing movement, which was close to that required for gently painting blue across the paper:

Draw the bow   Let if flow   Through the sky   in Blue we go

We now aimed to further improve Neil's movement around the school. The Sarabande (see above) had begun to move too easily against his own rhythm. We developed 'The Season of Mars.' Its thirty bars were phrased irregularly (5-6-4 4-5-6) to keep him 'on his toes.' Upward phrases were in C major, whilst downward phrases were lowered by four flats:

Open 5th
* Chord of C

Season of Mars

Part 2

Round and   round the   seas - ons   turn - ing,

Spring will   rise from   ic - y   Win - ter's   ir - on   hold.

Then comes Sum - mer   and the   Fall,   Then comes Sum - mer

and the   Fall.   Round and   round the   seas - ons   turn - ing,

Spring will   rise from   ic - y   Win - ter's   ir - on   hold.

This contrast of tonality gave him energy especially when sung as a two-part canon. Neil would smile and step forward with enthusiasm. The art therapist used back projected slides of Raphael's Madonna images to reinforce the colour mood and Neil started working with yellow.

Musically, this was taken as a bright and instant quality. The moment he shook small bells, a cluster of notes followed on a hand lyre and we sang 'Yellow, yellow, yellow'!

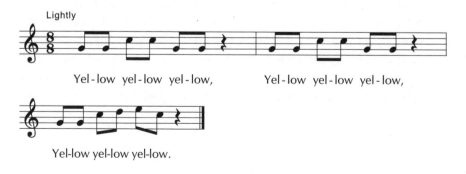

Lightly

Yel - low yel - low yel - low,   Yel - low yel - low yel - low,

Yel - low yel - low yel - low.

We now created a sound/colour form:

> Red   percussion
> Blue   sustained bowing
> Yellow   instant bells and lyres

This could be used actively or passively by Neil. It developed further. For example, 'Green' was created as a combination of blue and yellow in both sound and sight and then supported vocally. With his increasing awareness of colour and sound, Neil was ready to join Jane in attending a Colour Light (or Colour Shadow) Treatment group. The music therapy room was specially designed for this having large bay windows into which were fitted coloured 'gels.' By careful shading and placement of these, 'coloured light' is projected onto a large screen.

Standing between the light source and the screen, any movement is displayed on the screen as a coloured shadow. The process is difficult to describe but the effect is like painting with flowing watercolours. It can look both beautiful and dramatic. The colours come alive and are no more fixed than the weather. The overall design is overseen by the art therapist. The movement behind the screen, although not eurythmy as such, can certainly benefit from the skills of a eurythmist. It is brought together with specially composed sound and music played behind the pupils who are sitting by candlelight in the darkened room. A programme is designed with the individual children or groups in mind, using music, speech, colour and movement. One has to be careful not to 'overload' the pupil's sensory experiences but to harmonize them.

Jane and Neil come into the therapy room. They have been attending together on a twice-weekly basis just before the end of the school morning. They sit quietly facing the screen. Just before the lyre begins to play, Jane clearly sings the first tone. How does she manage to do this? She continues throughout the session with spontaneous and unpredictable harmonies, whilst gazing at the screen. Neil is also absorbed in the moving colours. He yawns, relaxed but attentive. It will be the end of a good morning at school. There is a sense of harmony and community in the room. All of us are part of this healthy, healing process, which in itself reflects the wider scope of life and work in the environment of Camphill.

7. Art Therapy

JENNIE TANSER

Artistic expression is something that transcends the need for language, and is a direct expression of the soul of the creator, coloured by his cultural upbringing and his own personality. It goes further, however, for lying behind the observable physical phenomena, there is an additional dimension — the realm of the spiritual. Art as therapy makes no distinction between a child with special needs and a child whose development is unhindered by learning difficulties. Through a deep love for the individuality of the child, the therapist aims to help and support him by acknowledging the uniqueness of his being and giving him the courage to discover meaning to his life and fulfil his destiny. Through the artistic therapeutic process illness and trauma can be addressed indirectly, by means of a gentle working rather than fully confronted, thus connecting with the inner imbalances, confusions and disturbances of the human soul.

In helping to support the child to discover and nourish his inner development, it is important to distinguish between interference and intervention, allowing the individual to progress towards making a connection with his own healthy healing forces, so that these can grow and develop, and enable the attainment of a degree of inner independence which allows him to trust in life itself.

Since primarily art therapy addresses the individuality of the child, it is clear that there is no overall methodology. Each series of exercises, which are created for the particular child and his condition, have their artistic basis in the fundamental laws of colour and form. It is important, therefore, to work with a clear understanding of one's aims, which are based on the diagnosis given by the doctor. This provides the 'illness picture' and careful observations of the child's habits and dispositions, with respect to his life experiences. The relationship of the therapist to the child is of the greatest importance, and even the best devised exercises have no meaning without a warm and caring attitude towards the child.

Anthroposophical art therapy developed from the work of Margarethe Hauschka, a medical doctor, who was inspired by indications of the potential of painting for therapy, which had originated from consultation sessions held by Ita Wegman and Rudolf Steiner. This work began in Boll in Germany and was later developed in Britain where a training in art therapy was offered by Vera Taberner, a pupil of Margarethe Hauschka in 1963. Art therapy is therefore based on the philosophy and ideology of Rudolf Steiner.

The therapist does not analyse the child's painting in an intellectual sense but looks for certain artistic phenomena. How has the colour been used — is it strong and dense or weak and pale? How is form manifested, and in what manner has the child built up the painting? Answers to these questions allow the therapist to come to a diagnostic picture, which then provides a clue as how best to proceed with the therapeutic process, which aims to help the child develop his own initiative and move towards an inner equilibrium to aid the realization of his full potential.

Engaging in art therapy is not just an opportunity for self-expression in the sense of simply making manifest one's subjective feelings. It allows the child to move towards truths which lie beyond the personality, and are expressions of one's true inner self. It involves the lifelong search for an answer to that most elusive and complex question, 'Who am I?'

In this process the child is encouraged to move at his own pace, within the parameters of his own soul capacities. In the therapeutic process there is no expectation that the child will possess an 'artistic talent.' As far as the results of the exercises are concerned the therapist is always looking for the *potential* in the painting, for this can lead to the next exercise to support his further development. It is important to place the emphasis on what the child is able to achieve and to recognize any hint of change. If we miss these indications we lose the opportunity, which the child is offering us to guide the process forward. The soul is never static and our thinking, feelings and how we translate these inner perceptions into practice are always changing. A child is constantly in the process of 'becoming.'

The key question is how to find the right therapeutic task. With a child there are often many issues to be addressed. First, a simple beginning must be made before it becomes clear which direction to take. Only when a working trust has been established can the therapist gently 'challenge' the child in order to see whether he can begin to use his own initiative more freely. Naturally, this is only possible if the child's interest has been caught so that he engages his own ego in the process and finds the art work pleasurable. The therapy may extend over several weeks, and sometimes blocks of sessions may continue over a period of months with intervals of time in between.

One of the first things to address is any disturbance in the child's breathing pattern which very often is out of balance. There are many ways to do this. One of the most helpful for the child is to endeavour to establish a rhythmical brushstroke. The paper is made damp and the brush is drawn across the paper in a slow, one-directional, rhythmical movement: the gesture is initiated from the movement of the arm rather than the wrist so that the chest expands and the breathing is regulated.

Working on damp paper with the fluidity of the water element gives the greatest chance for the colour to be moved around freely providing an infinite variety of possibilities for expression. Colour itself has an intrinsic healing power and working with the laws of colours in the spectrum gives a strong basis for therapeutic work. William Wordsworth expressed this beautifully in the words: 'My heart leaps up when I behold a rainbow in the sky ...'

Our heart, the centre of our being, is moved by the natural harmony of colour in its purest form, so that when the child paints the rainbow colours he receives an echo of spiritual truths. For some children it is sufficient to create colour moods, whereas others are able to develop motifs emerging from the colour. All emotions have their own echo in the natural world — the energy of the wind, the surge of the tides, the lifting of the light at sunrise. Consequently, in working artistically with these changing elements and rhythms of the year, the child begins to feel a greater connection to the world in which he is striving to find his place. Working on dry paper and adding translucent layers of colour gives a further dimension, which offers the possibility for older children to develop their faculties of judgment, discernment and discrimination, thus strengthening the ego. This way of working is referred to as veil painting because it involves building up many layers of colour, which give the impression of superimposed coloured veils.

There are various ways in which drawing can be applied: *observational drawing* can help the child make a deep connection with his environment: *charcoal drawing* enables the young person to evaluate his world with all its elements of light and darkness of feeling and the grey tones that lie in between: and, *form drawing* which deals with strong linear expressions of right and left, up and down. The striving towards balance not only concentrates and focuses the mind but also heightens an awareness of spatial orientation and rhythmical movement.

Therapeutic use of working with clay encourages the child to strengthen and regenerate his will forces through modelling; working directly with an element taken from the earth itself. This gives a grounding and steadying support because the child must use both his hands, enabling him to develop his formative forces in creating a form of three dimensions.

The whole theme of working with children of any age is that of building up and encouraging self-esteem. However, a distinction should be made between working with younger and older children. It is obvious that the nature of the artistic exercises will be different depending on the ages of the children. For example, a young child should first of all paint with the purity of primary colours only then move towards secondary colours, and later incorporate the dynamic effect of complementary colours. As he comes into the teenage years he moves from colour to work with black and white, and later returns to colour again. Whilst there is a connection here with the Waldorf curriculum, one may deviate from these guidelines with art therapy according to the needs of the individual child.

With very young children one can begin to help them develop a sense of responsibility, albeit unconsciously at first, for their own life and destiny. Their receptivity to colour is more acute than that of adults for it is not 'dis-coloured' by intellectual or analytical perceptions. Therefore, the therapeutic effect of the colour itself is extremely powerful and can through its direct experience fulfil a deep soul need. The activity of painting is usually a great joy for the child, since when he is young he is entirely unselfconscious. He is not so caught up with the need to have a finished painting: indeed he often delights more in the changing colour of the water as the paint has that magical effect.

However, as a child grows into puberty and discrimination begins to develop, self-consciousness shifts the emphasis from the activity of painting towards the need of the young person to achieve an end result, so that he can give the painting the stamp of his identity and be recognized as its creator. This change comes about when the older child becomes more aware of the difference between his developing inner life of attitudes, feelings and the impressions, which are coming towards him from outside. A process of separation occurs, which can throw him out of balance and it is here that therapy can provide a steady and strong support. To strengthen that centre allows the young person to rise above a handicap, which can often be hard to bear. For a child who finds difficulty in expressing himself through the spoken word, working with colour, images and forms gives release to his feelings. Working with colour also loosens or activates the soul so that areas of unconscious feelings may be touched which require great sensitivity on the part of the therapist.

SAM

Sam was twelve years old, very sensitive with a strong tendency towards hysterical behaviour. All external influences affected him deeply, resulting in feelings of inner chaos, since he lacked the ability to discriminate and so protect himself. Consequently he easily became overwhelmed, both in his thinking and emotional responses. He had been a deprived child in his very early years, lacking any real loving care and had been subjected to physical abuse. He later developed strong behavioural difficulties where he displayed aggressive behaviour, which resulted in peer group problems. One aspect, which I decided to work on, related to the fact that he always needed more and better material goods than anyone else. For example, his bike had to have more gears than anyone else's bike!

He loved stories and would listen eagerly with wide eyes, sucking his thumb just like a small child, and as a story progressed it was evident that he had entered into the story with his whole being. He would straighten up in his seat when the hero had to combat danger, for Sam had become the hero himself. Taking the lead from this reaction to story-telling I decided to use a story in a pedagogical sense. I wanted to tackle his overwhelming need to have the best of everything because of course he would never be satisfied and would remain frustrated. I chose the Brothers Grimm story of *The Fisherman and his Wife,* where the wife wishes first of all for a cottage then demands ever more grand dwelling places, until eventually she ends up in her hovel again.

The other aspect I wanted to address was Sam's lack of self-discipline, which led him into trouble. Each painting he undertook had the same elements: sky, hill, sea and the magic fish. Because of his constitution Sam found this repetition hard to tolerate, but as the sessions went by he began to resist less. 'Do I have to do the hill again?' became 'What colour shall I paint the fish this time?' The sessions lasted several weeks and when the story finished we looked together at all the paintings that had been laid out on the floor. Sam was amazed that he had achieved so many fine paintings and was able to point to each episode and tell me the relevant story. It was three weeks before his birthday and he told me that he wanted all the Game Boy toys available in the shops because he needed them all. When I didn't respond to this, he looked at me doubtfully and said: 'Well, maybe I only need six!'

The next series of sessions came when Sam was almost fourteen and was entering the phase of puberty when further confusions heightened his already troubled constitution. At this stage a fairy tale would not have been suitable, although he did still ask for a story. I chose the Native American myth about 'Scarface' where an orphan boy is subjected to taunting and a lack of understanding from his peers, but when the orphan boy overpowers his first bear he is shown respect and treated as a hero. Interestingly, Sam identified with the bear and he filled most of his painting with the bear standing on his hind legs towering above 'Scarface.' At this time Sam was also having eurythmy as he often walked with the gait of the self-conscious adolescent with toes turned inward. This was how the bear, the hunted one, was also pictured. The story of 'Scarface' deals with issues of rejection and courage and follows the journey the young man must take and the great trials and confrontations he must undergo, before finally winning through, after having been courageous and true to himself. Here is an example of how a young person, like Sam, can be reached without direct confrontation from a figure of authority, a situation which often provokes extreme reaction during adolescence.

The last time I worked with Sam was when he was sixteen. He was deeply resistant to all approaches, everything was either tedious or boring and he felt misunderstood by everyone and this was causing him particular pain. I felt it was time for him to focus on something scientific, which might lead him to deal with his unharnessed emotional issues. Observation of spectrum colours through a prism caught Sam's interest and he was amazed by the brilliance of the colours particularly where they revealed themselves between light and darkness, but painting these colours was another matter. Painting was now boring. I tried introducing him to form drawing linking it initially to certain linear designs on one of his CD covers. During this time Sam would come into the therapy room and immediately sink into a comfortable chair with an exaggerated sigh. All effort was just too much and motivation was at a very low ebb. However, dynamic form drawing, which seeks to focus the artist's concentration and works on a logical basis, had enough novelty to it for several sessions that for a while he made good progress, despite his initial boredom.

Then one day Sam announced: 'Jennie this art therapy is ruining my life!' Teenage drama was at its height now. I felt that to finish the therapy at this point would not be helpful so I decided to round it off in a positive way. I found a picture of a piece of sculpture — a man sitting still and dignified and looking out far into the distance. I thought that this might resonate somewhere with Sam in the midst of all his reactionary turbulence.

We copied this figure in clay and I worked with him because I felt a lack of self-motivation was a strong factor at this point. It was not an easy process because there was still the proffered resistance, but I felt it worthwhile to continue because now and again, without knowing it, Sam showed his engagement with the process by spontaneously standing back to view the figure and saying 'Oh, it's beginning to look quite good.' However, this remark was quickly followed by 'Oh, it's so boring.' The figure was eventually finished and Sam wanted to show it to his houseparents, but at the last minute his natural feelings of creativity and pleasure of achievement were overtaken by a negative reaction which sadly did not allow him to show it to his houseparents. But underneath I felt he had touched his truer feelings, which were at that time swamped by his genuine struggle toward self-identification.

BEN

Sometimes an integrated multi-therapeutic approach is required when it is evident that no single approach is enough to help a child in a severe crisis situation. Ben's crisis manifested itself in disturbing behaviour of an aggressive and sexual nature. Approaching adolescence was clearly causing him to struggle to find his way through this new phase of life. Medical staff including a clinical psychologist, houseparents and co-workers, a counsellor, plus various therapists all worked with him, and at that time he was under constant supervision. This group 'effort' was put in place for a year with art therapy sessions offered twice a week.

The first exploratory drawings, where he was encouraged to draw pictures of his immediate surroundings, clearly indicated the driven nature of misplaced sexuality, which was eventually diagnosed as 'unsocialized conduct disorder.' Added to this were complications arising from the fact that he had foetal alcohol syndrome, which can promote a premature awakening of sexual drives. His self-esteem was very low and at times he felt himself to be worthless. His next drawings related to his family. His parents adopted him when he was 2³/₄ years

old and had always been extremely supportive of their son through tre-
mendously difficult times. When portraying his older brother, sibling
rivalry was clearly indicated.

Initially, what I decided to address was his self-preoccupation, where
he had tied himself in knots through confusion and anxiety and now
seemed trapped. The aim was to see if through precise objective observation of the phenomena of the natural world it might be possible to
counterbalance his over-emotional behaviour, and build up his centre
and inner strength. The procedure involved inviting him to look at the
open view from the wide therapy room window when he arrived, and
then before leaving to say what had changed. In this way he gradually
developed a real interest in what was outside himself, which was both
beautiful and true. The painting exercises linked to this approach also
required exact observation so that his whole focus was directed towards
an objective perception of natural phenomena.

This was followed by colour experiments, which required a scientific
approach rather than any expression of subjective feeling, which might
perhaps have led back to his initial drawings of his pathology. Gradually
he became more confident and so we moved on to veil painting. He
found this difficult to begin with, for this was another threshold to be
crossed. This phase covered the last six months of the year and it was
impressive to observe how he was more and more able to make his own
decisions and judgments, and was able to respect his own perceptions in
this complex and more thoughtful, meditative and concentrated form of
painting. Each painting took several weeks to complete and so required
the discipline of continuity and application. It was important for his
own feelings of self-worth that he wanted to frame his paintings for his
parents. Thus, for Ben it had been quite a tough year when he had had
to face himself and all his difficulties in new and challenging ways. He
eventually left school a more balanced and responsible young man.

Conclusion

These are just two examples of how a child can be supported through
an artistic therapeutic process. The guided exercises have a flexibility
which provides a secure route along a path which the child travels
with the therapist. *The artistic process in itself is the healing element*
— slowly progressing and changing in direct response to the child's

needs. Art therapy for the growing child helps provide a positive future direction in which the artistic activity brings harmony to that which has become habitually unbalanced and one-sided, transforming uncertainties and awakening new faculties of imagination. I believe that the arts will come to play an increasing therapeutic role as our society moves towards a deeper understanding of those qualities, which must be developed to allow people to become truly human. To be creative in a healthy way is for the child to confirm and verify his sense of self and to be able to say: *To be creative is to be myself.*

8. Therapeutic Speech

DONALD PHILLIPS

What is therapeutic speech?

A person can reveal their state of wellness or illness by speaking. It can be heard in the way sounds are spoken, how the breath is used and how sentences are constructed, and since movement is integral to speaking, movement and stance also reveal a person's state of health. However, health can also be positively affected by engaging consciously and artistically in the speaking process (Denjean-von Stryk & von Bonin 2003). Speech, therefore, has the dual nature of revealer and healer, and therapeutic speech seeks to exploit this fact for beneficial outcomes.

Therapeutic speech is an artistic therapy for both speaking and non-speaking children and adults, based on the anthroposophical view of the human being. It uses as its artistic media the sounds of speech, voice, speech rhythms, movement and breath. It originates from creative speech, an art of speech based on the ancient art of recitation and drama which was renewed and then fundamentally redeveloped in the early twentieth century by Rudolf Steiner and Marie Steiner-von Sivers, an accomplished actress of the Russian and French stage (Douch 2004).

Many speech exercises used in therapeutic speech today were first used in 1919 in the first Waldorf School. The exercises were developed to help teachers overcome deficiencies in their own speech, aid their stamina for classroom teaching and help children in their overall development. These and other exercises were further developed for use by actors. In the early 1930s Martha Hemsoth (1887–1936), a singer by training who had also completed creative speech training, began applying creative speech principles in the clinical setting, in co-operation with Dr Ita Wegman. However, their promising and potent collaboration did not last long, as Hemsoth died as the result of a tragic accident. For many years this put an end to the development of therapeutic speech in the clinical setting . In the succeeding years, therapeutic speech has been able to thrive and develop wherever there is co-operation between physician and therapist. This is especially true in the curative education and social therapy arena where the need for therapeutic speech is more obvious. (Denjean-von Stryk & von Bonin 2003)

What are the principles upon which therapeutic speech is based?

Therapeutic speech is unique in its approach to health care combining as it does the principles of creative speech with the principles of anthroposophical medicine, child development, Waldorf education, general anthroposophy and general science. A person engaging in creative speech not only works with elements such as rhythm, effective breath and voice use, sound quality and text content but also develops an awareness and control over gesture and movement, much like an actor would do. By fine-tuning the speaking 'instrument,' poetry, with its subtle nuances and dramatic text, comes alive and the speaker is able to grasp and express the finer aspects of poetic imagery and literature. In this way the speaker strives to achieve beautiful speech by finding their own 'true' voice with which they feel at home.

The same elements, which are cultivated in the artistic process, are transformed for use in the therapeutic process, the only difference being that they are directed to the individual speaking rather than an audience. When we take a closer look at what occurs when speaking we see the meeting of two dynamic systems within the human being: the nerve-sense system and metabolic system. The metabolic, with its warmth and will nature, rises into the circulatory processes, while the cooling and thought nature of the nerve-sense system streams downwards into the breathing (Phillips 2001). These two systems meet in the rhythmic system of circulation and breathing where the speech process seeks to bring balance. While they have a reciprocal relationship, one system can be more active than the other at different times. For instance, some words incline towards thinking, while some tend more towards the will. In every sentence there is a continuous alternation; however, there must be a striving for balance and this is the key to therapy (Lorenz-Poschmann 1982).

WORKING WITH RHYTHMS

One way to strike this balance is by working with rhythms. All rhythms are comprised of a combination of long parts (—) and short parts (˘).

Rhythms can be grouped into falling or rising rhythms: falling rhythms begin with a long part and bring a cooling and relaxing effect, while rising rhythms begin with a short part and warm and invigorate. Examples include the trochee (— ˘) and dactyl rhythms (— ˘ ˘), which are falling, and the iambic (˘ —) and anapaest rhythms (˘ ˘ —), which are rising.

Many rhythms used in therapeutic speech are harmonious in their structure and some are specific in their application, such as the amphibracus rhythm (˘ — ˘) and hexameter verse for cardiac disorders. The hexameter is especially harmonious and was developed significantly in ancient Greece. The great orator, Homer, is said to have spoken or sung all his great epics, such as *The Odyssey* and *Iliad,* in hexameter verse. A line of hexameter has a structure of six dactyl metres or feet (one dactyl metre is comprised of one long part and two short parts), plus two metres given over to inhalation (one at the beginning of each line and one in the middle at the caesura). This creates eight metres of dactyl per line, including the two breaths, and gives a 4:1 ratio of pulse to breath. This 4:1 ratio is considered the most harmonious relationship between pulse rate and breathing rate.

— ˘ ˘ — ˘ ˘ — ˘ ˘ — ˘ ˘ — ˘ ˘ — ˘

// These were the words of the king, // and the old man feared and obeyed him;
// Voiceless he went by the shore // of the great dull echoing ocean.
// Thither he gat him apart, // that ancient man, and a long prayer,
// Prayed to Apollo his lord, // son of gold-ringleted Laito:
// 'Lord of the silver bow, // whose arms gird Krissy and Scila,
// Hurl on the Greeks they shafts, // that thy servant's tears be avenged.'
// So did he pray, and his prayers // reached the ears of Phoebus Apollo.

(From *The Iliad* by Homer)

— ˘ ˘ — ˘ ˘ — ˘ ˘ — ˘ ˘ — ˘ ˘ — ˘

// This is the forest primeval. // The murmuring pines and the hemlocks,
// Bearded with moss, and in garments // green, indistinct in the twilight,
// Stand like Druids of eld, // with voices sad and prophetic,
// Stand like harpers roar, // with beards that rest on their bosoms.
// Loud from its rocky cavern, // the deep voiced neighboring ocean
// Speaks, and in accents disconsolate // answers the wail of the forest.

(From *Evangeline* by H.D. Longfellow)

Recent scientific investigation has shown the hexameter verse positively influencing the synchronization of respiration and heart rate oscillations, while also affecting change in heart rate rhythmicity and cardiorespiratory co-ordination (Cysarz *et al.* 2004; Bettermann *et al.* 2002). As well as having a calming and cooling effect, the hexameter is also used to harmonize and strengthen rhythmical processes in humans (Cysarz *et al.* 2004).

Arhythmic verse, which uses stresses instead of rhythm, is also beneficial in many circumstances. The main style which is used is alliteration. Alliterative verse usually has four strong stresses in a line, with two to three being alliterative, where the same sound is repeated. Gripping the alliterative sound by speaking it strongly has an awakening quality and is especially helpful to children around the ages of nine to twelve years when they begin separating themselves from the world and become individuals in their own right (Steiner 1988).

                    v*   v
          They bore him out to the boundless ways,
                 v   v   v
          Schilding the Great, the giver of gifts.
                  v   v
          There at the shore standeth the ship,
           v   v   v
          Icebound and eager a wingéd arc.
                 v   v   v
          They laid him there, their beloved Lord,
           v   v   v
          Many there mourned him, Earls of might.
                 v   v
          They laid him there in the wave-stream's lap,
           v   v   v
          Birnies and blades on his bosom lay.

          (From *Beowulf*)

While speaking obviously involves the use of the breath, the correct use or misuse of the breath can largely determine a person's overall health. In a world of sensory over-stimulation people are forced to 'breathe in' many sense impressions in quick succession. There is little chance to digest what has been 'breathed in,' let alone 'breathe out' completely. This over-stimulates the nerve-sense system and illnesses such as panic/anxiety disorders, stress related disorders, cardiac disorders and breathing disorders can result.

* v = alliterative stress

Today, it is exhalation that is in need of development. The exhalation process, which engenders life forces within it, is connected with the metabolic system, and helps counter the deadening effects of the over-stimulation of the nerve-sense system. By developing exhalation, therapeutic speech seeks to bring the nerve-sense and metabolic systems into balanced correspondence. This is achieved by deepening or widening the breath and by speaking on the freed stream of breath. In this way the inhalation process is also trained to respond appropriately to outer stimuli with the result that the amount of inhalation is determined by the needs of the exhalation. The inhalation process is then freed from the chain of over-stimulation and can then develop to 'breathe in' pictures, ideas and inspirations in a healthy way. When therapeutic speech breath exercises are practised correctly people feel relaxed, revitalized and feel they can 'breathe again.'

CONSONANTS AND VOWELS

During speaking we also make extensive use of sounds, but in all speaking, it is single sounds that make up the words we speak. These can be differentiated into consonants and vowels. It can be argued that consonants have a connection with the structure of the outer environment, while the sounding vowels are more intimately connected with one's inner environment.

Consonants can be allocated to the elements of earth, fire, water or air. For instance, sounds which have an impact quality to them, such as **B, P, M, D, T, N, J, CH, G, NG** and **K,** are similar to the rocks, stones and earth on which we walk. In therapy, speaking them gives form, structure, strength and firm ground upon which to stand. Fire can be experienced in sounds which are blown, such as **W, F, V, S, Z, SH, TH, Y, CH** (as in loch) and **H.** Through the warmth of the exhaled breath these spoken sounds help warm what is cool and bring direction into life. The sound **L** has a liquid or wave-like quality. When spoken this sound brings the possibility for flow and movement in the liquid aspect of the body where there is sluggishness or stagnation. The airy sound **R,** when sounded with a trill, can establish movement in the breath, lifting heaviness into buoyancy. Thus, by speaking a particular consonant or using a consonant grouping, a healing effect can be achieved.

The consonants can be further grouped according to their area of articulation. A qualitative difference exists between the formation of the more sensitive lip sounds (**B M P W**), the clarity and directing quality of the dental sounds (**L N D T**) and the strength and warmth qualities of the palatal sounds (**G K H Y NG**). These three areas find their parallel with the spirit, soul and body, respectively. Between these three main articulation regions there are two others: the interplay between lip and upper teeth (**F V**) and tongue and teeth (**S Z SH**). Thus, therapeutic speech divides the speech organs into five distinct regions based on the reflection of the human being as a whole. In therapy the articulation regions are observed by the therapist as a means of diagnosis and are used to intervene in an illness by strengthening the appropriate region(s).

Vowels, on the other hand, are the vehicles through which the voice (soul) can express itself, through painting and by weaving colours between the forming consonants. Each vowel has a distinctive quality and soul mood, which carry the tone and melody of language. For instance, in the vowel **a** (as in *father*) the experience of wonder comes forth (Steiner 1959). In the **e** (as in *gate*) a crossing takes place, consolidating a boundary between world and self, while the sound **i** (as in *sheen*) shines clearest of all vowels and gives inner strength and light. Coming to the lips, the sound **o** (as in *gold*) gives the quality of astonishment or surprise and **u** (as in *true*) brings with it the ability to go through difficulty with one's whole being. The way a vowel is sounded can have a direct correlation to a disturbed organ. This aids the therapist in further understanding the condition of the patient and helps in diagnosis. Further, a division can be made with the vowels, separating them into light, pointed vowels (**e, i**) which are connected more with the nerves, and full, dark vowels (**a, o, u**), which are related to feeling and will. The main aim of any therapeutic treatment is to bring the vowels into proper flow and by so doing stimulate the life processes. Also, by training the vowels, the forces of the personality are strengthened and released (Denjean-von Stryk & von Bonin 2003).

How does therapeutic speech differ from speech and language therapy?

Therapeutic speech is holistically oriented, observing how speech reflects the human being as a whole. It also recognizes speech as a revelation of the inner human being. In general, the global picture is more important than the mere functional aspects of speech; however, by exercising the functional aspects the global picture is affected. For instance, by enhancing particular sounds or sound placements a change on a global level can be produced. Conversely, by executing certain movements or gestures while speaking, a functional change in one's speech development can be brought about. In many cases the root cause of a functional speech disorder is to be found in the imbalance between the two dynamic systems mentioned earlier. Illnesses of many types are exhibited through a person's speech and by exercising speech the forces which gave rise to the illness are brought back into a balanced dynamic relationship with the whole.

Speech development begins as early as prenatal life. The embryo hears the mother's speech, feels the heartbeat and breath rate. All speech development and capacity depends on learning to hear. Only through active hearing can one learn to speak (Steiner & Steiner 1978). Once the child is born obtaining nourishment is a chief activity: suckling is the first step in speech development. The lips and tongue are strengthened, toned and co-ordinated. All functional aspects of feeding are functional aspects of speech development and soon babbling ensues. When the baby learns to crawl and move about babbling gives way to more meaningful sounds, and the more precise motor co-ordination of lip and tongue. It is as if the baby is crawling through their speech organism. Upon standing upright and walking, the toddler is free to develop meaning-filled speech. The rhythmic system is now literally open to the world and the toddler begins the naming phase of speech and language development. Soon verbs and adjectives follow, phrases turn into small sentences and then sentences begin to tell stories. Speech itself has learned to walk and the child is off on their journey of discovery in life.

But what happens if any of these windows of opportunity are missed? There are ample opportunities for speech development to be side-lined. Dulled senses, genetic disorders and over-sensitivity to stimuli are some causes. As speech is a barometer for the overall development of the child, the child's speech is affected. In therapeutic speech the focus of any treatment includes addressing the developmental features, which the child has not fully mastered or has missed out completely. Treatment includes revisiting those missed developmental stages through activities, games, role play, movement and sounding in order to help seat the development of the child more firmly. Once these steps have been addressed the child is prepared and ready for direct speech intervention.

Therapeutic speech is important for children and young people because it works with the forces of speech development in aiding child development. As every child goes through similar stages of development and can slip into various stages at will through play, they readily accept and work with a therapeutic speech treatment programme. They experience it as fun, exciting, challenging and special, while their parents are happy that their child is being addressed as a whole individual.

What does therapeutic speech involve in practice?

Therapeutic speech treatment involves speaking individually-tailored sequences of specially developed speech and voice exercises, combined with movement and gestures. There are five groupings of exercises, each one giving a different therapeutic effect. Below is a listing of the five main exercise types and their effect.

Type of exercise	*Effect*
1. Articulation	Activates awareness of the speech organism
2. Breath	Deepens or widens the breath
3. Agility	Produces agile speech
4. Sentence formation	Warms and enlivens the metabolic processes
5. Vowel	Correctly places the voice

Poetry is spoken for its rhythm, breath use and content, and because it serves as a means of expressing emotions or describing the world. The two poetry styles, which are used frequently in therapeutic speech are recitation and declamation. In recitation, events or stories are re-cited. The great epics of Homer, Longfellow *(The Song of Hiawatha)* and Kingsley *(Andromeda)* are a few examples. Speaking recitation poetry is akin to painting a landscape picture: it is full of bountiful colours and yet is objective. The process of recitation encourages horizontal breathing and widens the breath, while at the same time giving a cooling and rhythmic effect to the speaker.

Declamation, on the other hand, expresses experiences and declaims one's feelings. Many people do not realize that most of modern pop music is written with declamatory lyrics. The most notable exponents were the Romantic poets — Blake, Keats, Shelley, Coleridge, Wordsworth — who often expressed their feelings about external events, and how they inwardly experienced them, through poetry. A person speaking this style of poetry develops richness in their life of feeling. They learn how to express 'feeling-pictures' with all the colours of their soul. Speaking in a declamatory fashion is similar to expressionist painting, which adheres to laws of form yet gives freedom of expression. Therapeutically, speaking declamatory poetry warms and invigorates, while deepening the breath and encouraging vertical breathing.

For non-speaking individuals, movement, gestures and rhythmic activities are central to treatment. As therapeutic speech follows the pathway of speech development, it recognizes the important first stages of non-verbal communication. Movement and gesture are thus incorporated to help the non-speaking person fully develop at this stage so they can progress to the next stage of meaningful sound production. This is characterized as the babbling phase, the playful sounding of speech accompanied by more meaningful gestures. At this stage animal sound imitation is important, as is sound imitation (onomatopoeia), which associates singular sounds or sound blends with everyday activity sounds (e.g., chopping vegetables, bubbling soup, cutting grass, chopping wood, etc.). Combining gesture and sound simultaneously helps develop greater co-ordination and consciousness, which in turn facilitates functional development in the speech organs.

Cognitive processes also develop when consciousness is enhanced, thus enabling the appropriate use of sounds and words for verbal communication. Rhythmically, the beat is established first, followed by rhythmic co-ordination during the course of various exercises. This enhances development significantly as it establishes boundaries between the person's inner and outer world and supports better breathing habits overall, thus reducing stress, anxiety and ill health. As speaking is a rhythmic activity, speech capacities often improve at this stage with the result that language development takes place. Nouns are usually the first words to be acquired in language development, followed by verbs and then adjectives. Phrasing follows from single words, after which short simple sentences are constructed. These sentences grow to eventually colour in the fullness of life.

STEVEN

Steven is now a sixteen-year-old boy with an autistic spectrum disorder. He is tall, thin and possesses a large head. I first began seeing Steven when he was twelve years old and he gave the impression of not being in control of his arms and legs. His arms would swing back and forth, at times his upper body would rock and he appeared unaware of his legs. When I first met Steven his only use of speech was direct echolalia, repeating what someone had just said, but when he copied he did not copy exactly because of a fair amount of cluttering in his speech. Cluttering is characterized by rapid or irregular speech rate, omissions and inversions of sounds, syllables and words. It manifests as a disorder of fluency, timing and articulation (Heitmann *et al.* 2004). He did not have directed, meaningful or cognitive speech. He seemed aloof and it was difficult to communicate with him. Eye contact was poor and he also displayed violent outbursts when he was placed in an unfamiliar situation, or had unfulfilled expectations. His ability to communicate his needs to others was poor, which frustrated him and his carers thus isolating him further.

We began by working on establishing an inner feeling for beat and timing in order to develop his inner sense of listening without the immediate repetition. Taking advantage of his echolalia I had him repeat a small poem after me line for line while bouncing a big ball back and forth. The aim was to produce a directed 'push' of the ball with enough force to bounce it back to me, thus developing his own conscious impulse for speaking. This proved very difficult at first. He would simply drop the ball and it would land at his feet. But after showing him how to thrust the ball forward, using demonstration and hands-on help, he began to 'push' the ball to me. I would say 'Push the ball' and he would repeat this and then weakly push it towards me. Over time he gradually developed more force in his throw and was able to bounce the ball to me at ever increasing distances. Ball bouncing also helped his response time increase, which in turn helped the listening activity.

To help him speak on his own initiative, we worked with picture cards of everyday objects. He could then begin focusing on a picture and name the object. This helped train his nerve-sense system to direct his attention, develop his cognitive recognition and nurture his speech impulse to respond appropriately to outside stimuli. Eventually his attention span began increasing, while his echolalia started to decrease.

The introduction of alliterative verse helped Steven work consciously with his arms, hands and legs by involving them in the speaking process. To help him capture each word we would step over rods placed on the floor at stepping distance apart. Once this was achieved we were able to take the vital shift to stepping only during the alliterative sound, thus effecting a self-awakening in him. We also began throwing a juggling ball to help with directing his speech. At first he needed hands-on help to teach him how to throw a ball underhand. He tended to hold the ball with his fingertips, which indicated a lack of ability to be engaged in self-directed activity. He had to learn how to hold the ball in the palm of his hand before releasing it, allowing it to roll off the fingertips as he threw it. Coupled with this we spoke a small speech exercise together which was designed to develop his listening capacity and integrate his speaking and movement. The latter is especially important for self-directed speaking. His echolalia had initially hampered efforts to develop his listening skills but as we worked with this exercise his listening improved, and his timing of throwing and speaking simultaneously also improved.

Steven began making big breakthroughs in speaking and communication around the age of fourteen, opening the world up to him. He began asking questions, showing interest in his daily schedule, initiating small conversation and answering questions put to him. Over the past two years he has continued expressing himself in speech with greater confidence and his ability to engage his whole self in our speech sessions has continued to improve. His ability to express and understand his emotions still remains limited. This will be a further area to address in our speech work together.

Barbara

Barbara has Down's syndrome. She is fourteen years old and I have seen her regularly for seven years. As a young girl she possessed a sunny disposition, a likeable personality and a genuine openness to her surroundings. She had a good speech impulse rising from her metabolic system but her language and concept acquisition descending from the nerve-sense system was more impaired. Her language skills were at the level of a one to two-year-old child. She used mainly nouns and gave one or two word answers to questions. Her articulation at a word level was good, having all the sounds independently, including most sound blends.

Her speech had only begun at five years old but her main difficulties lay in the area of differentiating senses and language acquisition (Phillips 2001).

Our initial starting point began with the early stages of speech acquisition. Working from the development stage at which she felt most comfortable we played with sounds, words and gestures much as a one or two-year-old year-old would do. Nursery rhymes and simple poems were used for their rhythmic content and the imaginative playfulness of sounds. They also served as a medium to develop the sense of hearing/listening and being able to discern the difference between 'P' and 'B,' or 'T' and 'D.' Gestures were used which supported experiencing and 'seeing' the differences in these and other sounds.

We tackled verbs and activity next. As she still lacked the proper grammatical structure for her to be effective in language, we began to approach this area by playfully stepping to a beat in a poem. This brought more awareness to her limbs, which helped her use and understanding of verbs to grow. Again gestures accompanied poems, discerning between flying and walking, smiling and crying, etc. Running alongside our active development of verbs, we worked with verb picture cards to help reinforce grammatical structure development. Learning to differentiate the pronouns of he, she and it; and being able to include the active verb ending 'ing' helped her gain a better grasp of language use. Once verbs were better established we progressed to prepositions, learning to differentiate between on, under, next to, between, in front of, behind, etc. Once again this was achieved by acting out these words and concepts in poetry and verses through movement and gesture. This activity was supplemented with picture cards in order to help improve her sentence structure.

By this stage Barbara's language use and structure had improved significantly in the therapy setting. It was only a matter of confidence for her to transfer these new skills to her everyday life. Her ability to discern sense impressions also developed. Her sense of rhythm improved, which helped her to establish a healthier correspondence between nerve-sense and metabolic systems. Not only had her speech development improved but she had taken significant steps in her overall development. Her next trial was to be the period when the child inwardly experiences a separation from the surrounding world in which it had previously been integrated (Steiner 1988). For most children this takes place around the age of nine to twelve years, but for Barbara it came around the age of eleven to twelve. To help her with this challenge we began working with elements of alliteration, first through movement then through combining speaking and movement. This awakened her co-ordination abilities and revealed her hidden individuality, which expressed itself in a strong and sure voice. Picture cards now took back stage while poetry and storytelling came forward; the overall aim being the integration of movement, speech and language use.

The second part of the nine-year change was characterized by a shift from grasping the alliterative to harmony in the hexameter. Hexameter verse harmonizes blood circulation and breathing thus creating support for the next stage of development — adolescence (Steiner & Steiner von Sivers 1981). For Barbara this proved especially important for her rhythmic system development. We began simply. I spoke the hexameter verse and for each half-line we passed a rod between us while seated. This simulated the breath being used and moved across the space between us while speaking. After becoming familiar with the text she joined in speaking while passing the rod back to me. The next step involved stepping to the text's beat and being precise and focused. She tended to dream at this stage, and her steps did not always keep to the beat, but after some practice her focus improved and she could step to the beat more consistently. Once the beat was better established we focused on expressing the rhythm which is our current activity. While standing and speaking we pass the rods between us on the long parts and between our own hands on the two short parts. A sort of standing dance results and we are carried by the spoken rhythm. After establishing an inner feeling for the rhythm we begin speaking the text while stepping to the rhythm in a circle around the room. Her engagement in the activity is strong, although dreaming off at times she continues to enjoy the sessions.

9. Riding Therapy

ROBIN JACKSON

The horse

When you are tense, let me teach you to relax.
When you are short tempered, let me teach you to be patient.
When you are short sighted, let me teach you to see.
When you are quick to react, let me teach you to be thoughtful.
When you are angry, let me teach you to be serene.
When you feel superior, let me teach you to be respectful.
When you are self absorbed, let me teach you to think of
       greater things.
When you are arrogant, let me teach you humility.
When you are lonely, let me be your companion.
When you are tired, let me carry the load.
When you need to learn, let me teach you.
After all, I am your horse.

— Willis Lamm (1997)

History

The earliest record of treatment using horses was apparently found in Chinese manuscripts dating from 3000–2000 BC. Hippocrates (460–377 BC) pointed out riding's healing rhythm in both its harmonious emotional effects as well as its purely physical benefits. At that time it was acknowledged that riding was more than a means of transportation; it was also seen as a way of improving the health and well-being of people with disabilities. Followers of Hippocrates saw horse-riding activities as a panacea and recommended it as a treatment for all sorts of maladies. Xenophon (435–354 BC) is quoted as saying: 'The horse is a good master not only for the body but also for the mind and for the heart.' In 1569 the Italian Girolamo Mercuriale wrote on 'The Art of Gymnastics' and mentioned the value of horse riding. In 1600 the English physician, Sir Thomas Sydenham, wrote: 'The best way I know to improve morale and to strengthen muscles is to ride horseback several times a day.' The first study of the value of riding as therapy was reported in 1875 when the French physician, Chassaign, prescribed pony riding as a treatment for a variety of conditions, and concluded that riding helped in treating certain neurological ailments. He noted improvements in posture, balance and joint movement as well as a striking improvement in morale.

Riding therapy was offered to wounded soldiers from the First World War at a hospital outside of Oxford. Miss Olive Sands, a physiotherapist, had taken her horses to the hospital in order to provide riding facilities for soldiers who had been disabled in the war. In 1946, following two outbreaks of poliomyelitis riding therapy was introduced in Scandinavia. By the 1950s British physiotherapists were exploring the potential of equitherapy to treat many other types of handicap.

A seminal moment in the development of therapeutic riding occurred during the 1952 Olympics in Helsinki, when Liz Hartel, an accomplished horsewoman who had been stricken with poliomyelitis in 1943, won the Silver Medal in the Grand Prix Dressage. After surgery and physical therapy had allowed her to walk with crutches, Hartel had been determined to ride independently again and as a result of daily supervised riding sessions her muscle strength and co-ordination had significantly improved allowing her to return to riding.

In the early 1950s Elsebet Bodthker, a Norwegian physiotherapist and an accomplished horsewoman, met Liz Hartel and noted her physical progress, in particular the psychological benefits that Hartel derived from riding. Bodthker began to teach her own polio patients to ride, using both basic equestrian exercises and those used by physiotherapists in clinics. As a consequence of the achievements of Hartel and Bodthker a number of European enthusiasts began exploring the possible benefits of therapeutic horseback riding. Hartel's achievement was clearly the catalyst for the formation of therapeutic riding centres across Europe and America.

Riding therapy has since been used with persons diagnosed with cerebral palsy, functional spinal curvature, developmental delay, Down's syndrome, multiple sclerosis, sensory integration dysfunction, traumatic brain injury and learning or language disabilities. A 1989 survey of practitioners in Germany and Austria indicated the following distribution of disabilities for persons receiving this intervention: cerebral palsy

(27 percent), orthopaedic disabilities (20 percent), multiple sclerosis (19 percent), post-traumatic spasm disorders (19 percent) and hyperkinetical syndrome (15 percent) (Heipertz-Hengst 1994). In a more recent survey practitioners from twenty-four countries provided a similar rank order of persons with disabilities frequently treated by riding therapy: cerebral palsy, traumatic brain injury/post traumatic stress syndrome, multiple sclerosis, hemiplegia, developmental delay/Down's syndrome, sensory integration deficit and spina bifida (Copeland-Fitzpatrick 1997).

The horses

One horse that has been a particular favourite for riding therapy in the Schools has been the Haflinger. It is tempting to call a Haflinger, which stands at between thirteen and fifteen hands high, a 'pony' when in fact it is a tough, strong and hardworking horse — a native of the Tyrolean Mountains in Austria. In its native country it is sometimes referred to as a 'prince from the front and a peasant from behind.' This is because of the size of its muscular hindquarters. The Haflinger has a well-shaped head, sometimes reflecting its remote Arabian ancestor, with a small, almost delicate muzzle, wide dark eyes, a friendly and intelligent expression, set on an elegant neck. His striking chestnut coat can be blonde or chocolate brown, and the blonde mane and tail is ideally snow white, quite heavy with the mane often falling double on the neck.

The Haflinger descends from a race of mountain horses that have grazed the Alps for centuries. These horses were used as all-round helpers of Austrian farmers. Only horses that could be handled by all members of the family were kept and bred, resulting in the docile and friendly nature of the modern Haflinger. After World War Two the breeding was taken over by the Austrian government and it has become one of the most strictly selective and examined of warm blood breeds in Europe. Breeders who have turned to Haflingers comment not only on their undeniable appeal and people-oriented personalities, but also on their intelligence, boldness and resilience. They learn quickly and are sensible, attributes that have earned them a place in the world of therapeutic riding. Perhaps, most of all, the Haflinger is a friend and companion. Over the centuries of living so closely with people, the Haflinger has developed a temperament that is not simply unflappable but actively outgoing and engaging. It is said that 'Haflingers can do anything, with a smile!'

The bond between horses and children with an intellectual disability

It has been suggested that there is a special bond between horses and children with an intellectual disability (Albert 1981). When a horse is in the presence of a child with an intellectual disability, it has been noted that there is a sudden and visible change in alertness and a change in the position of the ears. Joe Royds, who was manager of Mencap's Riding Fund in the UK, argued that there appears to be some kind of communication between horses and children with an intellectual disability. He cited the case of one horse that had been barred from two pony clubs because it was a kicker and biter but whose behaviour with the children with an intellectual disability could not be faulted.

Royds also observed that horses seem able to remember their encounters with the children. He told the story of an autistic child who was put on a novice chaser and who so enjoyed himself that he started to sing. The boy saw the horse two years later after a three-mile novice chase and he put his hand over the sweat rug as he had done on his previous encounter. There was a remarkable transformation as if the horse recognized him and remembered the incident with pleasure. The horse then walked quietly to the stable with the boy. Even the stable boy noticed the change in the horse. It was also Royds' belief that horses discriminated in favour of small children and children with a disability.

The romantic explanation advanced was that there was some peculiar primitive bond that centuries of 'civilization' have knocked out of the rest of us. Royds recalled one incident, which concerned a child with Down's syndrome who had never seen a horse before. The moment that the riding hat was on his head he broke loose from his teacher, rushed out of the bus and started blowing up the horse's nose. How did he know to do that? Could it be because his feelings and sensibilities were highly developed? A possibly more down-to-earth explanation involves the possession of heightened senses of touch, warmth and, particularly smell. Is it a coincidence that about one in ten of children with an intellectual disability who mount a horse for the first time without prompting bury their face in the horse's mane and inhale?

Riding therapy at the Camphill School

This section is based on a paper written by Bernd Ehlen, a former riding therapist at the Camphill Rudolf Steiner School, and are printed here with his kind permission.

Riding therapy is prescribed for children at the School as a result of consultations between doctors, teachers, houseparents and therapists. There may be a variety of reasons for prescribing riding therapy. Usually a block period of six months is allocated and the child has riding for a period of about twenty minutes two or three times a week. The therapy takes place in an enclosed purpose-built riding school. Before these facilities were built riding therapy took place in the open, which had a number of drawbacks, not least the fact that it could only be offered when the weather was fine which meant that it was difficult to ensure regularity, continuity and meaningful block periods of treatment.

Prior to therapy sessions, the therapist prepares the horse so that when the pupils arrive the horse is in a responsive and obedient mood. Before the child approaches the horse, a suitable hat is fitted, which has a specially designed chin strap that prevents the child from removing it and ensures that it cannot fall off. It is important that the therapist undertakes a comprehensive assessment to determine each child's stage of development. For some children therapy begins with an attempt to groom the horse. The initial approach is very tentative and gentle, with the therapist's voice instilling confidence in both the child and horse. The gentle grooming involves stroking the horse's back and putting the child's face against the body of the horse so it can take in its warmth, softness and smell. To begin with, the children ride bareback. The horse is fitted out with a purpose-designed roller which is made of leather or webbing material and which is placed on the horse's back and secured around the girth by two straps. The roller is fitted with a number of metal D-rings to which side reins are attached. This equipment is necessary as the side reins are linked to the horse's head and the positioning of the head of the horse is important for therapy. The horse is also equipped with a bridle and bit. No reins are used at this stage other than the side reins for the positioning of the horse's head.

After the initial introduction of the child to the horse, the child mounts with the help of the therapist. At this point the horse or pony is on the lunge. After mounting, the child is asked to lean forward to stroke the horse's mane and neck reaching out as far as the ears. This is to establish the child's confidence while he is mounted. No special methods of strapping the child in, or holding the child's hands, are used. From the very start all therapeutic riding is unaided. Because of this, high standards of training for therapists are needed. After good contact between child and horse has been established, the therapist will command the horse to 'walk.' It is led by the lunge and the hand of the child who is receiving therapy is not held.

Gradually, the distance between therapist and horse widens until the therapist is in the middle of the arena and the horse is walking in a fifteen-metre circle. After this opening session, the child progresses to the middle session, which may consist of confidence-building exercises, such as freeing the hands from the roller, followed by rhythmic arm movements or butterfly turns on the horse, either while the horse is standing or in motion. It may also include catching and throwing balls or bean bags of varying sizes and weights, or catching and throwing back copper rods approximately 60 cm (2 ft) and 15 mm (5/8 in) in diameter. For other children, the main work may consist of working on the breathing rhythm and at this point the horse is invited to trot. At this stage the freeing of the hands from the roller may be attempted. For some older children and young adults the 3/4 rhythm of the canter may be used but this has to be done on a selective basis.

After the middle section of the therapy, the horse is brought to a 'stand' followed by a concluding moment where the child lies backwards on the horse with his arms hanging down in a totally relaxed and easy breathing manner, the horse totally motionless. The child is asked to close his eyes and lie for two or three minutes in complete silence totally still on the horse. After this, the child dismounts, pats the horse and if possible leads it back to a corner of the arena to be tied up. After a moment's break the next pupil arrives. The total session usually lasts around twenty minutes, sometimes half an hour. The maximum number of pupils that a horse is asked to take in a row would be four.

As the riders progress and gain confidence, the lunge line is removed and the horse moves freely in the arena, being commanded by the voice of the therapist. The removal of the lunge line gives the child the feeling that he is in control. For some of the older children and young adults who have progressed in their riding skills, and are physically more able, saddle and stirrups are introduced. Initially the saddle is used without stirrups, stirrups may be added later. At this stage great stress is laid not so much on speed but on precision handling with an emphasis on control.

Benefits of riding therapy

The possible physical, psychological, social and educational benefits that children may derive from riding therapy have been comprehensively outlined by the Strides Therapeutic Riding Centre in California. These benefits have been summarized and are set out below. There is no suggestion that all children receiving riding therapy will obtain these benefits. Indeed there will be a minority of children who, for one reason or another, gain no benefit at all. It is, however, difficult to think of another form of therapy that offers so many possible benefits.

THE PHYSICAL BENEFITS OF RIDING THERAPY

— *Improved balance.* As the horse moves, the rider is constantly thrown off-balance, requiring that the rider's muscles contract and relax in an attempt to rebalance. This exercise reaches deep muscles not accessible in conventional physical therapy. By placing the rider in different positions on the horse, different sets of muscles can be worked by stopping and starting the horse, changing speed and direction.

— *Strengthening muscles.* Muscles are strengthened through increased use. Even though riding is a form of exercise, it is perceived as enjoyment and therefore the rider has increased tolerance and motivation to lengthen the period of exercise.

— *Muscle stretching.* Sitting on a horse requires stretching of the adductor muscles of the thighs. This is accomplished by prestretching prior to mounting the horse and by starting the rider off on a narrow horse, gradually working to wider and wider horses. Riding with stirrups with heels level or down helps to stretch the heel cords and calf muscles. By encouraging the rider to maintain an upright posture against the movement of the horse, stomach and back muscles can be stretched.

— *Improved coordination.* Riding a horse requires a great deal of coordination in order to get the desired response from the horse. Since the horse provides instant feedback to every action by the rider, it is easy to know when the correct cue has been given. Repetition of the movements required in controlling a horse quickens reflexes.

— *Respiration/circulation.* Although riding is not normally considered a cardiovascular exercise, trotting and cantering increase both respiration and circulation.

— *Appetite/digestion.* Like all forms of exercise, riding stimulates the appetite; the digestive tract is also stimulated, increasing efficiency of digestion.

— *Sensory integration.* Riding stimulates the tactile sense both through touch and environmental stimuli. The movement of the horse stimulates the sense of balance as it changes direction and speed. The olfactory system responds to the many smells involved in a stable environment. Vision is used in control of the horse. The many sounds in a stable involve the auditory system. All these senses work together and are integrated in the act of riding.

THE PSYCHOLOGICAL BENEFITS OF RIDING THERAPY

— *Improved self-confidence.* Confidence is gained by mastering a skill normally performed by people without a disability. The ability to control an animal much larger and stronger than oneself is also a great confidence builder. Exercise in the fresh air helps to promote a sense of well-being.

— *Increased interest in outside world.* For those confined by a disability, the world tends to shrink in size. Riding increases interest in what is happening around the rider, for the rider is able to explore the world from the back of a horse.

— *Increased interest in one's own life.* The excitement of riding and the experiences involved stimulate the rider, encouraging the rider to speak and communicate about the experience to others.

— *Improved risk-taking abilities.* Riding is a risk sport. The rider learns to master fears through the act of staying on the horse, as well as attempting new skills and positions on the horse.

— *Development of patience.* Since the horse has a mind of its own, the rider has to learn patience as he or she attempts to perform skills on the horse when the horse is not cooperating. Repetition of basic riding principles also helps the rider to develop patience.

— *Emotional control and self-discipline.* The rider quickly learns that an out-of-control rider means an out-of-control horse. Shouting, crying and emotional outbursts upset the horse, which in turn can frighten the rider. Riders learn to control these emotions and express them appropriately.

THE SOCIAL BENEFITS OF RIDING THERAPY

— *Friendship.* Although riding can be a solitary activity, it is normally performed in groups. Riders share a common love of horses and a common experience of riding which is a good foundation on which to build a friendship.

— *Development of respect and love for animals.* Horses require a great deal of care and attention as a consequence of which riders find themselves bonding with the animals. They develop an interest in them and learn to care for them. They learn to put the needs of the horse first.

— *Increased experiences.* The variety of experiences involved in riding is endless. From grooming and tacking up to trail riding, from learning the parts of the horse to going to horse shows, the rider is constantly exposed to a wide range of experiences.

— *Enjoyment.* As riding a horse is fun, riders experience excitement and pleasure every time they come for a lesson.

THE EDUCATIONAL BENEFITS OF RIDING THERAPY

— *Remedial reading.* Before one can read, it is necessary to recognize differences in shapes, sizes and even colours. These can be taught easily on horseback, as part of games and activities. There is often less resistance to learning when it is part of a riding lesson.

— *Remedial maths.* Addition and subtraction can be taught through games involving throwing numbered foam dice and adding and subtracting the numbers. Because the concepts are taught through games, resistance to learning is decreased.

— *Sequencing, patterning and motor planning.* Something as simple as holding and using a pencil requires a great deal of motor planning. Knowing which comes first in a sequence of events is an important part of most activities. These and other similar skills are taught on horseback through the use of obstacle courses and many other games and activities.

— *Improved eye-hand coordination.* Eye-hand coordination which is necessary for such skills as writing are taught in tacking up the horse, as well as various other activities and exercises.

— *Visual spatial perception.* This includes our awareness of form and space, and our understanding relationships between forms in our environment. Included in this area are directionality, space perception, form perception and visual sequential memory. Both reading and mathematical concepts involve visual spatial perception. It has been argued that visual spatial perception improves as a natural result of control of the horse.

— *Differentiation.* The rider learns to differentiate significant from less significant stimuli in the environment. An improvement in this area occurs as the rider learns to concentrate upon the needs of his horse and those things that may influence it as opposed to other extraneous factors.

Conclusion

Whilst the kind of physical, psychological, social and educational benefits that have been identified are immediately recognizable to all riding therapists, there have been calls for more scientifically rigorous research to be undertaken to demonstrate the effectiveness of riding therapy (McGibbon 1997; Macauley 2002; Rolandelli & Dunst 2003). At the present time there are relatively few refereed journals which carry comparative research results showing what makes riding therapy beneficial, or even what particular aspects of the activity are most effective (Bertoti 1988; Brock 1988). Whilst applauding the call for more research to be carried out, a note of caution needs to be sounded, for it can be argued that there are certain aspects of the nature of the relationship between man and horse that will always defy scientific scrutiny, and remain immeasurable and immutable.

10. Eurythmy Therapy

ANGELA & JOHN RALPH

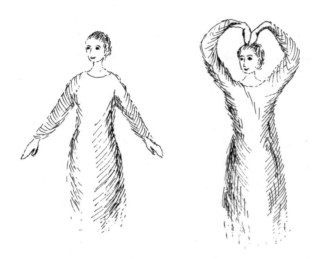

Eurythmy is an art of movement inspired by Rudolf Steiner at the beginning of the twentieth century. Originally it was developed as a performing art, first appearing on the stage in Steiner's Mystery Dramas during 1912. It soon became apparent that this newborn child of anthroposophical culture could develop fruitfully in other areas of work. When the first Waldorf School was opened, eurythmy was part of the curriculum from the very beginning. It was included to complement the intellectual activity of other subjects, and give pupils the opportunity to enrich their experience of subjects such as geometry, ancient history, poetry and music through movement lessons relating directly to the main lesson themes.

Development of eurythmy

The eurythmy teachers of the first Waldorf School soon noticed that children with concentration, movement or developmental difficulties benefited from their lessons. Individual problems were alleviated through the regular practice of eurythmy. These pioneering eurythmy teachers approached Rudolf Steiner and asked him to tell them more about eurythmy's therapeutic potential. This inspired a lecture cycle by Steiner (1983) to doctors and eurythmists, and so the first artistic therapy within anthroposophical medicine was born.

This happened in the last years of Steiner's life and eurythmy therapy remains the only artistic therapy where Steiner gave the indications and exercises himself. When Steiner talked to the curative educators in 1924 eurythmy therapy was one of the main therapeutic interventions. In the following years, a number of eurythmy therapists deepened and developed the work.

Eurythmy is currently practised in the following areas:

— in Waldorf Schools and curative education classes, such as in the Camphill Rudolf Steiner Schools;
— on stage as a performing art;
— as a therapeutic medium;
— in recreational classes;

— as an enhancement to study and aid to self-development in education and training in higher education;
— in organizations at all levels, from workers to higher management, to enhance team-work, self-management and decision-making, often known as *Eurythmy in the Workplace.*

It is also practised within the Camphill Schools and many other curative education establishments:

— as a medium to convey stories, myths and inspirational themes in a religion lesson for pupils who have limited access to the spoken word;
— as a passive or an active therapeutic medium for small groups, including Listening Space Therapy, and Coloured Light Therapy.

What is eurythmy?

Eurythmy gestures follow the innate laws of speech and music. The inner qualities of speech and music are made visible, not the feelings aroused in the listener. The eurythmist makes visible the inner life hidden within what is heard. In *speech eurythmy* there are arm gestures for each sound, outwardly expressing the inner movements of the larynx. There are also movements that follow the grammar, soul moods and colours, which may be interwoven with the sounds. The movements are choreographed according to what is heard, rather than written. The eurythmist determines which sounds are emphasized in a word, so some gestures may appear more fully than others. All these movements are presented as the individual eurythmist moves across the floor in geometric and other forms arising from the text. The performance of eurythmy may include one or more soloists and possibly groups in chorus. Steiner (1923) argued that:

> one can use the entire human body in such a way that it really carries out those movements which are otherwise carried out by the organs connected with speech and music. Thus there arises visible speech, visible music — in other words, the art of eurythmy.

In *tone eurythmy* the possibilities for movement can be found in the music's beat, rhythm, pitch, melody, intervals, chords, phrasing, silent rests and loud and soft dynamics. The eurythmist listens to the music, finding which facets predominate and then combines appropriate movements to reveal their innate musicality. Individual instruments may be represented by one or more eurythmists. The path of choreographed forms supports the process of rendering the music visible, the interaction of the instruments and harmonic progression.

Although eurythmy gestures are strictly disciplined there is still considerable artistic freedom in articulating the various elements most clearly for the audience. It is perhaps one of the more perplexing aspects of eurythmy that eurythmists do not express personal feelings or a response to the music by the choreographer, as is frequently seen in modern dance. The challenge is to move beyond personal limitations or disabilities for the speech and music to become objectively visible. In a similar way a piano player may develop the skill to allow the music of Beethoven to sound freely without the player's personality intruding. As the pianist learns the piano as an instrument, so the eurythmist learns skilful technique as well as developing a mobile body as an instrument. The ability to overcome personal limitations in movement comprises an important aspect of the self-development of anyone who practises eurythmy, and this aim is integral to eurythmy's potential to address disharmonies in our constitution therapeutically.

Eurythmy therapy

Anyone can receive eurythmy therapy on the advice of an anthroposophically trained doctor. It may be prescribed for acute or chronic physiological illnesses, terminal illness, psychological and stress related problems, as well as for the wide range of conditions encountered in education and curative education. Eurythmy therapists undergo a rigorous and thorough training, in addition to a four-year foundation training in eurythmy. Some of the exercises and movements used therapeutically are modified from those used in *artistic eurythmy*. Movements relating to speech are more commonly used in therapy than those relating to music. Often only three or five different gestures are used in one session. Repetitions of single gestures or sequences of gestures are practised in order to produce a healing effect in the bodily organization.

Eurythmy therapy sessions are usually carried out on a one to one basis, addressing a particular medical problem or constitutional imbalance with an individually tailored approach. A rest period after each session enhances the healing effect as this gives the practised movements the further possibility to resound or echo inwardly, while the body is outwardly still. This is often experienced strongly by the resting person who may also fall asleep.

Eurythmy therapy in curative education

Eurythmy therapy has been offered for many decades in Camphill Schools. We can address many of the physiological and psychological conditions of our pupils through eurythmy therapy, such as Autistic Spectrum Disorder (ASD), Attention Deficit Hyperactivity Disorder (ADHD), epilepsy, genetic disorders and various effects of trauma or neglect. All these conditions involve mild or severe movement disturbances.

The ability to imitate is not a prerequisite for eurythmy therapy. Passive movements, where the therapist gently guides the arms of the pupil, are also beneficial. Pupils who are supported by the therapist to complete the movements often prefer humming or singing to accompany the movements rather than spoken words or sounds. Lightweight copper rods or copper balls are used for rhythmical exercises. The warming property of copper can help to warm up cold hands, and so allow more conscious awareness of hand movements.

Within the holistic environment of Camphill, where other therapies and approaches are used in mutually enhancing combinations, eurythmy therapy can be of great benefit. The healing effect of eurythmy therapy is seldom immediate, although it may be experienced powerfully. The physical body of each person responds at its own pace. Ideally eurythmy exercises are practised more than once a week over a whole term or even longer. Many pupils, especially those who have a programme of passive movements, continue to practise eurythmy for many months or years.

The team that works with each pupil meets regularly with a Camphill doctor to review the pupil's progress and consider the next steps. It is here that the appropriate therapies are selected following a diagnostic assessment, and the right balance and sequence of therapies is chosen. For half a year a pupil might have eurythmy therapy and massage; for the next half year, therapeutic art and riding therapy may address the same issues.

CASE STUDY

When Norman came to Camphill he had little speech. He echoed back what was spoken to him, seldom initiated communication, avoided eye contact, and preferred to observe rather than being involved with people. He found it difficult to engage his hands in any activity, did not imitate movements shown to him and had limited fine motor skills. For four years Norman had intense therapeutic input, including twice-weekly eurythmy therapy. Today Norman speaks in full sentences. He looks at people and has an enthusiastic interest in everybody. He is less reluctant to work with his hands and can imitate movements almost exactly. Because of the rich therapeutic input from other therapies and the general healing approach of Camphill life, it is difficult to determine how specific elements have contributed to Norman's tremendous progress. Every aspect of curative education has played its part.

The power of movement

Surprisingly, eurythmy remains little known in the field of other movement therapies. Eurythmy and eurythmy therapy have attracted few resources for specific research, however we can draw on existing research into general movement and kinaesthetic learning. Rudolf Steiner saw the potential of eurythmy therapy as a core intervention in curative education, and gave specific advice about children in lectures to the first Curative Educators in 1924 (Steiner 1998). Today neurophysiological research has made tremendous discoveries that show how movement stimulates the development and functioning of the brain throughout childhood and beyond.

All forms of exercise stimulate the oxygen flow to our head, and even when we smile a subtle adjustment to the chemical cocktail in the brain is induced. Regular movement exercises not only help with movement disturbances, but also address other learning disabilities, cognitive, emotional and psychological issues. All our nerves and senses are stimulated when we practise movement. In eurythmy there is no competitive element so those who are shy or anxious about failure can be encouraged to become confident enough to practise movement alone, or to integrate within a group of pupils with various abilities.

Movement and sporting activities are integrated into school life everywhere. Young growing bodies need practice and discipline to learn co-ordination, refine motor skills and accomplish dexterity. The exercises used in eurythmy therapy offer a focused approach to specific conditions in a supportive environment. Group work in eurythmy can be tailored to include all abilities in elegant artistic creations in movement. Groups of Class 12 pupils in Camphill Schools have often performed eurythmy as part of their graduating presentations.

Many different movement-related therapies are available to help children, adults and senior citizens with a wide range of problems. The regular practice of martial arts and other movement disciplines has become commonplace as people seek an enhanced experience of well-being to compensate for long days of inactive deskwork. Yoga and other well-known forms of stretching and movement claim many general and specific health benefits. Many people appreciate the importance of learning how we use our own bodies in movement, and what we can learn from our bodily feelings. It has been shown that even the over-seventies benefit from regular movement exercises to improve co-ordination and mental alertness. Unreliable memories begin to respond more readily again, and an improvement in the general quality of life is recognized. It seems that we never grow out of the chance to make a difference in our lives through movement and exercise. It is also clear that some of the most powerful benefits of movement and eurythmy are experienced by young growing children.

The practice of eurythmy in organizations all over the world has led to the realization that people who have regular eurythmy sessions become increasingly able to manage themselves at work. They may also show increasing initiative, so that one experienced eurythmist warns organizations with whom she works that such results may change the way the organization works.

Movement stimulates mind and body

The close relationship of body and mind is generally recognized. It is important that we perceive our own movement accurately in order to avoid clumsiness. Research has shown that our mind responds to actual experiences and imagined experiences of movement in much the same way. A modern gymnast practises in stillness through visualization while learning a new skill as well as slowly rehearsing the actual movement.

Our bodies affect our minds as much as the mind is able to affect the body. There are movement-related neurons throughout our brain that are actively stimulated when we think. Our movement reaches right into our thinking organ, and can arouse the dexterity of our thinking. If we become constrained by habit to a few narrow clichés of movement our quality of life can be affected. For this reason an important element of therapeutic eurythmy is to strengthen the individual experience of a variety of healthy fluid movements. Our pupils need to practise and perceive fluent articulate movements and gestures. Eurythmy is rich in its variety of possibilities.

It is not only our minds that are invigorated by movement. Our pulse and breathing rate changes in the presence of movement, even if we do not participate. When we listen to music and watch dancing or marching, we are moved inwardly. This process, known as entrainment, makes us want to dance and is widely used in piped music applications to relax us or help us work faster. It is not our aim in eurythmy therapy to seduce our pupils unconsciously into healthy movement, but to involve them consciously and actively in developing themselves. We aim to work in partnership with our pupils through a therapeutic and educational process, and they are included actively in their programmes of eurythmy therapy. Sometimes they may take the initiative to ask if they can have some more eurythmy therapy sessions.

It is through the effort and experience of body movement that therapeutic changes are brought about. The body is empowered to heal itself. The eurythmy therapist can target specific areas of the body and mind with exercises that work towards the harmonization of problematic, unbalanced conditions. Eurythmy exercises synthesize a combination of movements and focus the efforts towards specific parts of the body. As has been discovered through sensory integration, our sense organs of balance and proprioception must be exercised and refined to enable us to skilfully synthesize our perception and movement (Ayres 1979).

> It is the full activation and balance of all parts of our mind/
> body system that allows us to become effective, productive
> thinkers. With full development of the neocortex and its

> integration with the rest of the brain's structures, we are
> able to creatively play with ideas, use fine motor skills to
> present them to others, and reach out as human beings to
> the world at large. (Hannaford 1995, 95)

Mainstream education has long recognized the benefit of movement as a prelude to study and to aid concentration. Brain Gym* has been developed in North America, and spread throughout the world. Brain Gym exercises are derived from sound neuro-physiological research, often aiming to improve mental focus and overcome the confusions of dyslexia and dyspraxia. Many of these exercises closely resemble eurythmy exercises, and do not require extensive training to be taught effectively. Children learn to experience the beneficial effects of moves like the *hook-up* and may begin to use them spontaneously. We are fascinated and delighted by the enthusiasm of Camphill pupils for eurythmy. Co-workers sometimes comment on the tremendous anticipation of a youngster on eurythmy days. Eurythmy gestures are sometimes used playfully in games, and non-verbal pupils are unanimous in choosing the T-gesture for communicating 'eurythmy.' So a new silent expression for eurythmy has entered our vocabulary of meaningful gestures.

Enthusiasm for eurythmy

Eurythmy is best understood through experience. Everyone in the School has an opportunity to try some eurythmy. Groups of co-workers are often invited to be creative together in eurythmy. When people combine their movements into a meaningful gesture, sometimes creating a word together in eurythmy, a profound experience of inclusive achievement unites us all. This is as true for children as for adults.

Eurythmy is a source of enjoyment. Some of the greatest enthusiasts of eurythmy are children and young adults with severe movement disabilities. They become able to experience eurythmical movement without their usual inhibitions, and often shine in gratitude afterwards. We have always made regular eye contact during eurythmy from pupils diagnosed with Autistic Spectrum Disorder.

---

* Brain Gym is a registered trademark of the Educational Kinesiology Foundation.

We have watched the characteristic walk and body posture change gradually in many pupils over the years, and we see this as an outer expression of hidden inner changes that have been brought about through eurythmy combined with other approaches within curative education. Our pupils make visible the healing power of language, music and movement and that is just what eurythmy aims to do. We who live and work with the pupils cannot do eurythmy better.

11. Crafts

SUSIE KOERTING

—·—

> The density of nerve endings in our fingertips is enor-
> mous. Their discrimination is almost as good as that of
> our eyes. If we don't use our fingers, if in childhood and
> youth we become 'finger-blind' this rich network of nerves
> is impoverished-which represents a huge loss to the brain
> and thwarts the individual's all-around development. Such
> damage may be likened to blindness itself. Perhaps worse,
> while a blind person may simply not be able to find this
> or that object, the finger-blind cannot understand its inner
> meaning and value. (Bergstrom in Mitchell & Livingston
> 1999, 9)

True education aims to serve the needs of the whole human being.
Head, heart and hands are brought into a particular relationship with
each other in practising handwork and crafts. In the lessons pupils
have the opportunity to 'tangibly grasp' the world and give expression
to their latent creativity. Handwork and craft activities help educate
pupils in the nature of different materials and processes involved.
There is also the therapeutic aspect of the activity from which the
pupils benefit, for it is the very nature of handwork and craft activities to bring order to the materials used, and to bestow order upon
the maker. In practising his craft a potter not only leaves his imprint
— his thumbprint on the clay — but is also inwardly impressed
by the creative process at work. In addition to the educational and
therapeutic benefit that crafts can confer, there is the opportunity to
acquire different manual skills, and for older pupils to be introduced
to the experience of real work. Apart from the therapeutic contribution that crafts offer, involvement in craftwork presents the pupil with
the challenge of working from the idea for an object (abstract) to the
finished product (concrete). In this process the pupil is made aware
of human attributes, both at an emotional and intellectual level, that
are involved in the creation of an object.

Craft activity

> Tell me, and I will forget.
> Show me, and I may remember.
> Involve me, and I will understand.
>
> — Confucius, 450 BC.

Craft activity is part of a holistic approach that provides opportunities for learning in the classroom, households, therapy sessions as well as in craft settings. Craft activity aims to promote in young people with special needs a strong, responsible and respectful relationship with their environment, other living beings and themselves, through active use of all the senses and an engagement of the will. The purpose of crafts is to:

— give pupils opportunities for creativity and self-expression;
— encourage pupils to express their choices, preferences and ideas;
— engage pupils in creative processes that require patience and determination;
— encourage pupils to become 'masters of their own action' leading to the ability to create items that are useful to others;
— introduce pupils to working;
— provide a frame of activities in which pupils can learn to relate and interact with others;
— introduce pupils to the importance of team work;
— guide pupils to create products that are of practical value in daily life.

In the workshops pupils have the opportunity to explore different materials and learn craft-specific techniques and skills. This can be a positive and motivating experience. Many pupils are proud when they hold items in their hands that they have made. Through craft activity fine/gross motor skills may be enhanced and hand-eye co-ordination strengthened. Working with different colours, smells and textures adds to the therapeutic qualities of the craft activity practised in Camphill Schools.

Handwork and craft activity are key components of the Waldorf curriculum. They offer possibilities for activities and tasks that lead the pupil towards becoming a creative, skilled and moral being. The Waldorf curriculum is the inspiration for the curriculum taught at Camphill Schools. Since the 1940s craft activity has been an integral part of the anthroposophical curative education curriculum, and is placed in the curriculum in such a way that it accompanies pupils throughout their education.

NURSERY

The educational emphasis in the nursery is to introduce children to 'learning' in a creative and playful way. Children are supported in developing their learning capacity by joining activities that stimulate their natural desire to copy and imitate. The playful and innocent need of young children to imitate is essential for the development of those capacities that allow human beings to become moral individuals and responsible world citizens. Children attending a nursery in a curative educational setting are encouraged to learn to use their hands in age-appropriate creative activities. Through these simple activities children become familiar with their surroundings in a playful way.

CLASSES 1–3

Children aged seven to nine are naturally curious and interested in what is happening around them. They are eager to join in with activities, are keen to listen to stories and want to learn. Steiner stressed the importance for children in engaging in focused and rhythmical activity with their hands. He singled out knitting, as he believed that this manual activity led to an enhancement in the child's faculty of judgment. If education can harness the tireless curiosity and energy of children, then their ability to focus their thinking, and merge their inner experience with taught knowledge will be enhanced. In Steiner's view the ability to knit was not enough. He argued that it was important to teach children to make objects that had purpose, meaning *and* beauty.

At around the age of nine years children grow more sensitive to their surroundings and become more aware of the difference between themselves and those around them. This can be a sad and lonely experience, as it is the first step from childhood towards greater self-consciousness. One way of helping the child to feel part of mankind and feel 'at home' is literally to create a house. Part of the curriculum in Class 3 relates to house building. The many different handwork activities involved in house building are introduced: woodwork (e.g., sawing, rasping, and hammering); making bricks out of clay; brick-laying; decorating, etc. Children also get involved in the planning and building of 'their' house.

CLASSES 4–9

From Classes 4 to 9 the different processes involved in making objects are learned. It is at this point that they progress on to craft activity and later on to work. Children learn that things are not created from one minute to the next but that everything needs its own time to come into existence. It is accepted that the qualities of patience and determination are almost as important as the acquisition of practical skills and abilities. At this stage children may learn to engage in simple woodwork and carving. They may make pictures, soft-toy animals or balls from felt, leather or other material. Children are introduced to a variety of materials and techniques and learn to measure, count and produce an item of beauty.

CLASSES 10–12

At Camphill, craft activity is offered to older pupils in recognition of the fact that it helps introduce them to the realm of work in a creative and therapeutic way. At this age young people have the potential to absorb large amounts of factual information but unlike other young people of this age, our pupils do not gain their knowledge from books or computers but need some form of practical activity to experience new realms of learning. The principal task of the craft instructor is to help a pupil develop his or her talents so that they may be used to serve humankind.

Craft areas

Each craft workshop at any one time can take from two to six pupils — all of whom may have different degrees of ability and level of need. One important approach in curative education is to identify and respond to the potential of the individual. This approach holds true for all craft activities. As each craft activity uses particular materials and tools, it provides the pupils with an opportunity to experience different therapeutic qualities. The purpose of all the craft processes is transforming material into objects which have an aesthetic and practical purpose. Within the School, placements are possible in the following craft areas:

— Felt Making
— Candle Making
— Weaving
— Pottery
— Woodwork
— Metalwork
— Tool refurbishment

FELT MAKING

For felt making the pupils are taught to prepare a raw fleece which involves sorting it, removing dirt, and then washing and drying it. After teasing, which necessitates loosening and separating the wool fibres, the wool can be carded. Once the wool has been carded, it is ready to be felted, spun or dyed. In the workshop the wool is used for felting two- or three-dimensional items. The carded wool is first arranged into a pile of three to four neatly prepared layers which are placed criss-cross on top of each other. The pile is then wrapped in netting and laid on top of a few towels. Warm, soapy water is added and gently spread over and through the pile. The delicately arranged wool fibres are then reduced to a flat piece. It is at this point that the felting process begins. The hands move rhythmically over the surface of the piece — adding water or soap as needed. During this process the wool fibres interlock and are bound together permanently. To make the piece even denser, it is rolled in a bamboo mat and milled in a sheet or towel with hot water. The finished piece of felt is then rinsed, dried and laid out flat. To complete the process the felted piece can be decorated or sewn into a variety of objects, such as bags, pouches, clothing, dolls, toys, etc.

The pupils are encouraged to participate in all stages of the process, but they will do so according to their ability and needs. There are many possibilities in this craft where pupils can express their own creativity, for example, by choosing a shape or item they wish to make, or by creating colourful patterns or pictures with the wool. Felt working requires in pupils an ability to concentrate on their task and to direct the application of their will. At the same time the process has a soothing effect conducted as it is within a warm and peaceful working atmosphere. Whilst it is an activity which is stimulating to the senses, it also lends itself readily to group work. Working with wool, which is a pleasant, soft and warm material, provides comfort and joy to the pupils.

CANDLE MAKING

In this workshop pupils learn to make candles out of pure beeswax by using the dipping method. The candles are popular in the households in Camphill Schools where they are used on a daily basis. During the Christmas season, the demand for candles is very high. During a typical candle making session pupils will prepare for the dipping by:

— choosing a roll of wick of an appropriate thickness;
— measuring and cutting several ends to the length required;
— attaching weights to the wick to produce a straight candle;
— threading the wick on wooden dipping boards;
— placing them in simple sequence on a dipping rack.

All these activities take place around a large table in the centre of the workshop. Pupils learn to work together and to appreciate each other's contribution as they work in a team. Dipping candles involves pupils walking from the dipping rack to the wax pot, carrying the emerging candles with great care and at a slow pace. The growing candles are then slowly dipped in the wax and taken out again as slowly. Finally, the candles are placed on the rack to cool down before their next dip. The candle making process takes time and requires concentration, persistence and a great deal of patience. In addition to producing candles for orders, pupils are encouraged to choose other candle-making activities and to decorate candles in an individual way. Candle making is not only a very appealing craft for pupils but also provides an attractive activity for local craft fairs and open days.

WEAVING

In this workshop the pupils obtain experience in plain weave and possibly pattern weave. As far as possible they are involved in creating useful textile articles such as tablecloths, table runners, bags and

Floor loom

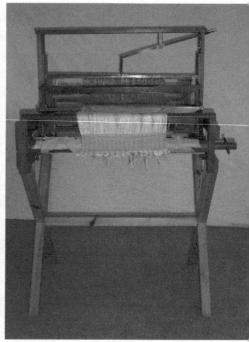

Table loom

Inkle loom

Tapestry loom

cushions. Cotton and linen yarns, as well as commercial and homespun wool, are woven into fabric, using floor looms, table looms, inkle- and tapestry looms. Basic weaving knowledge is gained at a simple loom by demonstrating the alternating over and under thread process. According to the skills and interests of the pupil further work is chosen. The aim is to help pupils to weave independently. In the weaving process an appreciation of colour combination is fostered. Because of differences in ability it is often necessary to share weaving tasks. Part of the work may be done by the pupil and another part by a helper. The pupil's contribution to the end result — however small — is always the important consideration. Weaving necessitates an orderly working process. Weavers sit at their work and perform a range of tasks involving a specific sequence of movements. There is the back and forth movement of the beater, the right to left movement of the shuttle and the up and down movement of the levers. Through this process pupils are likely to gain a heightened sense of spatial awareness.

POTTERY

The Pottery Workshop aims to give pupils practice and understanding of basic pottery techniques. They are guided to work on a task individually or as part of a group. Pupils are given the opportunity to experience working with different types of clay and, using glazes, they can design patterns and decorations to finish their pottery items. In the workshop pupils are introduced to handling a variety of tools. These include tools for measuring, tracing, shaping and slicing or rolling out the clay as well as using moulds made from plaster casts. Using such processes, a variety of items can be produced, such as cups, plates, vases, jugs or pots. Some pupils can progress to more complicated procedures where they may learn how to 'throw' clay at a potter's wheel or use clay for sculpture. Pupils may also be taught to recognize different types of clay and their particular qualities; be aware of the variety of glazes and their uses; and, note the various techniques of firing clay. Pottery is also a valuable therapeutic activity for through it pupils may gain confidence, improve their fine/gross motor skills and learn about the importance of being motivated and enthusiastic about their work tasks. Pottery can be 'magical' for pupils. Witnessing a lump of clay being transformed into a recognizable shape can make the eyes of pupils light up with wonder and joy, which can create an inner healing.

WOODWORK

Woodwork lessons provide pupils with an opportunity to work with different types of timber in a variety of ways to produce attractive, useful and well-finished items. A strong emphasis is placed on the correct use, care and maintenance of hand tools — handsaws, rasps and files, sanding blocks, instruments for measuring and marking, edge-tools, hammers, screwdrivers, etc. The pupils might make a darning egg using rasps, files and sandpaper. A bowl is another object that is often made, and provides an interesting contrast to making the egg. In making a bowl, material is removed which leaves a negative or concave shape quite different in character from the convex form of the egg. However, on turning the bowl upside down, it is then necessary to make a complementary convex shape. Pupils are encouraged, wherever possible, to make objects to their own design, as long as the object fulfils some practical and useful function. A wide range of skills can be taught in wood-working, for example, measuring, drawing, cutting, carving, spatial awareness, number work, the following of instructions and plans, identifying timbers and knowing their appropriate or traditional uses.

METALWORK

The Metal Workshop aims to give pupils an understanding of, and practice in, the basic techniques of metalwork. The pupils are encouraged to design their own work pieces and are given the opportunity to work with different soft metals — copper, aluminium or brass. Occasionally, iron may be used in blacksmithing. When pupils practise metalwork, they are taught to handle the variety of tools required for this craft. These include tools for measuring, tracing and cutting as well as the use of wooden moulds and various hammers. Under supervision pupils learn to use a gas torch in order to soften the item on which they are working. Safety measures are always observed.

Pupils might be engaged in making a bowl, candleholders, jewellery or plates. Able pupils can learn to engage in more complicated processes. Items, such as fireplace tools (e.g., tongs, pokers) can be made as well as candlesticks, copper balls, metal sculptures or pictures. The list is almost endless! Metalwork is a craft in which the direct engagement of the will is needed. To work on a piece and to finish it requires patience, determination and persistence, qualities which pupils with special needs often find difficulty in acquiring. The involvement of hard/cold material (metal) with fire makes metalwork an attractive craft. It is very gratifying for craft instructors to help pupils to complete beautiful items, which then go into the households where they serve a valued function in the household's daily life.

TOOL REFURBISHMENT

The School actively supports the work of Tools for Self-Reliance (TFSR), a charity that organizes the collection, refurbishment and distribution of hand tools to Third World countries. The refurbished tools are assembled into tool kits and distributed to developing countries. The TFSR Workshop is part of a network in Britain, and provides an opportunity for senior pupils to be trained in basic tool refurbishment. The related educational programme looks at the history and use of hand tools, intermediate technology and international social and economic issues.

A pupil will disassemble a tool noting all the different parts and the way in which the tool had been put together. The cleaning of parts is carried out using sandpaper, wire brushes, de-rusting and de-greasing agents. For the refurbishment of wooden parts the following tools may be required: rasps, sandpaper, saws, wood chisels, gauges, sand belt machines, electric drill and twist bits. A range of techniques is employed. For example, in refurbishing hammers it may be necessary to detach, repair and replace handles with appropriate wood. For the refurbishment of the metal parts, the following tools may be required: files, wire brushes, screwdrivers, spanners, electric wire brushes, grinding machines and welding apparatus. The process of metal tool refurbishment may also involve de-rusting, sanding to clean surfaces, completing repairs to fractures. On completion of the refurbishment pupils are involved in box making, then working through a checklist to ensure that all the tools have been packed in the kit and, finally, a letter of goodwill to the recipients is included in the tool kit.

The recycling and refurbishment of old and broken tools into good-as-new ones can be an encouraging, positive and challenging experience for senior pupils with special needs. The repaired tools are assembled according to trade: there are kits for blacksmiths, builders, joiners and even shoemakers. These are then sent to developing countries to aid disadvantaged people. This aspect of the work gives additional value to it and motivates the pupils to use their hands and work in a precise and reliable way.

Conclusion

Bergstrom has cogently and convincingly highlighted the consequences of neglecting the role of craft activities in the school curriculum:

> If we neglect to develop and train our children's fingers and
> the creative form-building capacity of their hand muscles,
> then we neglect to develop their understanding of the unity
> of things; we thwart their aesthetic and creative powers.

Those who shaped our age-old traditions always under-stood this. But today, Western civilization, an information-obsessed society that overvalues science and undervalues true worth, has forgotten it all. (Bergstrom in Mitchell & Livingston 1999, 9)

12. Camphill Medical Practice

MARGA HOGENBOOM

The care and diagnosis of children with special needs is a relatively new professional activity. It was only in 1866 that Dr Langdon Down described people with Down's syndrome for the first time. Dr Down also made a classification of the different causes of intellectual disability. The involvement of doctors has been central to the development of classification systems for children with special needs. Autism, now one of the main causes of learning disability, was independently identified and described in the Second World War by two doctors — Dr Kanner and Dr Asperger (Woodward & Hogenboom 2002). Many syndromes like Angelman syndrome and Prader-Willi syndrome carry the name of the doctor who first described the condition (O'Brien & Yule 1995). The central involvement of medical doctors in the care of children with special needs slowly changed towards the end of the twentieth century to the extent that doctors were only involved in the initial diagnosis and treatment of conditions such as epilepsy.

The education and care of children with special needs is now carried out under the supervision of educational psychologists and social workers, while the diagnosis and treatment of children with behavioural problems usually involves input from a clinical psychologist. This represents a shift from a medical to a psychological model in the care and education of children with special needs. This contrasts with the situation at the beginning of the twentieth century when the cause of intellectual disability was thought to be physical in character with a strong inherited component. After the Second World War, increasing emphasis was placed on the impact of dysfunctional mothers and families as the cause of disorders, particularly autism. At the time of writing, scientists once again have a strong interest in exploring the genetic component in the causation of intellectual disability, neurological functioning and the role of neurotransmitters. What is missing is a clear theory and praxis that permits the creation of a bridge between the medical and psychological approaches. In the School the physical, medical, psychological and spiritual aspects of the child with special needs have always been seen in holistic terms.

The role of doctors in the School has been prominent since the pioneering days. Dr König had worked as a successful physician in Vienna before coming to Scotland. A large group of young doctors was to join him later. As is the case in other schools the doctor now plays a less central role, although the medical therapeutic aspect is still essential to the approach to, and treatment of, the children in the School. This is seen not only in the involvement of the medical officer in the curative educational reviews and in the manifold therapies the children receive but also in the training of curative educators to be aware of the child's diagnosis, his physical health and the interaction of the bodily processes in the child's development and education.

The Camphill Medical Practice

The Camphill Medical Practice is situated within Murtle Estate in Bieldside. It can probably boast one of the best views from any waiting room. The Camphill Medical Practice is a National Health Service practice, and until 1990 the doctors were part of the Camphill Rudolf Steiner School, when the practice became independent. In 1999 the Camphill Medical Practice won the Innovative Practice Award from the Royal College of General Practitioners for its integrated and radical approach to Primary Care.

The Practice originally started as a place where medical care was given not only to pupils from the School but also to co-workers and villagers from Newton Dee and other Camphill communities. Over time this has been broadened and now patients from the local neighbourhood come as well as many referred patients from practices all over Scotland. The speciality of the Practice is the anthroposophical treatment of children and adults with special needs and people with cancer. The practice has 1000 patients on its list of whom 300 have special needs. On top of this, the Practice sees around 200 patients every year who are referred by other practices.

Anthroposophical medical treatment is a form of complementary treatment based on orthodox science, which aims to expand the diagnosis and treatment through knowledge of the spiritual side of a human being. Illness is seen as an imbalance which can be addressed and a new, heightened state of well being created.

At this point in time the Practice has two doctors, one practice nurse, a practice manager and two receptionists/secretaries. All are employed by the National Health Service. The Practice is also a registered charitable organization which employs an art therapist, eurythmy therapist, speech and movement therapist and massage therapist with a facilitator to co-ordinate all the therapeutic work. A counsellor and music therapist are also affiliated to the Practice. The pupils of the School use the Practice as their first point of contact for any medical problem. The doctors or nurse will see the child or young person and decide what is needed. As it is a NHS practice a referral can be made, if required, to the local hospital. Aberdeen is fortunate in having a good University Hospital with a new children's hospital. The Practice has good relations with the various hospital departments.

Since we specialize in children with special needs, it means that the doctors are well aware of how to approach the children and the kind of problems they will meet.

JAMES

James, a non-speaking child with challenging behaviour, is screaming this morning and is distressed. The GP examines him in his room with the support of two carers. The diagnosis is an irritation of the eardrum. He settles after the use of some complementary remedies and a painkiller.

The nurse is an expert in taking blood from all pupils and manages to make this event a positive occasion. She uses 'magic' creams and a 'butterfly' as a needle with the result that the child hardly notices a thing.

MAGGIE

Maggie is a young woman with Down's syndrome who has a phobic fear of needles. Because of problems with her thyroid she needs blood tests every two years. In the past this could pose quite a problem. Now the nurse and GP visit her in her home and she is proud of the fact that she can now cope with the test.

When the children are at home the local community paediatrician or paediatric specialist undertakes the ongoing supervision: this continuity of care is important as the child returns home every holiday.

When children go through a medical and/or behavioural crisis, the GPs are at hand to offer daily support.

Lizzie

Lizzie is a child with autism who has epilepsy and is severely deprived. She has picked up a viral infection, has a sore throat and is refusing to drink or eat or even take her epilepsy medication. She is having more seizures and fits. Hospital admissions are always very stressful for her as she hates being touched or forced to do anything. With the close daily support of the GP, and medical advice from a consultant, the carers are able to manage to guide her through this crisis.

The General Practitioners in the Practice are medical officers to the School, which is an important aspect of their work. The medical officer is involved in the admission of the pupils, where there are medical problems, and with the ongoing assessment and review process of the pupils. Another key aspect of the medical officer's role is to be aware of the well-being of the pupils. The involvement of the therapists with the pupils is a further feature of their role. The School has its own Therapy College involving a total of twelve different therapists. Where a therapy is not available in the School, a pupil can receive therapy from one of the therapists in the Camphill Medical Practice. Two of the therapists, the speech therapist and the rhythmical massage therapist are both based in the practice but also work in the School.

The medical officers are involved in teaching on the BA in Curative Education Programme which ensures that the curative educators have a firm grasp of the importance of bodily processes and their influence on the spiritual development of the child. They are also actively involved in research regarding children with special needs; for example, the influence of supplements on children with Down's syndrome and research into the beneficial aspects of horse riding.

Pupil profile

A fascinating and unique aspect of the Camphill Schools is the great diversity in the pupil population. Most of the children who come to our school have been examined extensively by a local paediatrician and psychologist. Their problems are as wide ranging as their abilities, extending from the severely handicapped child, who needs full time care in every aspect of his life, to the highly intelligent, but emotionally disturbed, youngster who, hopefully, will later find his way independently in life, marry and hold down a job.

Some of the children who come to us have genetic syndromes associated with an intellectual disability. Down's syndrome is the most common of these conditions but there are also children with Angelman syndrome, Fragile X syndrome, Taybi Rubenstein syndrome, Rett syndrome, microcephaly and Cri du Chat syndrome. Other children have syndromes, which do not have a genetic basis. This group includes children with epilepsy, hydrocephaly, foetal alcohol syndrome, foetal alcohol effect and cerebral palsy. There are some children who have a complex mixture of different problems.

CARL

Carl is a nine-year-old boy with poor vision, hyperactivity, hydrocephalus, a drain and epilepsy. He is on a major tranquillizer and anti-epileptic medication. Slowly he is calming down, his tranquillizer can now be stopped and his parents are delighted at the fact that he can now sit through a concert and enjoy it.

There are children with a mild intellectual disability who have had a disturbed childhood. Some have suffered sexual and/or physical abuse and deprivation and have difficulties in forming trusting relationships with others. Where a relationship comes too close, these children may test it to the limit and even seek to destroy it. This is a very challenging group to work with as many of these children have a record of failed foster placements behind them. Some of these children have been damaged by alcohol during their mother's pregnancy leaving them with many problems, particularly the ability to control their feelings and actions. Many children in this group have added problems such as hyperactivity, inattention and dyslexia.

The largest group at this time comprises children with autism or autistic spectrum disorder. However, although children may have a diagnosis of autistic spectrum disorder, the condition presents itself in different ways. Many children with Asperger's syndrome are bright, intelligent and verbally proficient but have severe social impairments and anxieties and often present challenging behaviour. Another group exhibits the more typical features of autism being non-speaking and having no understanding of body language. This is often coupled with challenging behaviour due to their anxiety and need for sameness. Other children fall in-between these two categories.

Some children may have no diagnosis on arrival, except the broad diagnosis of having an intellectual disability. However because of the experience and expertise of the medical team, it is often possible to arrive at a diagnosis.

LILY

Lily was a fourteen-year-old girl who came to us for an interview. Her parents described how hard they had had to work in the first six years of her life to establish a relationship with her. She clearly had a moderate intellectual disability, a stiff way of walking and sharp facial features. The doctor involved in the interview noted her facial features and tested for Rubenstein Taybi Syndrome. A geneticist later confirmed this tentative diagnosis, which gave her parents a measure of inner peace to know why Lily had problems.

Changes in referral pattern

It is interesting to look back at an early Annual Report which describes the different children, their problems and how they responded to their placement in the School. In 1962 there were 209 pupils (65 percent boys and 35 percent girls). Many of the children came from England (90 percent) with a small number from abroad (5 percent). Trying to group children according to diagnosis is not so easy. The majority of the pupils at that time had multiple handicaps or severe personality disorders:

— 25 percent of the children had autism with IQs ranging from 30 to 120
— 16 percent of the children had emotional disorders (e.g., aggression; hyperkinesis, anxiety)

— 9 percent had behavioural disorders
— 29 percent had sensory defects (e.g., visual, hearing)
— 23 percent had a motor handicap (e.g., cerebral palsy; hemiplegia)
— 8 percent had severe epilepsy
— 6 percent had Down's syndrome

Nowadays, the largest group of children who come to the School are on the broad autistic spectrum. They all have difficulties in social inter-action and problems with verbal and non-verbal communication. The implications of these changes are obvious. This large group of children needs very skilful handling and often one-to-one care. It is a pity that because of new regulations that children can no longer share a bedroom, for sharing provided an opportunity for social development as it gave the anxious child the experience of feeling safe and being part of a special group.

The present policy of keeping children with special needs in their local school may be beneficial for many children but there will always be a group who require a consistent therapeutic approach in order to flourish. These children, who can be very challenging for their fam-ily, need residential care. One of the consequences of the policy of inclusion is that when pupils eventually arrive at the School they need a highly specialized form of care. Too often children are referred to residential schools after a succession of previous placements has failed and this fact complicates the task of helping the child feel secure. Early intervention is increasingly recognized as being extremely important and many parents now actively seek a therapeutic placement at an earlier stage in a child's life. Much younger children are now being admitted to the School with the result that the nursery provision is in the process of expansion.

Holistic nature of treatment

The School is unique insofar as the emphasis is not on education alone but on healing education. In order to facilitate this healing process, an accurate diagnosis has to be made. As discussed earlier, children arrive with a range of diagnoses, for example, Attention Deficit Hyperactivity Disorder (ADHD), Autistic Spectrum Disorder and Angelman syndrome. It is our experience that whilst these diagnoses are important, they do not tell the whole story. In order to gain an understanding of all the problems with which a child is struggling, it is necessary to undertake a much more comprehensive diagnosis. This diagnosis is not made by the medical officer alone since the process requires the assessment and observations of teachers, house co-ordinators, curative educators and therapists. After an initial settling-in period by the child, all the professionals involved in the care and therapy of the pupil come together to share their observations.

The physical body of the child is observed. Is the child small or large for his age? Is his body well formed or are there signs of a congenital problem? Does the child have any physical illnesses? Are there any strong one-sided characteristics and, if so, do they form part of a syndrome — for example, the sharp nose of a child with Angelman syndrome; the small nose of a child with Down's syndrome; the protuberant ears of the child with Fragile X syndrome; the small head of a child with microcephaly. The purpose of such an observation is to assess how some of these physical features may impact on the child's self-image.

How vital are the life forces of this child? Is he pale or does he have rosy cheeks? Is he easily tired and irritable or is he dreamy and far away? How good is the child's memory? Is it so overdeveloped that the child can forget nothing or is the memory only situational, so that the child can only remember what to do in the toilet, once he is in the toilet? What about the bodily rhythms of the child? Are there regular bowel movements or, as is common in children with autism, does the child hold back from going to the toilet for long periods of time? What do we know about his sleep patterns? Poor sleep habits are often a major contributory factor in admitting a child to a residential school.

The quality of the child's physical movement needs to be noted. Are the movements of the child fluent or not? Does the child move too fast and does he rock to and fro? Are there signs of dyspraxia? Are the fine and gross motor skills appropriate for his age, or are they not well developed? Is the child right- or left-handed and which eye, ear and leg is dominant? Is there any sign of cross dominance? Is the child oversensitive in picking up all the emotions swirling around his environment or is the child not sensitive at all? Is the aggression displayed a sign of confusion, anxiety, fixation or lack of control? Are there medical explanations for the behaviours displayed — for example, epilepsy; mental illness; schizophrenia? The final aspect, which is examined relates to the biography of the child and his inner development.

These are the different aspects of the diagnostic picture that is formed. The aim is not to arrive at a fixed diagnosis but rather to create a living image which allows all the professionals involved to improve their understanding of the child and thus know better how to approach him, and determine which therapeutic measures are likely to be required in the house or school. It allows the therapist to identify the problems, which need to be concentrated upon, and guides the medical officer in her choice of complementary remedies for the child.

This review process is a continuing and informal one and starts from the moment a child is admitted. The curative educator commences the process. Once a term the medical officer liaises with the house co-ordinators regarding the progress of individual children. The medical officer also speaks with the therapists to see if there are any questions, or to review the therapeutic processes. Once a year — or more often if there are concerns — a formal review process takes place which involves the house, school, therapies and medical officer. The insight gained in this assessment process is reflected in the annual review, which is held with the parents and other concerned professionals.

The profession of anthroposophical doctor in curative education

In Britain there are no specialist medical practitioners who deal with children and adults with special needs. That role is shared between the doctor, psychiatrist for people with special needs, paediatric neurologist and community paediatrician. In Holland it is recognized that the medical care of children and adults with special needs requires a specialist training and expertise: thus there is a three-year training course for specialists working with people with special needs.

The medical officers in the School work as medical practitioners and have undertaken medical training. They have also created their own

training programme by attending conferences with other doctors working in similar institutions in Europe, and by living and working closely
with children with special needs. This insight is augmented by study and
contact with different professional organizations for specific conditions,
such as autism, Fragile X syndrome and so on.

As a doctor for children with special needs, it is important to be
aware of different aspects of their well-being and potential medical
problems. A common problem is over-sensitivity to touch, which
requires the doctor to approach the child with gentle movements, and
to speak to the child with a soft voice. Small physical problems like a
sore throat can have a huge impact on the well-being of a child. With
a sore throat or tonsillitis it is painful to swallow and some children
refuse to take any fluids or food. After a few days of refusing food and
drink the situation can become dangerous so that the children need
active encouragement, which may involve the use of a syringe to help
them to drink.

A doctor for children with special needs also has to be aware of the
special complications that children and adults with certain syndromes
can have. For example, children with Down's syndrome have a higher
risk of visual and hearing problems, can develop an underactive thyroid
and can be at risk of subluxation of the neck with associated neurological problems. Children with Fragile X syndrome are at greater risk of a
heart valve prolapse and children with Prader-Willi syndrome are at risk
of being severely overweight. If a child presents with aggressive behaviour it is important to eliminate any physical reason — for example, ear
infection, constipation, reflux in the oesophagus. With autistic children,
the doctor needs to be aware of possible gastrointestinal problems,
which can be quite common.

Prescribing anthroposophical remedies

A visitor to the School may notice that many children receive a 'potion'
before their meals. The use of anthroposophical remedies is part of
the treatment of the pupils; they are remedies made from minerals and
plants. The remedy will often be potentized, which means 'rhythmically
diluted' so that only the smallest trace of the original substance is left.
All the plants are grown organically and the remedies are manufactured
by companies, which specialize in anthroposophical medication.

Such remedies may be prescribed in the following circumstances. If a child has an acute illness, for example, a painful red ear and it is medically safe to use complementary remedies then anthroposophical remedies will be the first option. The doctors often prescribe Apis (Bee's sting) or Belladonna (Deadly Nightshade) for acute infections. A bee sting gives localized redness and swelling: a potentized remedy of Apis deals specifically with those symptoms. Poisoning from Belladonna leads to dilated pupils and a flushed and bouncing head: again a potentized, rhythmically diluted remedy can help with fever conditions.

Some children who have chronic conditions like epilepsy, constipation or sleeping problems take remedies, which are prescribed alone, or in combination with, conventional drugs. Anthroposophical remedies can be safely combined with conventional drugs. The medical officer will also prescribe remedies to help the general, educational therapeutic process of the pupil. A child may be pale, look frail and have a poor appetite. In addition to ensuring that the child has enough sleep, the doctor can prescribe *Argentum per Bryophyllum* a gentle remedy, which helps restore the well-being of the child.

Nutrition

An important aspect of the therapeutic impulse is the provision of a wholesome diet, with as a much organic food as possible and food with few or no additives. Fresh milk is brought daily from a local Camphill community farm and bread is usually baked daily in a neighbouring Camphill village community. The school gardens produce some of the vegetables. Nutritious food can bring significant improvements in a child's physical and mental well-being. Many modern diets are totally unsuitable for children given their high salt content and the additives in fizzy drinks, ready-made meals and sweets. Each day the children in Camphill Schools eat freshly prepared food. This can be a challenge for some children, especially autistic children who may have lived on a limited diet of macaroni cheese or sausages and crisps. These children need to be shown a lot of patience in order to help them widen their food intake. However, it is important that they are still occasionally offered their favourite food. Some children arriving at the Schools have special diets, for example, a casein free or gluten free diet. Where it is clear that this is medically beneficial for the child the diet will be followed.

The future

The problems presented by the children in the School are constantly changing, and as medical officers we have to respond to these changes. One way of doing this is through research and collaboration with other professionals. One particular challenge is the education of young doctors entering the profession as medical officers; a rewarding but complex role. A start has been made by having regular visits from medical students for a few weeks at a time. It is also our hope to:

— establish training practice for General Practitioners;
— expand consultancy work for children and adults with special needs;
— undertake further research into the effects of dietary intervention and the use of supplements with children with Down's syndrome and Autistic Spectrum Disorder ;
— research quality of life issues with children with special needs;
— publish findings of our research in professional journals.

13. The Built Environment

DENIS CHANARIN

We all make the journey from birth, through childhood, to adulthood and for some it is a difficult journey. For those who seek to guide the child on this journey, it is important to recognize that the buildings and landscapes in which we live affect us deeply, and can influence our efforts to create an enlivening therapeutic environment. I make no apologies for the fact that I believe passionately that good architecture has the potential to improve our lives, encourage harmony and well-being and enhance our sense of being alive. The way the built environment is shaped can help calm the agitated and distracted child and can awaken the withdrawn child. It can foster a sense of belonging and encourage the healing relationship between a fragile and vulnerable soul and the world around it.

We experience the world through our senses. When we reach out and touch something — whether a stone, a tabletop or the surface of a pool of water — not only do we experience the object but we also awaken something in ourselves; our sense of 'self,' our 'ego.' As we grow up this ego gradually takes hold of our will, thinking and feeling — the ego takes control, connects with the soul forces, integrates thinking, feeling and actions and anchors them in a healthy and true relationship with the world. The child needs to develop confidence, inner strength and a sense of morality, while retaining a sense of wonder and respect. With this goal in mind there are two particular aspects of the built environment surrounding the child that I want to explore. How do we create a sense of belonging, a sense of 'place?' How can the spatial qualities of architecture — the forms, proportions, colour and materials — enhance therapeutic work?

Let us, first of all, explore how we can help a child to feel that they belong. How can we create a local environment which is comprehensible and where the child can feel safe and at home?

If we experience the world as chaos, it can appear a frightening place. Creating a sense of place, of order, can bring the world into an intelligible whole. It is both a physical and a soul experience to be able to orientate within the world. For a child, naturally more vulnerable and sensitive, having a sense of how the world fits together and is interrelated is important. That is why children love to build a *toy* farmyard or a village — a world that is containable and embraceable. We all need to create such 'mental maps' in order to place ourselves in the world. We need to be able to say: 'This is where I live, this is where I belong and this is my home.' Understanding the concept of the 'mental map' helps shape the process of planning, albeit a single building or a whole school estate. That does not mean that everything should be the same, but that there should be unity and natural cohesion.

On the more intimate scale of design, the need to create a sense of place is as important. A tree trunk, a low wall, some steps, even a change in level, is enough to begin to delineate personal territory and define a sense of partial enclosure. Children love to turn the space beneath a table into a cave, or the hollow inside a garden bush into a den. They want a sense of enclosure — a sense of containment helps bring them security and a feeling that this is 'my space.' From that safe, personal place, they can venture out to meet the world. Fairy stories often repeat this theme of going out into the world. For most of us, and even more for the vulnerable child, the need to work from a position of security is important. At every level of design, whether a bed corner in a bedroom, a classroom or a school house, an architect will look to define or suggest spaces, which enhance a sense of personal space and a sense of security.

It is important for children to learn to be part of a group and a community. Sometimes these opportunities are formal occasions like school assemblies, festivals and plays. We can design buildings in a way which helps children approach such events in the right way, and recognize the kind of behaviour that is expected of them.

The informal and unstructured nature of community life is as important as participation in formal events. Social life can happen anywhere. Children learn from seeing how adults behave. Whether waiting for transport, bumping into people outside the office or making a drink in a kitchen, each occasion can become a social event in its own right. For informal socializing to work there need to be suitable props. It may be the provision of a covered porch outside an entrance door, the foyer of a school or hall, the bay window in the dining room or the seat in an alcove off a passage. Good architecture must respond to the needs of the community and contribute to its well-being. Community life is created by the ease of movement between individual and social, between private and public, and the building design can both clarify and facilitate this need.

How do we experience architecture? Entering a mighty cathedral the soaring scale and volume are mirrored within us and create an inner attitude of awe and reverence. However, when we are in a low confined space we can feel crushed and claustrophobic. The outer space is mirrored within the soul; there is a corresponding inner spatial experience. It is not simply dimensions that we are responding to but the *quality* of the space. Its proportions, forms, sculptural shapes and colours, all combine to create a subtle, yet complex, inner resonance.

'Organic' architecture has grown out of this understanding and the belief that man must find himself in and through harmony in nature. The term 'organic architecture' encompasses a wide range of styles ranging from the incorporation of discrete stylized motifs drawn from nature, to buildings which appear to be a kind of hybrid growth of plant and creature. At one end of the spectrum are designers such as the Scottish architect, Charles Rennie Mackintosh, who used stylized and decorative motifs inspired by forms found in the natural world. At the other end of the spectrum are buildings that appear to have grown out the ground as a living organism, where each surface, curve and bulge is like an exotic sea creature. Antonio Gaudi is an exponent of this more exuberant style.

We no longer live in trees or caves but *build* our homes and by doing so impose order and meaning on our environment. Whilst some wonderful and exciting work is being done today, what is required is not a 'style' in the form of a set of aesthetic rules governing design but an architecture which arises out of an understanding of two things. First, the forces that shape the natural world also shape the human being, We need to understand the forces that form the natural world and allow that insight to generate the shapes and forms of our buildings. Second, by understanding how the human being is affected by form and space, proportion and shape, we design in such a way that enlivens the soul, resulting in architecture that lives, breathes and enhances the forces in living things.

As we move through a building we experience changes, even when we are motionless our eyes still move about. The expansion and contraction of the space around us enliven our experience. Harmony comes not from absolute stillness but from elements that maintain the balance of breathing in and breathing out. Through the subtle metamorphosis of shapes, angles and planes we can create forms, which are invigorating. We do not create curves for the sake of it, as if rounded forms are intrinsically 'better' or 'friendlier,' but we generate forms, which arise out of clear meaning and understanding of their purpose.

Goethe described architecture as 'frozen music' and the analogy of architecture to music is very helpful. As we respond to the intervals of the musical scale and experience certain combinations of tones and notes as harmonious or discordant, so the scale and proportion of the spaces around us also acts upon us. At their most refined the Gothic cathedrals and the buildings of the Renaissance embody subtle mathematical relationships and harmonies, point and counter-point and the interplay of vertical and horizontal, which is the built equivalent of a Bach composition.

Whilst there is a rigidity in repetitive rectilinear forms, it does not follow that all right angles should be banished. Excessively-sculptured, or moulded, architecture can be equally oppressive. Buildings speak to us — they make statements and we consciously or unconsciously understand what they say. The wide steps leading to the Corinthian columned portico of a courts of justice proclaim: 'Be in awe, you enter an important building!' However, a low overhanging roof set on a row of columns made from round timber tree trunks, with a set of honey-coloured stone steps leading to an entrance, with wooden bench beside the door, say: 'You are welcome.' If architecture speaks to us, it should use a language that makes sense and that we understand. Architecture should not be overbearing and impose itself on us. For the child buildings should encourage a range of emotions, moods and experiences; awe, delight, work, mess, order, formality and informality.

The relation between inside and outside is important. We need to connect with, and not be cut off from, the world around us. However, if too much is opened up the space flows out and the balance between containment and openness is lost. The child is drawn away from the room they are in and their consciousness flows outside. When designing in the context of curative education, it is important to be aware of how a child's attention can be drawn away to the outside and how, as a consequence, they can find it difficult to concentrate.

For some children the act of crossing a threshold can cause difficulty, for others the need to see a goal is important. The transition between one space and another is an important consideration in design. Moving through a building or between buildings is a minor journey. Let us imagine a journey. We take a path which curves around a pond, then we go up some steps and as we do so our hand runs along the smooth oak handrail, we enter an enclosed passage and catch a glimpse of distant hills ahead, the path then turns away and drops down through a gateway which opens to stepping stones canopied by overhanging tree branches, then we go up and across a narrow bridge over a stream to a door. At one point we can see into the far distance, at another point our attention is guided to the red maple bush close to our feet. The quality of light changes as we progress — at one moment we have open sky the next moment leaf dappled shadow. The path has led us through a richly tapestried world both natural and man-made. We eventually reach our goal but not before having had a 'wonder-full' experience.

Colour and the way it is applied creates soul moods. To argue that colour is a matter of individual taste is to miss the significance of the use of colour in supporting and enhancing the creation of a therapeutic environment. Small differences in hue or tone can significantly and delicately alter the way we experience, and are affected by, colour. As space and music are echoed as inner soul experiences, so colour can affect the soul in a manner more subtle than the crude notion that 'red is enlivening and blue is calming.' In trying to create a therapeutic environment, all the elements surrounding a child should support the healing qualities of that environment. For example, in working with colour a special technique of applying translucent washes has been developed. As natural light falls upon a surface, the colour experience is a gentle, rich and subtly varied one. In contrast, the application of a single bright opaque colour gives a dull effect, whilst the translucent wash vibrates in a calming, yet harmonious, way.

There are many other elements — materials, textures, and the quality of natural and artificial light — which shape our built environment. Vitruvius, the Roman engineer, wrote that architecture must embody three qualities: firmness, utility and delight. In short, buildings should not fall down, should serve their purpose and should be enriching at a spiritual level. The ideal is to achieve the practical requirements for which the building has been constructed, as well as to create buildings that lift architecture above the simply functional, and by doing so occasion delight, raise consciousness and generate fun and wonder, which is part of the business of being truly human. Architecture can connect us to what is deepest in ourselves and to the world around us. It is a magical and mysterious event in space and can be part of the healing environment that we strive to create around the child.

14. The Natural Environment

FRED HALDER

We are part of the earth and it is part of us,
the perfumed flowers are our sisters.
The bear, the deer, the great eagle, these are our brothers.
The rocky crests, the meadows, the ponies — all belong to
the same family,
you must give the rivers the same kindness you would give
to any brother,
the air is precious. It shares the spirit with all the life it
supports.
The wind that gave me my first breath also received my
last sigh.
You must keep the air and wind apart and sacred, as a place
where we can go to taste the wind that is sweetened by the
meadow flowers.
The earth does not belong to us. We belong to the earth.
What befalls the earth befalls all the sons and daughters of
the earth.

— Native American-Indian Chief Seattle, 1900s.

The setting of the Camphill School

The Camphill Rudolf Steiner School, Scotland, is situated in the Dee Valley, in north-east Scotland. To the north, the gently rising side of the valley is hardly noticeable. On reaching its top there is a smooth undulating landscape composed of a series of hills each more pronounced than the last. It is a patterned landscape cultivated by generations of farmers, who have toiled unceasingly on stony and hungry soil. To the south, we face the River Dee and the steep north-facing slopes of the valley, which rise up to a bleak upland area made up of much less favoured farmland and harsh moorland, before the land eventually falls away to the richly fertile lands of Kincardineshire. To the east, the River Dee flows quietly through lightly-wooded banks and into the grey and once fish-rich North Sea. Finally, to the west, are the foothills of the Cairngorms, that mighty granite intrusion, from whose plateau at 1200 m (4000 ft) the

River Dee is born. Here, the purest and softest water bubbles forth before descending rapidly in alpine style to lower altitudes. The character of our landscape is dominated by granite: the stones picked off the fields are granite; the dykes separating the fields are composed of granite boulders; the hungry, free-draining alluvial soils are granitic in origin; and, most of the older houses are built of granite. One further feature of the landscape, about which most people comment, is the quality of the light. Whether it is in winter when the sun is low or at the height of summer, the intensity of the light, when combined with the magical luminosity of the omnipresent silica, defies description. Each of the three estates that comprise the Camphill Rudolf Steiner School — Cairnlee, Camphill and Murtle — has its own unique character.

CAIRNLEE ESTATE

Cairnlee Estate is almost a small housing estate in its own right. Situated in the village of Bieldside on the south-facing slope of the Dee Valley, the Estate extends to 3.5 ha (8.5 acres), and accommodates not only part of Camphill School but also Camphill's Simeon Care for the Elderly. The grounds of this small estate possess a surprising number of features, including a small vegetable garden, an orchard, a small copse of willows grown for basket-making and a compact area of well-maintained grounds. The established conifers on the Estate's southern boundary provide an evergreen barrier to the adjoining housing estate, whilst the belt of deciduous trees to the north provides welcome shelter from the Arctic winds. Notwithstanding the fact that the Estate is surrounded by luxury housing, a calm atmosphere prevails.

CAMPHILL ESTATE

Camphill Estate is situated three miles further to the west of Cairnlee Estate. It occupies an alluvial mound extending to 10 ha (25 acres) and is located on the flood plain of the Dee Valley. This was the first Camphill estate and comprises several substantial granite-built houses as well as modern school accommodation, all set in secluded wooded grounds. Many of the trees are grand and imposing specimens and provide more than just physical shelter, for they give the Estate its uniquely peaceful atmosphere. The eastern half of the Estate is given over to woodland, whilst Camphill House enjoys a southerly aspect on top of a small rise

Gardener's Cottage, Murtle Farm

overlooking the Dee. To the east of Camphill House lies the sheltered, tranquil Rose Garden: a particularly peaceful area, which contains the ashes of many former longstanding co-workers of the Camphill Movement. The Estate also has a small walled garden which is extensively worked by pupils and co-workers, as well as a sensory garden designed to stimulate the senses of smell, touch and sight.

MURTLE ESTATE

Murtle Estate, the largest of the three estates, occupies over 40 ha (approx. 100 acres), and is located on a knoll some 30 m (100 ft) above the valley floor. From the House there is a splendid view of the Grampian Mountains to the south-west with the distant munro, Lochnagar, clearly visible. The River Dee, whose shore we share, engages in a lively meander against our fields. The fields are protected by a substantial embankment which shields them from most of the flooding. Murtle Estate is surrounded by farmland and an inner perimeter of woodland, most of it located on steep escarpments facing the Dee and Murtle Burn. Located within this perimeter are the family houses, school accommodation and Camphill Hall. There is also a large walled garden, which lies marginally

Walled garden, Murtle Farm

above the Dee flood plain. A disused sand quarry is now the location of the farm steading. The manicured parts of the estate, the extensive farmland, the steep woodland and the less tamed areas contribute to its overall diversity, which is evidenced further by the great variety of trees found on the Estate, including native birch, Scots pine, yew, hazel, wych elm and willow as well as non-native beech, chestnut, sycamore, lime and a host of firs and spruces.

Environmental therapy

It would be surprising if the beauty and tranquillity of these surroundings did not have a beneficial and therapeutic effect on both the children and adults who live and work there. Research has shown that the 'natural' environment of a country landscape can have a greater healing effect upon individuals than the arid and soulless redbrick and concrete surroundings of the urban environment (Ulrich 1984). Being enveloped in such surroundings not only helps to awaken an interest in the environment but also provides direct experience in the maintenance and development of the estates.

It is evident from our own observations that horticultural activities in the kind of peaceful surroundings that our estates offer are beneficial to the mental, emotional and social health of pupils and adults. It has also been noted that a group engaged in horticultural work often becomes more cohesive; verbal and non-verbal communication is stimulated and social interaction increases (O'Reilly & Handforth 1955).

Pupil participation

The gardens, where vegetables and flowers are grown for use within the schools, is one area where active participation by pupils is possible. For both educational and therapeutic purposes, the gardens offer an excellent opportunity to foster a child's connection with the natural world. This can be done by enabling him to participate in the essential activity of producing, what is euphemistically referred to as a 'primary product,' more commonly known as food! Even pupils with severe disabilities are able to benefit from their involvement in the process of growing a plant: whether through preparing the soil; sieving soil for seed modules; or sowing two lettuce seeds in a single module. Each pupil, with the help of a co-worker where necessary, can play an active and meaningful part not only in producing the lettuce, which is eaten in his house, but also in gaining satisfaction from being involved in the process of germination and growth, tending, harvesting and delivering something as essential as food. Other children may be involved in weeding or in writing labels (to keep track of seeds sown), and a myriad of other operations, which are less obviously essential.

CASE STUDY

Malcolm was a delightful fourteen-year-old boy, small for his age, who was also deaf and unable to speak. He loved to be outdoors and liked to have company around him, although he seemed oblivious to others when engaged in his tasks. Despite his disabilities he was exceptionally observant and able to distinguish between weeds and cultivated plants quite easily once he had been shown the difference. Malcolm was able to weed small beds of seedling vegetables to perfection at that very early and critical stage. He derived an obvious sense of achievement and delight when the task was successfully completed.

Camphill House, Camphill Estate

Murtle House, Murtle Estate

Camphill Hall, Murtle Estate

Craft Studio, Cairnlee Estate

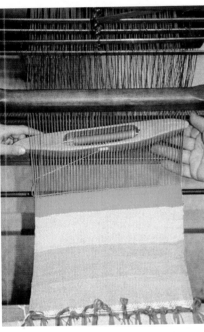

Craftwork

Laverock, Loch Arthur

Pottery and Craft Workshop, Delrow

Gardening involves not only growing vegetables but also an engagement in all the stages that precede and follow that process. It might be a more peripheral activity like compost-making for the vegetables; or growing flowers for the various flowerbeds on the estates, raising tree seedlings or selling produce at the Open Day. Each of these activities links the pupil to the natural world.

The biodynamic farm

Karl König (1960) noted that one of the foremost tasks ahead of the Camphill Movement would be the care of the land:

> gardens today and farms today are ruined and exploited by mechanized work and chemical fertilizers. The soil over the world is like someone who suffers and cries out for help and healing. It is to be hoped that the Movement will find the right helpers to create remedial work in this field, too.

The farm on the Murtle Estate produces beef and lamb, cereals for livestock and vegetables for consumption within the School. The biodynamic farming methods used on the Estate are not so vastly different from organic farming methods (Sattler & Wistinghausen 1992). When asked: 'What is the difference between organic and bio-dynamic agriculture,' I usually reply: 'Biodynamic farming is an enhanced form of organic agriculture!' From a biodynamic perspective each farm should be regarded as a self-contained and self-sustaining organism. There should be the minimum of external inputs to enhance fertility and these inputs should be generated from 'within' the farm! We aim to use biodynamic/organic food for its increased taste, enhanced life-forces present within the food and vastly reduced pollution. The danger of adding potential pollutants unnecessarily to the soil was highlighted in 2005 by Professor Vyvyan Howard, at the Seventeenth Annual Soil Association Conference. He argued that since no amount of research will ever determine the detrimental effects of the thousands of pollutants released into the environment, let alone their infinite combinations, the best alternative under these circumstances is to avoid them as far as is reasonably possible.

Where livestock is kept, closed herds are an essential ingredient of biodynamic farming. The various applications of compost starters or enhancers — more often referred to as 'preparations' — should all be produced on the farm. Unfortunately, producing some of these preparations on a biodynamic farm is no longer permitted as a result of European regulations.

Particular emphasis is placed on having livestock in as stress-free an environment as possible where their handling and feeding is concerned. The beneficial effects of this approach can clearly be seen in the end products — the taste, texture and ease of cooking of the meat. No prophy-lactic treatment is given to the livestock and antibiotics are used only in exceptional cases. We seek to take from the land only that which it yields freely and is needed to sustain the farm's continuity. Not only are the 'preparations' applied in extremely dilute (i.e., homeopathic) quantities but, wherever possible, their application is intended as an enhancement of the life-giving forces within the soil and crop. Whilst experience and old estab-lished agricultural practice form the basis for day-to-day decision-making on the farm, account is also taken of planetary influences on such activities as sowing, cultivating or applying preparations (Thun, M. & M. 2005). However, it should be stressed that the link between preparations and cos-mic dynamics is only effective where balance and harmony are maintained (Sattler & Wistinghausen 1992). Sustainable husbandry practised in this way amply repays the extra investment of energy and resources!

Research

During the past five years Murtle Estate has collaborated with the universi-ties of Aberdeen, Edinburgh and Newcastle in a number of international research projects, which have included examining the antibiotic resist-ance of organic beef cattle, as well as a project on the blight management of organic potatoes. We were approached to take part in these projects because Murtle Farm is recognized as a long-established, organically-cer-tified farm. I believe it is important that we make our facilities available to mainstream research and assist in such endeavours where appropriate.

Work experience

In a farm environment some of the older pupils are able to gain a unique and valuable form of work experience that is not driven by economic impulse and exploitative methods. The seasonal rhythms provide the necessary impulse in livestock and crop production. Through working on the farm pupils are exposed to a process of resensitivization, where they are made aware of the needs of the land and where, at the same time, they have to accept responsibility for the animals and plants in their care. If the cattle are not fed on a daily basis during the winter, then they will die. Pupils who are actively engaged in working alongside farm staff rapidly become aware of such harsh facts! Pupils are also encouraged to recognize that just as man is dependent on the fruitful produce of the land, so too the land is dependent on the good stewardship of man. This concept of reciprocity is central to the philosophy and practice of curative education, namely, that one should give in return for what one takes.

Pupils who may initially regard farm work as tedious can, over time, not only come round to liking it but also enjoy the activity and wish to repeat the experience.

CASE STUDY

A group of six reasonably capable boys aged fifteen to sixteen were asked to help mix and barrow concrete at a prepared site. The concrete was required to construct a bridge thus facilitating tractor access to a newly-acquired field. With varying capabilities amongst the group the response was mixed but on the whole positive. Rising enthusiasm and a sense of urgency once the work had begun yielded astonishing results. Ten tons of concrete were mixed and barrowed during the day, far beyond our expectations. Their sense of achievement was immense.

Every so often the former pupils, now grown men, who were involved in the above enterprise visit the School and invariably recall this event with pride! This example provides a clear demonstration of the importance of having a genuine purpose for any work proposed. Since the bridge had to be built for the benefit of the Community, it also reinforced the sense of belonging to the Community.

CASE STUDY

Ronald came to us as a withdrawn twelve-year-old who would willingly converse with some of his peers but was very hesitant with adults. His interests were building and plumbing even at that early age. When asked what he would like for his birthday present, he replied: 'A bag of cement!' This he duly received on the appointed day. Subsequently, he took an interest in the tools necessary for this trade, invariably always choosing the very best. Ronald took an increasing interest in mechanical and electrical items and slowly became more vocal, when allowed to assist in repairs and maintenance of mechanical items, such as a small tractor used on the farm. He displayed great aptitude and ability in this area, and was always present when this type of work took place. Ronald finished school and was taken on as an apprentice plumber/electrician on the Murtle Estate for a time. He attended college as part of his training and became fully qualified. It is extremely rewarding to know that Ronald now runs his own successful plumbing and electrical business and is also a fully-qualified gas installation engineer.

The farm at the heart of the community

It was Karl König's view that the farm should be at the heart of the community. This is certainly the case in some Camphill communities, for example, Botton Village in Yorkshire. However, this is not feasible within a school setting. Barkhoff in a lecture given to Camphill farmers and gardeners in January 1989 argued that the farmer's decisions at the beginning of each day should determine the work in that community setting. He argued that the farm was the 'dynamo' of the community providing not only food and drink but also an educational activity that was linked to the many life processes not obvious to those living in an urban environment.

Chief Seattle's statement at the beginning of this chapter is important because it stresses the fact that we do not own the land. 'The earth does not belong to us, we belong to the earth.' We are guardians of the land and the environment that is entrusted to us. We must, therefore, fulfil this responsibility by caring for it. Hence the application of biodynamic farming methods, the respect and reverence for the livestock, crops and soil, and all those who over the years have contributed to the health and well-being of the Estates.

This reverence should also be extended to the way that we prepare the produce for the table. Our increasing use of organic/biodynamic food, the culinary expertise reflected in the house menus, the physical presentation of the meals, the taste and nutritional value of the food, should all add to the feeling of well-being. Meals should not simply be times set aside to eat food but should be social occasions, which are celebrated. Sadly, in this day and age, family meals are no longer the norm. Meals should be convivial occasions, when respect is shown for what one eats which can be done through offering a grace at the start and finish of each meal.

ISLANDS OF RECOVERY

The following extract is from a talk given by Karl König to an Agricultural Conference in 1963:

> I very much hope that more and more land can be acquired, not to start everywhere a village but to start on every piece of ground which from now on is coming into our care, a harmonious and balanced spot of health. These will be islands of recovery where a given number of people for a given number of fields and woods and with a given number of animals live, work and breathe together. I personally would see this as one of the main tasks of the agricultural impulse within the Camphill Movement.

Karl König 's notion of 'islands of recovery' is of particular interest. On one level this can be interpreted to mean bringing back to health the impoverished lands, which have been acquired. But on another level the agricultural impulse is needed to create a balanced and harmonious environment within which people can live and breathe. In short, it is the land which provides the heartbeat and rhythm for the community. Representing the Camphill Rudolf Steiner School as an 'island of recovery' is perhaps not too fanciful a notion as that indeed is its purpose.

Critics often comment upon the fact that Camphill communities are located in remote rural settings — islands — which are alien to the everyday experience of most people who are drawn from urban backgrounds. What this criticism ignores is the fact that such settings can provide essential nourishment for mind, body and spirit, those human elements that curative education seeks to address and nurture. Thus the quality of the physical environment in which curative education takes place is of crucial importance.

15. The BA in Curative Education

NORMA HART & ANGELIKA MONTEUX

The BA in Curative Education (BACE) is a practice-based training offered by the Camphill Rudolf Steiner School in partnership with Aberdeen University. It seeks to integrate theoretical teaching with practical experience in the curative education areas of care, education, therapeutic activities and crafts. The teaching is informed by the philosophical principles of Rudolf Steiner, which adopt the view of the human being as a biological, social, psychological and spiritual entity. In its interdisciplinary character, the BACE represents a challenge to traditional concepts of professional training. The Programme is exceptional, too, in being the only instance in the UK of a nationally recognized care qualification that is offered in partnership between a Higher Education Institution and a service provider.

The role of the School is central to the day-to-day running and ongoing development of the Programme, which is at the forefront of the School's pioneering activities. Students live and work in this community where almost everyone is engaged in continual, planned learning and development.

The Scottish and international contexts

In Scotland over the last ten years, government policy regarding qualification and registration requirements for co-workers has presented significant challenges to the Camphill Schools. In March 2003, following a significant period of review and development, the BACE and its associated awards (Certificate and Diploma) were successfully accredited as professional qualifications for curative educators. The Programme was recognized by the Scottish Social Services Council as an appropriate qualification for workers in *any* care setting in Scotland, and this was the first time that a qualification in curative education was professionally recognized in the UK. The Programme is also recognized by the Council for Curative Education and Social Therapy of the Medical Section of the School of Spiritual Science at the Goetheanum in Dornach, Switzerland.

In 1949, recognizing the importance of personal and professional development, Karl König developed a comprehensive training programme for curative educators. The Camphill Seminar in Curative Education, as it came to be known, was a holistic community experience. Along with the co-workers and pupils, König sought to develop the School as a community of practice, where team learning and a shared vision, as outlined by Senge (1990), played an essential role. From the beginning he succeeded in creating an active learning culture, where co-workers were encouraged to study the work of Steiner and where guided and intensive research, integrated with ongoing practice-based learning, helped to inform the development of the principles underpinning anthroposophical curative education.

König had a modern vision of *community,* based on Steiner's research into social organisms, which is evident in the formulation of what Steiner called the fundamental social law:

> In a community of people working together, the well being of the community is greater the less the individual worker claims for himself the proceeds of the work he has done and the more he makes these over to his fellow workers. Similarly he allows his own needs to be met out of the work done by others. (Steiner 1919, 50)

The practical embodiment of this vision secured the development of the BACE as a learning community.

König regarded an ethical approach to learning, and the idea of connectedness, as central. This is clearly reflected in his own words, which are quoted in the Camphill School's prospectus:

> It is the conviction of those who work in Camphill that beneath the outer physical handicap, emotional disturbance or failure of motivation, each child's inner eternal being remains unimpaired and whole. They are not handicapped children, but children who bear a handicap. We, as co-workers, can help them better if we recognize what they have to teach us. We can effect more of a change if we ourselves are willing to change.

This approach underlined the importance of learning and constant development, which is essential to the Camphill ethos and is very much alive today in the learning community of the BACE Programme.

The BACE and Curative Education

Anthroposophical curative education cannot be defined as a professional discipline in the usual sense of these words. It is a complex activity, where a range of disciplines, such as education, care, therapy, medicine, various arts and crafts, come together and are united by the shared task of creating a holistic approach to the support of those who suffer an imbalance in the integration of body, soul and spirit. In order to be effective, the above disciplines need to work closely together, to communicate with one another, and share knowledge and insights.

The aim of the BACE is to develop the knowledge, values, attitudes and practice that comprise curative education. For the purposes of the programme, curative education has been defined as:

> ... a multi-disciplinary, professional approach concerned with the physical, emotional and spiritual well being of children and adults with complex needs. It encompasses care, education, craft and artistic activities and a medical, therapeutic element. (BACE brochure 2005)

The multi- and interdisciplinary philosophy underpinning curative education allows for a deep creative approach, based on the formation of a common context of meaning and identity. This approach has been described by Wenger:

> As people pursue any shared enterprise over time, they develop a common practice, that is, shared ways of doing things and relating to one another that allow them to achieve their joint purpose. Over time, the resulting practice becomes a recognizable bond among those involved. (Wenger 1999 in Capra 2001, 94)

This sense of identity formed by common practice, when combined with a commitment to ongoing learning, mean that the School can be fairly described as a group:

> ... of people who share a concern or a passion about a topic and who deepen their knowledge and expertise in this area by interacting on a regular basis. (Wenger *et al.* 2002, 4)

What makes this Programme unique is the fact that students 'live the course' in the residential community setting provided by the School. The BACE has developed from within this community of practice with its rich learning opportunities to become a thriving learning community (Lave & Wenger 1991). In this setting, which does not recognize the usual professional barriers, the ongoing learning experience of the students is a communal activity in which many people, including the pupils, participate (Palmer 1997). The community orientation also provides continuous feedback and close supervision of work at all levels, and offers an opportunity for the concurrent acquisition of theoretical insights, practical skills and personal growth. This community aspect is one of the Programme's defining characteristics.

The professional training in anthroposophical curative education is structured over four years on a part-time basis and encompasses: the integration of anthroposophical and non-anthroposophical knowledge and understanding, with practical experiences of sharing life with children and adults with complex needs; the use of arts as a medium for self-expression and personal development; and an exploration of the holistic approach of curative education.

The students

The BACE attracts an international student group from Britain, the European Union and non-EU countries. The Programme is open to applicants over the age of nineteen years who have had experience of working with children and/or adults; possess the ability to undertake a programme of study at this level; show an interest in working within a therapeutic community; and, where their first language is not English have successfully completed the International English Language Testing System (IELTS) Level 6, or equivalent. Priority is given to students with previous experience of work in a curative educational setting.

While the majority of students live and work within the School, there are also students working in associated Camphill adult communities. For all Camphill sponsored students, the university fees are paid by the Camphill community in which the student lives. Tuition, board and lodging are provided free and the students receive pocket money for personal expenses.

The Programme is unique inasmuch as it brings together sixty to seventy students from all over the world, of whom more than ninety percent are from outside the UK, and who have different outlooks, life experiences and values. This diversity contributes to the richness of the experience of all who live, study and learn in Camphill communities — children and young people/adults, students, teachers, houseparents, therapists, doctors and craft instructors. The motivation of the student for personal and professional development must be seen within a community context, where mutual responsibility and interconnectedness are essential prerequisites of daily life.

The teaching and tutor team

The BACE as a learning community extends beyond the School to the associated Camphill communities and Aberdeen University. The Programme is delivered mainly by experienced curative educators from the School and associated communities. University staff contribute to teaching and assessment in all three Stages and in Stage III undertake the teaching and tutoring of the research/project work for the final dissertation. Former students are now joining the tutoring groups, strengthening and renewing the teaching and learning process. Regular meetings of the tutor groups provide opportunities for review and reflection and the development of the group itself. Student representatives attend these twice-yearly meetings, as a means of ensuring an ongoing dialogue between students and tutors.

Learning, teaching and assessment

In the original seminar, learning was to a large extent informal although there were classes, lectures and study groups (Tight 1996). Students acquired practice-related professional skills in the setting of the house-community, classroom or craft workshop and learned from the example and attitudes of more experienced co-workers. The most important assessment instrument at that time was the 'Final Seminar Talk.' This was a community event symbolized by all the participants sitting in a circle. The whole community was represented in a non-hierarchical way, with students participating on equal terms.

STAGE I
120 SCQF 7

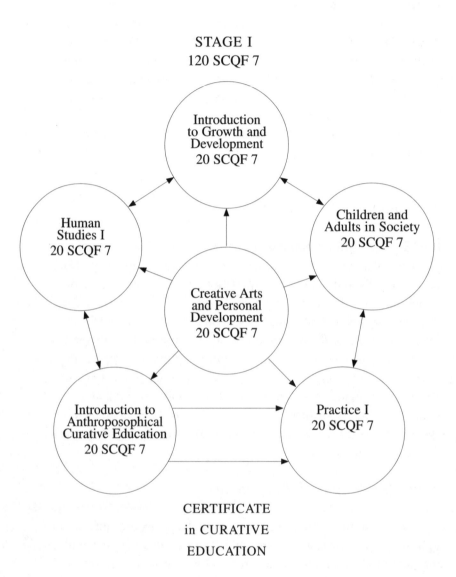

Introduction
to Growth and
Development
20 SCQF 7

Human
Studies I
20 SCQF 7

Children and
Adults in Society
20 SCQF 7

Creative Arts
and Personal
Development
20 SCQF 7

Introduction to
Anthroposophical
Curative Education
20 SCQF 7

Practice I
20 SCQF 7

CERTIFICATE
in CURATIVE
EDUCATION

*Personal
Qualities:*   empathy & questioning
                feeling
                responsiveness

STAGE II
120 SCQF 8

STAGE III
60 SCQF 8
60 SCQF 9

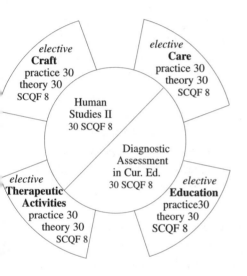

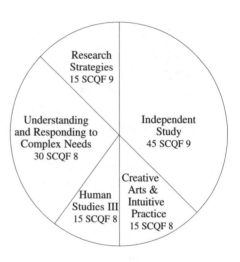

DIPLOMA
in CURATIVE
EDUCATION

BA in CURATIVE
EDUCATION

activity & responsibility
willing
pro-activity

initiative & research
thinking
research

Just as the process of undertaking the seminar was developed as a holistic community experience, so too was the final ceremony. All tutors involved with the student over the three years were present and anybody else the student cared to invite. Those attending also included co-workers, who had shared aspects of community life with the student. The student would then describe their experiences, strengths and areas for development and evaluate their learning. Following this self-assessment, others would add their points of view and reflect on the student's progress. The ensuing conversation established the final agreement regarding the award of the Camphill Diploma. The outcome of this event was summarized in a written 'Appreciation.'

These methods of teaching, learning and assessment remain integral to the BACE to this day. They help foster an awareness of the whole community context in which the Programme is offered, of its non-hierarchical interdisciplinary approach, and the opportunity it affords for the integration of theory and practice on a daily basis. However, there is now an explicit consciousness of the methodology used, the knowledge that needs to be acquired and the practice skills and qualities required. This has enabled the Programme to successfully stand up to the rigorous systems of academic and professional assessment and quality assurance, which are demanded in higher education in Scotland and by the Scottish Executive. The Programme:

— offers a flexible approach to learning which is learner-centred;
— encourages self direction giving the student increasing responsibilities for their own learning and development over the three stages;
— values the contributions of all and promotes teamwork and community building;
— employs teaching methods which stimulate reflection, enquiry, analysis, problem-solving and creativity;
— employs a variety of learning contexts, for example, through the use of the arts (including drama, music and painting);
— uses a wide range of assessment methods (e.g., group work, seminars, action inquiry, small scale investigation, project work, portfolios, etc.).

Prior to the BACE, there had been little reference to, or use of, non-anthroposophical theory or approaches in the training of curative educators. However, by the 1980s that had changed. There was a realization that it was as important to pay attention to the boundaries of the Community as to their core, and to make sure that there was enough activity at these boundaries to renew learning. Wenger (1999) observed that communities of practice truly become organizational assets when their core and their boundaries are active in complementary ways.

Continuing with the Camphill Seminar, innovative though it was, could have led to complacency, stagnation and isolation, if there had not been a willingness to reach out to the wider community and its academic institutions for other sources of expertise and excellence. Building on the solid foundation provided by the original training programme, the BACE has developed and extended the training for the curative educator. The partnership with Aberdeen University, and the subsequent expansion of the learning community resulting from it, has added to the richness of the learning opportunities, and has encouraged the development of a more outward-looking and confident workforce.

The BACE as a learning community

Learning is finding out what we already know.
Doing is demonstrating that we know it.
Teaching is reminding others that they know as well as we do
We are all learners, teachers and doers.

— Verse used in Camphill craftworkshops

The concept of a learning community has been defined as groups of students and faculty working in partnership and focusing on themes that cut across several traditional disciplines (Angelo 1999). As in the original Seminar the process of undertaking the BACE has been developed as a holistic community experience, in which the learning is gained from taught sessions, supervised practice and day-to-day community living, which all go hand-in-hand. Since students are 'living their learning,' they are more conscious of the role of theory and its practical relevance and value.

What does the Programme offer students? It offers:

— a unique learning community environment ;
— the ongoing challenge and possibility for practical experi-
    ence and reflection in the supportive framework of daily life;

— a wide range of activities providing opportunities for students of all learning styles and temperaments to use their existing gifts while developing new talents;
— a recognition of the reality of spirituality in giving purpose and meaning to the life and work of the curative educator.

The concept of a learning community also highlights the connectedness evident in the Programme in which everyone, students, tutors, colleagues and pupils, have a valued part to play, and where the professional approach of curative education transcends traditional disciplines and normal professional barriers.

The BACE and all related activities are held and supported by a community framework and a network of collaboration and mutual support. This can be seen as directly linking to the innovative work of current educational practitioners, who have argued that knowing, teaching and learning are communal acts (Palmer 1997).

The use of student-centred approaches to teaching and learning, such as problem-based learning, project and portfolio work, reflect this connectedness, by encouraging both interactive group learning and self-directed learning. With much of the teaching and learning occurring in the 'natural setting' of the students' everyday life, learning is necessarily experiential. From this comes the motivation to ask questions of other co-workers, tutors and pupils, to test out and apply what is learned. This is truly continuous problem-based learning.

The students

Students regularly share their assignments in discussions in their house evening, use their creative projects for the benefit of pupils, perform plays for pupils and co-workers as part of the assessment process, undertake small scale research projects taking forward knowledge and understanding and practice, continually deepen their knowledge and understanding of the pupils and their awareness of working as a member of a multi-professional team, and apply this in their day to day practice.

However, there is always the danger that the learning processes may remain unconscious, with students unaware of how, what and

how much they are learning, unless they actively engage in a process of reflection. This is an essential 'red thread' throughout the
four years of the Programme. To support this, students are required
to keep a Learning Journal in which they reflect on their learning,
raise questions and review and seek ways forward. It is designed as a
dynamic interactive process with tutors who read and respond to the
journal entries.

Through the ongoing interaction with others, support and feedback is
constantly available from colleagues, tutors and pupils, all of whom play
an important role in the processes of learning, teaching and assessment.
In fact, the entire community is involved in, and commits to, the support
of the student in a variety of ways. Some are more formal than others but
all are important. Support may come from a personal or practice tutor;
a colleague in the house/class/workshop who supports the student by
caring for their child when they are studying, or by listening while the
student shares ideas for an essay or presentation; the parent who is aware
the co-worker is engaged in study and consents to their child being vid-
eoed, and/or written about, for study purposes; and the pupil who plays
a part in teaching the student.

This well-developed system of student support begins when the community commits to sponsor the co-worker and finance their studies.
Each student has two tutors who are drawn from suitably experienced
and/or qualified colleagues in the community: *a personal tutor* providing academic and personal support and *a practice tutor* supporting and
assessing their practice.

However, within this community culture of training and co-worker
development, the priority is always to protect and promote the well-being
of the pupils. Inevitably there can be tensions. The tutors play a vital
bridging role between the student and the wider community, for example,
by helping the student balance the demands of the BACE for study time
with the needs of the community for co-worker time in a classroom with
a pupil. Working Agreements have been designed as a tool to facilitate
the ongoing communication between student, tutors and community. The
Working Agreement also addresses Steiner's concern that:

> In relation to the endless differences between individu-
> alities, it is barbaric to demand that all students should
> study medicine for the same length of time ... And when

it is demanded that every student must partake of a certain number of practical exercises, then one is creating through such a measure, chains for individuals who want to go their own way. (Steiner 1898, 16, translated by Angelika Monteux)

The Working Agreement Meeting is attended by the student, their personal and practice tutors and any other relevant person, for example, their house co-ordinator. The purpose of the Meeting is:

— to clarify the rights and responsibilities of all concerned;
— to support an open discussion regarding the learning needs of the student and the learning opportunities that are available;
— to determine the student's community responsibilities and the nature of the assessment process.

These Working Agreements are living documents, which are reviewed regularly and amended when necessary. Through their use, students are offered the possibility of choosing their own direction, as long as it relates to the given framework.

Continuous assessment is a key feature of the Programme and is a process which involves and affects the whole community. The assessment mechanisms are varied, creative and flexible and meet the relevant rigorous academic standards. The assessment tools include essays, oral presentations, group tasks, artistic projects and an open book exam. The Programme seeks to achieve an integrated assessment through the collaboration of Camphill tutors, the student's colleagues, University tutors and the pupils — all of whom come together to make a holistic and realistic understanding of the student's ability and potential.

In practice-based training, the assessment of practice is of particular concern. Curative educators need to acquire not only skills and competencies but also inner qualities and attitudes that will allow them to work in a flexible, creative and intuitive way. Community involvement is integral to this process and triangulation of evidence is a key feature. This allows direct observation by tutors, feedback from colleagues and pupils, as well as accounts from the students and their reflections in their learning journal. All of these are used as sources of evidence. The assessment of practice in Stages I and II involves the student meeting with his tutors. The event begins with an oral self-assessment and the presentation of supporting evidence. The tutors then feed in their views and from the ensuing conversation a judgment is reached — a process which is not dissimilar to the Assessment Circle used in the original Seminar.

Building on the foundation provided by the Working Agreements in Stages I and II, and recognizing the growing independence of the student, a Personal Development Plan is prepared by the student in Stage III, in dialogue with relevant tutors and invited others. This addresses all aspects of the student's work along with their community responsibilities, their personal and professional development, and at the same time looks forward to their future beyond the end of the Programme. This 'ending' process reflects the importance attached to the notion of interconnectedness, which is a feature of the holistic community experience. The personal tutor compiles a report from this meeting.

Experienced co-workers, who act as personal or practice tutors, are involved in the assessment of oral presentations, written assignments and practice. Members of the student's house communities and other colleagues are also involved in a variety of ways; for example, by commenting on work in progress and listening to rehearsals of oral presentations. The pupils may be aware that their co-worker is writing an essay or is waiting for the result of an assignment, or has just received a good or not so good result. Pupils may also know that they are being studied for the purpose of the BACE. The stresses of meeting submission deadlines and the joys and disappointments involved in the return of assignments also reverberate within the community, potentially affecting everyone in some way as pressure mounts or news is received.

Conclusion

The title of the original Campbell Seminar — *Community as a Path of Learning* — remains as relevant today as it was sixty years ago, with teaching, learning and assessment embedded in the life of the community and based on practical experience. The presence of the BACE students within the School's Community not only poses a positive and ongoing challenge to established practice, but also helps create and sustain a corporate learning environment in which the importance of training and continuous professional development is recognized. The School benefits enormously from sharing in the student's learning, their assignments and application of learning to practice. The Programme has brought new theoretical perspectives and insights which have informed practice and have contributed significantly to the continuing professional development of senior co-workers, who act as the principal teachers, tutors and practice supervisors for the Programme.

Comenius was a source of inspiration in the development of the learning culture of the original Seminar. To use Comenius's image of the orchestra, the learning community of the BACE is at its best when the individual players (students, colleagues, tutors and assessors), having practised their specific parts come together in a common effort to play a beautiful piece of music. Personal and professional development can be seen in terms of having the discipline to learn, practise and fine-tune one's own individual knowledge and skills, not with the aim of being a soloist but rather contributing one's personal learning and competence for the benefit of others, and working together towards the common goal of promoting the well-being of the pupils. The desire is to go beyond the immediate concerns of success and personal well-being and consider a wider framework of meaning in a community context, and is an essential ingredient of the holistic approach to teaching and learning within the learning community of the BACE.

If communities are to be effective then they need to follow the guideline formulated by Steiner (1920):

> Healing comes only, when in the mirror of each human soul
> the whole community takes shape, and when in the community the strength of each individual becomes effective.
> (Steiner 1920, 117)

16. A Community of Learning

PAUL HENDERSON

> Careful cultivation of the capacity to learn in the broadest
> sense, that's to say, the capacity both to acquire knowledge
> and to develop practical abilities, seems to offer a realistic
> way of tackling the pressing problems of our time. (Probst
> & Buchel 1997)

The above quotation highlights the crucial role that learning plays in
meeting the challenges we will encounter in the twenty-first century.
Individual, team and organizational learning are central to the effectiveness of any organization. It is essential, in the increasingly complex and
demanding care and education environment, to ensure that any training and development undertaken is relevant, accurately targeted and of
good quality. This requires a systematic approach to the identification
of learning needs, clarity about priorities and rigour in implementing
programmes.

The School has had a long tradition of studying and applying anthroposophical and curative education approaches. The wisdom inherent
in these approaches is constantly supplemented by study, research and
practice undertaken by a range of co-workers involved in academic study,
whether through the BA in Curative Education or other qualification-
based training. In recent years the School has embraced and integrated
many 'mainstream' ideas, concepts and practices as they seek to develop
curative education and facilitate community building. This openness to
learning exemplifies the School's commitment to continuous improvement. This chapter describes the crucial function that learning plays
within the School, and outlines how the community is responding to the
external and internal challenges it is facing.

The Camphill School as a learning organization

> The learning organization is an organization that is continu-
> ously expanding its capacity to create its future. For such an
> organization, it is not enough merely to survive. 'Survival
> learning' or what is more often termed 'adaptive learning'
> is important — indeed it is necessary. But for a learning

organization, 'adaptive learning' must be joined by 'generative learning,' learning that enhances our capacity to create.
(Senge 1994, 14)

According to Peter Senge, an organizational analyst, organizations have
to pay attention to the learning required to 'keep the show on the road,'
whilst at the same time making sure that people continually develop the
ability to respond creatively to new challenges. These facets of 'adaptive' and 'generative' learning are essential components for the School
and are both apparent within our training strategy. Senge stressed that
individual learning is a pre-requisite for organizational learning but that
individual learning does not guarantee organizational learning (Senge
1994). This may seem obvious. However, it is apparent that much of
what is *seen* as learning falls short when not undertaken within an organizational environment. It is, therefore, critical to make good connections
between the training activity and the individual's work setting to ensure
that the changes promoted by new learning are implemented. All too
often the impact of training falls flat when good ideas and intentions
become lost in the day-to-day, complex and demanding work situation.
It is equally crucial that any individual learning activity relates as clearly
as possible to the values, purposes and aspirations of the organization. In
developing the School's training strategy, we have sought to ensure that
the learning activities are relevant to the School's needs.

Putting learning into practice is a major challenge for any organization. Senge indicates that becoming a learning organization is not a
destination but a lifelong journey in which sustained effort is required
(Senge 1994). He argues that the learning organization is the means
through which we perceive the world and our relationship to it again.
Learning organizations, he contends, are places where people continually expand their capacity to create the results they truly desire, where
new and expansive patterns of thinking are nurtured, where collective
aspiration is set free and where people are continually learning to see the
whole together. The Camphill ethos, culture and organizational systems
possess many of these characteristics.

Burnes noted that: 'there appears to be considerable support for the view
that the pace of change is accelerating as never before, and that organizations have to chart their way through an increasingly complex environment'
(Burnes 2000). This is certainly the case for the School, and is evidenced
by the changing attitudes to residential special education, with the adoption

of the 'inclusive' education agenda and the greater emphasis by local and national authorities on inspection and regulation of services and workers. It is important that we re-energize ourselves to create a learning culture and environment. Only those organizations that are flexible, adapt to rapid change and can demonstrate quality of service are likely to survive. It is, therefore, essential that organizations engage 'the hearts and minds' of people, build their commitment to shared aspirations and motivate them to learn. Such organizations require a fundamental shift in the way they behave towards their workers. The capacity of an organization to learn will be influenced by its structures, attitudes to learning in the workforce, the extent to which reflective practice is encouraged, the kind of practical tools which are provided for the job, and the availability of guidance to workers for the situations they may face.

When organizations are asked what they believe is their most important asset they tend to respond: 'It's our people, of course.' Whilst this may be earnestly believed, there is ample evidence that this rhetoric does not match reality. The reasons for this are various and complex. It could be argued that a lot has to do with how people in organizations think work should get done. Simply training people for the task in hand is not sufficient. There is an increasing awareness that the world of work, in addition to providing the means to provide shelter and physical sustenance, must also contribute to our esteem, self-actualization and spiritual needs. The recognition of these is well rooted within Camphill where there is an inbuilt orientation towards the kind of approach that many organizations crave.

The strong underpinning principles of freedom and empowerment, which are evident within Camphill are ones recognized as critical elements in making organizations work effectively. It is self-evident to Camphill co-workers that unless someone takes on a task freely and is then given support and encouragement by his or her peers, it is unlikely that quality performance will result in the longer-term.

The Camphill School as a community of learning

Burnes argued that achieving learning organization status is something that very few, if any, organizations seem to achieve (Burnes 2000). Given that fact it would be arrogant to claim that the School can be described in such terms. However, it is true that there has been a long-standing commitment within the School to individual growth and learning through the various tasks a co-worker undertakes, and through his or her experience of community life. The combination of life and work within a community-building context has served to build, maintain and strengthen the capacity of the School to respond to challenges over the years. It would be appropriate to refer to the School as 'a community of learning' in which there is a commitment to individual and community growth.

Review Outcomes
— Training Group monitors
  and reviews Training Plan
— Training Coordinator
  facilitates evaluation
— Co-ordinators and Council
  receive report on Training
  Plan implementation

Assess Needs
— Support and Supervision
— Individual Learning Plans
— Inspection Feedback
— Registration Requirements
— Development Plan Process

Community of Learning
— Learning for personal growth and as-
  pirations, organisational development,
  task competence and qualifications
— Partnership between worker and
  community
— Fairness and Equity
— Regular Support & Supervision
— Annual Review and Learning Plans
— Assess, Plan, Implement, Review

Implement
— Training Co-ordinator takes
  action to create learning
  systems and opportunities
— Supervisors carry out
  supervision and annual
  review
— Individual puts learning
  into practice

Plan Action
— Co-ordinators approve
  needs and priorities
— Council agree Training
  Plan and Budget
— Training Group plan
  timescales and methods

The training process

A 'community of learning' can only occur where reflection on practice at individual and college/group levels is encouraged where learning across the organization is promoted, where organizational learning
needs are assessed on an ongoing basis and where annual reviews are
undertaken. Strenuous efforts are made to develop an integrated learning
environment that permits the development of both pupils and workers.
Emphasis is also placed on creating systems and promoting practice that
lead to quality improvement. The learning opportunities which are available vary considerably both in focus and delivery style and include a
mix of internal and external programmes. Some training activities, especially those relating to definite health and safety matters, are mandatory
and must be undertaken by all workers or specific groups of workers.
There is also a strong drive for the development of internal trainers and
facilitators in order to ensure that learning activities are relevant to the
organization.

All workers are encouraged to take responsibility for their own
professional development. However, responsibility is also placed on
supervisors, groups and colleges to help individuals identify and take up
relevant learning opportunities and to put learning into practice. Great
efforts are also made to ensure that decisions regarding access to training
and development are made in a fair manner using agreed criteria so that
every worker is treated equally in terms of access to training opportunities.

The regulatory context

We are living at a time of great change in the social care sector as a result
of the implementation of the Regulation of Care (Scotland) Act 2001,
which has led to greater regulation of social services in Scotland. Most
significantly it established two new executive non-departmental public
bodies. The Scottish Commission for the Regulation of Care, or the Care
Commission as it has become known, is responsible for the registration
and regulation of care services against national standards. The Scottish
Social Services Council (SSSC) is responsible for national workforce
planning, the registration of social services workers and the promotion
and regulation of their education and training.

New Care Standards, to which all care organizations are expected to
adhere, were introduced in 2002 and the School is now assessed against

these requirements twice each year. Whereas previously the respective authorities carried out care and school inspections separately, the Care Commission and Her Majesty's Inspectorate for Education (HMIE) now jointly undertake the inspection process. This is proving helpful in giving a broader overview of the School's operations, whilst providing specific feedback in relation to different aspects of curative education. This feedback is used as an important tool in helping the School identify training and development priorities.

It is a requirement that all residential care workers and managers in residential care register with the Council. A phased timetable has been set for the registration of all social services workers by 2010. To remain on the register in the longer-term (and therefore to be eligible to work in social services) workers must hold qualifications relevant to their job role. An analysis of the qualification status of co-workers who are required to register with the Council has recently been completed in the School and shows that most of those required to register from 2005 onwards are currently either qualified or are in training (e.g., the BACE or Scottish Vocational Qualification awards programmes). If co-workers possess the relevant qualification at the time of registering, they will gain full registration. Others not yet qualified will be granted conditional registration subject to completing the award before re-registration in three years (i.e. 2008/09).

Regulation for Early Years and Childcare workers is also being introduced, which will affect the School's Kindergarten provision. The SSSC qualification framework for this part of the social service workers register includes the BACE Programme qualifications. At present all those working in the Kindergarten hold a relevant teaching or BACE Programme qualification and will, therefore, be able to satisfy the qualification requirements when they are introduced in 2006.

As well as the individual registration requirements, employers and social service workers are expected to follow relevant Codes of Practice. These require employers to provide individual supervision and training and development opportunities to improve and maintain worker performance. In addition, employers must put in place properly resourced opportunities to assist workers to meet the Council's criteria for registration and continuous professional development. Workers are expected to take responsibility for their own learning by endeavouring to improve their knowledge and skills through participation in relevant training, education and supervision.

It is not only residential childcare workers that are seeking to gain relevant qualifications to gain professional registration. Regulation in other spheres of curative education is increasingly likely and in anticipation of this, teachers, craft instructors and therapists are seeking to obtain the necessary academic and professional recognition for their skills, talents and experience.

Whilst the School has a number of teachers registered with the General Teaching Council for Scotland (GTCS), there are several competent and experienced people who do not possess a formally recognized teaching qualification. Whilst qualification is not currently a legal requirement within the Scottish independent schools system — and there is an agreement with the GTCS that teachers already in post can continue in that role within Camphill — we are nevertheless taking steps to put relevant teachers through the state-recognized Postgraduate Diploma in Education (PGDE). This will serve to give our teachers the additional confidence that training can bring, enable them to register with the GTCS and more crucially contribute to improvements in the teaching practice and day-school education provision. Since craft instruction is unusual in schools outside Camphill settings, the role of the craft instructor has not been regulated by any specific body. This activity, however, is a valuable element within curative education and is recognized as such by Her Majesty's Inspectorate of Education and the Care Commission. The Schools have, therefore, taken steps recently, in liaison with the HMIE and the Care Commission, to specify the qualifications it expects of its craft instructors.

Anthroposophical therapists are not currently regulated by statute but it is anticipated that this will become a requirement within the next few years. A number of therapists have completed, or are currently engaged in, training programmes that will enable them to become registered practitioners in their chosen field. Some purely anthroposophical therapists are seeking external accreditation for their training and skills, although this is proving difficult. Where there are no relevant external professional bodies for specific anthroposophical approaches (e.g. eurythmy; therapeutic speech; riding therapy) it is hoped that the newly-formed Council for Anthroposophical Health and Social Care will gain recognition similar to that of the Health Professions Council, and will therefore be able to register anthroposophical therapists.

Training policy

The increasingly regulated environment demands that the School establishes a relevant, comprehensive, robust, reliable and flexible education, training and development system. The School's Training Policy sets out principles that guide training and development priorities, activities and expenditure, and establishes a framework for planning and decision-making. The policy also sets out a series of commitments to specific training initiatives (e.g., induction and supervision training for all) and clarifies how the training budget will be allocated in a fair and equitable manner, to fund individual, group and organizational programmes. It also sets out the responsibilities of individuals and groups relating to the effective operation of the training system. The core training which is offered includes specific training programmes for new workers, as well as training that everyone needs to receive in order to be able to perform their work safely and competently.

Supporting the co-worker within their work settings

As well as structured learning opportunities such as training courses, co-workers benefit from advice, guidance and opportunities for development and support from those more closely associated with their tasks, which is why supervision and team working are central to the work of the School. Every co-worker has a supervisor with whom they can discuss personal and professional issues that affect their work. The house evenings and various class, workshop and therapy meetings present regular opportunities for learning in connection with a range of issues affecting the co-worker. The central focus in all these meetings is the welfare and development of the pupil and how co-workers, whether working individually or together, can provide effective education, care and therapy for the pupil.

A new initiative is the introduction of a co-worker annual review and development process — similar to what elsewhere might be called an appraisal — to permit an annual reflection on individual contributions, and to create work and learning plans for the year ahead. In due course the learning needs which emerge from this systematic process will influence the School's training strategy and Annual Plans, as well as provide clarity for individuals about their own learning goals and activities. As part of the annual review cycle, the various colleges and groups will consider their particular learning needs and develop a plan for future development.

Conclusion

Learning facilitates change. What we seek to achieve in the School is a partnership between the individual and the organization for the benefit of the pupil. Learning is, therefore, not something undertaken for its own sake, it must facilitate the task of offering curative education within the context of the organization. The challenge for training and development in the coming years is to retain the essential elements of curative education, whilst incorporating best practice from the wider world.

17. Students' Perspectives

Pavlina Langerova, Czech Republic

My sister had spent one year at Beannachar, a Camphill training centre in Scotland, and through her I met people who were interested in working with people with special needs and also in Anthroposophy. I had had some experience with people with special needs, and it seemed a good idea to go to Camphill, a relatively safe place where things were provided for you but where at the same time you could learn a lot.

I had seen pictures of the Camphill training centre in Beannachar and heard a lot about it from my sister. I expected to live in a house with permanent co-workers (at that time still called house-parents), other co-workers like me and residents. I also expected to work in workshops and do most things with other people. I realized that Camphill was going to be a tough experience, hard work with challenges and I was prepared to feel down during the first weeks, but I promised myself that I would not give up. Instead I felt happy and at home almost immediately. I found myself in a beautiful place and was excited about everything during the first weeks and months. I met friendly and supportive people who helped me orientate myself. I met charming residents who needed my help and were prepared to receive it. They were open and tolerant of my imperfect English and of my total dependence on their guidance in the first days.

After my year in Beannachar, I went back to the Czech Republic, but soon decided to return to Scotland and enrol on the BACE course. I lived in Beannachar for the first year of the course, working with the young adults. Then I moved to Camphill Estate where I lived and worked with children for two years. For the last year of my course I moved to Cairnlee, another training centre for young adults, where I currently live.

I have been in Camphill for nearly five years and it is difficult to summarize briefly what I have gained, and still gain, from life here. These five past years have been an extremely important time in my life — a time of intense experience, learning and growing.

I came when I was twenty-four, a content girl who was eager to learn, with some interests and vague ideas about the future, but inside I had many fears, anxieties and doubts, so much insecurity, vulnerability and pain. Since starting the BACE my time in Camphill has been taken up with a process of becoming conscious of the reality of myself and the people around me. I had to experience many frustrations until I finally began to realize that they came from my inability to express feelings, thoughts, wishes and needs.

I have changed in the time I have lived here, and feel more mature and secure. Although one could say that I would have changed anywhere, I believe that living in Camphill has played an important role for me. Here I really have had no choice but to face my deepest insecurities and weaknesses and do something about them in order to take the next step.

I find it interesting that when I started studying for the BACE the most difficult thing for me was to be myself and be confident and clear about my views and my ability to express them. I wrote in my Learning Journal that I found it difficult to work in a team, to have inner certainty about what I felt and thought, and yet be tolerant, respectful and flexible in relation to other people and their views. Maintaining a balance between not giving up too much of myself and yet being open to others was most challenging for me. I was touched recently when I learned that, in my present house community, I am appreciated for my ability and courage to express my feelings with clarity, and that I am seen as somebody who is mature and in control of herself. I know how much struggling lies behind this and how much more I still have to learn.

Life in Camphill has taught me to empathize and communicate with people around me, to live with them and enjoy the experience. I have learned to see that they too act out of fear and insecurity, and that it is not my task to condemn them for it but to look for what is good in them and help them to find the courage to fight the insecurity and to shine. I have become more tolerant. I try not to judge people harshly but I still do and feel embarrassed when I find out I am wrong in my judgments.

We all have shortcomings and features that are difficult to cope with. They may be less obvious in co-workers, who are often good at hiding them. The pupils deal with extremes and do not hide them. They meet us with the full power of their personalities. In doing so they hold out a mirror for us to see what we would rather not see — our weaknesses that make it difficult for us to cope with what the pupils bring to us. They challenge us to develop, to learn to cope and to give them the support they need. It requires humility and courage to accept the challenge in the right way. We all do this for each other with different intensity.

My ability to see that the pupils are our equal partners in life has taken deeper roots in me over the years. Yet I would feel dishonest to say that I experience no division or difference between the co-workers and the pupils. Rather I consider our encounter a mystery and a part of a lifelong quest for understanding.

One outstanding feature of Camphill that I have enjoyed is celebrating festivals. Celebrating with many people whose heart is fully in the moment is deeply touching for me. The pupils and residents contribute to these moments in a wonderful way. I loved the first Easter I experienced in Beannachar. However, the everyday celebrations mean a lot to me, for example, coming together and singing. Sometimes the most mundane moments can be the most enjoyable ones — like spending time with somebody in a one-to-one situation and having a moment of real encounter with them, beyond the surface of their disability.

I will miss Camphill when I leave. Over the five years I have built relationships and connections that have helped me contribute something to the life of the community and to feel fulfilled by it. I have met people whom I respect and have learned a lot from; people who are open and willing to help me when I ask for help. It will be hard not having such a supportive framework around me when I go away. The pupils are of course the centre and purpose of the framework and play an essential role in it. Most importantly, they have allowed me to help them and feel needed, which has given me the fundamental assurance that there is a reason for me to be here.

Sharing life in households with pupils and co-workers is in my view the central and vital feature of life in Camphill. If the people responsible for running the house and guiding the less experienced co-workers are respectful, open and communicative the experience can be profound. They should strive to pass on the understanding, which lies behind the work in Camphill. I think it is going to be increasingly important that each individual should develop their own renewed understanding, which is alive and springs from their experience. Only in that way can living together be healing and enriching.

For me life in Camphill is clearly embedded in the seasonal cycles of the year. I consider Camphill a spiritual community. I find the respect for the forces of nature, and the attempt to bring together pagan and Christian traditions when celebrating festivals very precious. Anthroposophy adds another dimension to the picture, to the search for meaning and connection.

I believe that the daily rituals, like coming together in a circle to find a moment of silence and peace, are worth preserving, but they can only be imbued with meaning if they are understood and achieved together. Therefore it is essential to share experiences and thoughts in order to prepare for these moments and to carry them in the right way.

Camphill is about living in a community with special needs people, creating an extended family, finding a relationship with the rhythm of days, weeks, months and years and being open to give and receive, to learn and change.

> I know only one fruitful act and that is prayer.
> Yet I also know that every act may be a prayer
> If you give yourself through it
> In order to become.

> — Antoine de Saint-Exupéry

Gal Levy, Israel

When I arrived at Camphill 3 1/2 years ago, I thought I knew why I had come. I had finished the foundation course in anthroposophy and arts back in Israel, and it was clear to me that I was going to study music therapy and anthroposophy. It seemed to be quite a simple reason for me to come to Camphill, but that strong desire held other reasons, and only later have these reasons started to unfold.

The first encounter with the pupils and house life was very powerful. I had never worked with children and youngsters with special needs before, and I was filled with questions and wonder, and met some of my best teachers even before the BACE course started. The pupils showed me new facets of human experience, and in a direct — and sometimes challenging — way, helped me to learn and to change.

Even though I had many questions and could feel that my experiences had a lot to teach me, it wasn't enough to create a conscious learning process. The course helped me to bring some focus to my questions and clarity into my experiences. The work with the pupils and the course sessions supported each other.

Starting with observation, I learned how much more there is to life and how I usually see only a partial and distorted image of reality. I think a substantial part of the course is about learning to observe the human being from many points of view. Dealing with the infinite complexity of the human being, we were not given only one point of view but had to practise many 'tools of observation,' and were expected to choose which ones were most valuable for us to understand a specific individual at a certain time.

One such challenging individual that helped me deepen my understanding of human nature was myself. The course helped me to understand and to work with the children as well as to understand and work with myself. Themes like child development helped me to understand a pupil I was working with, and this understanding became more real when I recalled my own childhood experiences at a similar age. In trying to understand human perception I had to start from my own sensory experience, explore it and widen it, in order to try and understand how the pupils might experience reality differently.

Soon after the course started I realized that most of what I was learning was a step in a lifelong learning process. The course made me conscious of what I needed to learn and develop in order to be a curative educator. Through the course I started to gain clarity as to what I really wanted to learn; that is, the human qualities that are particularly needed in working with children with special needs. The children helped me to start and develop an ability to observe and listen, practise patience, empathy and courage. It is not something one can learn at a desk. I could only learn it by meeting the pupils, doing, and by making mistakes.

However difficult and challenging it was, I felt supported by the community throughout the course. The weekly talks with my housemother supported my work, my learning and my personal well-being. I felt that the talks with my personal tutor not only supported me academically but also offered a place where I could share and resolve difficulties. With the elective I received guidance and support from the music therapist and in the fourth year, I received further academic support from the university.

Even though I had experienced community life before coming to Camphill, being in Camphill showed me how much more I still needed to learn, and how significant community is for me and for others. The more I experience 'community' the less I understand what it is, and the more I want to experience it and to live it. Whilst at first I felt that only my house was my community, as time went by my awareness of the many circles that create 'Camphill' grew.

With time I have learned that even though life in the community can be complex and difficult, the awareness of these difficulties and the conscious effort to constantly create the community actually hold it together. Even though I was new to curative education and to Camphill I felt that the community, and particularly the experienced long-term co-workers, valued my questions, contributions and initiatives. I felt I could give something back to the community.

The encounter with the pupils, community life and curative education have filled me with the 'real reasons' for coming to Camphill. As a result of all the experiences and lessons I have had, I have almost forgotten the reason that initially brought me to Camphill, namely, music therapy. At one point I felt that the reason I came was simply to learn to be a parent.

In the middle of the second year the course splits into the three electives, and even though I was finally happy with my choice of music therapy, I also wanted to experience the education and care electives. I think that one of the strengths of curative education is the integration of care, education and therapy; however, it seems that Camphill is moving more and more towards 'professionally' separated tasks. The BACE course is alive, changing along with Camphill, trying to fit with the times and with people's needs. I think an effort has been made to keep the essence, and there is sufficient flexibility to allow for change.

Although curative education can be seen as a profession, it was clear from the beginning of the course that curative education is as much an art as it is a profession. Painting, drawing, modelling, music and eurythmy have helped me to deepen my understanding of the human being and also to explore myself as a means of becoming a better curative educator.

As time has gone by the role of music in my life, the community, the classes and the therapy room has become more significant. However, I try to see music from a wider perspective. I am so enthusiastic about music therapy now that I see music in everything. I try to listen to the musical interval when I encounter a pupil. I search for harmony in the house community. I am more aware of the daily weekly and yearly rhythms in life. I have a better understanding of the importance of silence and listening, both in music and in the human encounter.

While in the beginning my perspective was limited to the pupils I was looking after, with time I started to see my work in a wider context, as part of something bigger. As a result of going to the curative education conference in Dornach on behalf of the Camphill School, I started to have a sense that curative education was a world movement and my work is part of it.

Looking towards the future, I feel that even though I may leave Camphill, I don't think Camphill will ever leave me. Though I have gained experience and some knowledge, I think one of the most valuable things I received in Camphill are the sort of questions that motivate me and take me forward. These are questions about healing through human encounter, through community and through music. With these questions I return to Israel, hoping to find the answers in what I do.

18. Parents' Perspectives

Jack

KAREN AND CHRIS STEWART

One of the hardest things we have ever had to do as a family was to convince the authorities that our son, Jack, should go into residential care. We knew that this was what was needed if Jack was to have any chance of developing his potential. We were also conscious of the fact that we would have to live with the guilt we felt, as we were aware that a 'looked after' child was a child in care. Nevertheless, we wanted to act before we reached the stage of crisis intervention.

Recognizing that we really needed help was a major step, then to be bold enough to say 'No' when offered the wrong kind of help. We didn't mean to be 'difficult parents' but we knew our son better than anyone else and we wanted what was right for him. After one year of speaking to all the professionals involved in Jack's care and letting them know our situation, we were given support from a social worker after we had called for a multidisciplinary team meeting. Having to open heart and soul in front of that meeting in order to prove that I [Jack's mother], in particular, and our family, in general, were not coping was one of the most difficult things I have ever had to do. I would not wish to repeat the experience.

We have found it very difficult to come to terms with Jack's autism and have grieved for our child who will never have a normal future. We have also experienced a sense of guilt — 'What did we do wrong?' 'Is it our fault?' 'Was this something to do with our genes?' And at times, without discussing the matter openly, we blamed each other for things we may or may not have done.

We struggled to manage Jack's complex needs at home, knowing very little about autism or learning difficulties. From roughly two years of age Jack attended a good special school and we were members of the local Autistic Society. During this time we got very little sleep and were becoming more and more reclusive, as it was an easier option than having to handle the kind of bizarre situations that Jack's odd behaviour could occasion. For example, when doing something as simple as shopping, he would run up to a total stranger and feel her bare legs. He could not speak, had no awareness of danger, was hyperactive and had many obsessions. Attending a local playgroup when he was three to four years was supposed to help Jack integrate with other children but it only served to emphasize how different and disabled he was compared to his peers. As the weeks went by, it became harder to hold back the tears. We found that 'care in the community' meant isolation at home. The fact that Jack looked 'normal' made things worse, as onlookers would interpret his actions as simply being due to bad behaviour.

From two to five years of age Jack was obsessed with water and would love, given the chance, to paddle in the toilet or turn on the bath and sink taps after filling both with towels and flooding the bathroom. This meant fitting locks on the outside of the doors and having special thermostats installed to prevent him from burning himself. This all coincided with our attempts to toilet train him. This was not easy given Jack's lack of speech. We also had to get new lockable windows fitted as Jack enjoyed opening and closing things and was at risk of falling from an upstairs window.

At 5½ years, Jack used to enjoy jumping on my back and did so unexpectedly once when I was at the top of the stairs. We both went tumbling down the stairs and by some miracle neither of us broke any bones. But on other occasions, when we were not certain whether any harm had been done, we had to take Jack to Accident and Emergency. One such instance was when Jack fell off the back of the sofa landing on his arm. We explained his difficulties to the medical staff but still had to wait a couple of hours during which time his behaviour was attracting attention and causing us anxiety.

When Jack was three years old, we thought our back garden was safe as we had a four-foot wall around most of it, but he would just climb onto the wall and run along the top. We grew high trees but one day when he was left in the back garden whilst I was answering the front door, he crawled through a gap under the trees and ran out into the road in front of a van. Fortunately, I just managed to stop the van from hitting him. Trying to convince the community occupational therapist that we needed financial help to pay for the construction of a fence in order to keep him safe was another challenge!

Attempting to keep our house tidy was an endless nightmare. He would clear his books from the bookshelf and tip out boxes of toys on the floor but never play with them. As soon as I tidied them up he would move on to something else. It was a never-ending task, which I didn't have the time for. When trying to cook, tidy, etc. I needed to take Jack into the same room to ensure that he was safe. This soon became a habit, which developed into an obsession for he didn't like me being out of *his* sight! Jack almost ignored his dad and brother, only relating to me, which brought its own problems.

Due to the constant lack of sleep, lack of energy and lack of time to keep on top of things, home was not a place we wanted to invite people into and because of all the difficulties we were faced with if we went out, we found ourselves becoming increasingly cut off. We would pretend to our immediate family that things were all right, as we didn't want to worry them, but visiting was no pleasure as we were constantly checking that Jack wasn't doing anything that he shouldn't. Frequently he would break something, fuse lights, spill sugar or use all of someone's liquid soap and then get a skin rash as a consequence. We rarely did anything as a family, but on a really good day at a weekend we might go for a drive to a fast food restaurant. I have lost count of the number of family get-togethers we have had to decline.

We felt we had given our all. Jack was constantly watched over, attended to and kept safe but at the expense of our older son, Hugh, who always had to wait. At the time that Hugh started school, Jack was having a weekly assessment at the Raeden Centre. Juggling being in two places at the same time was one thing, but coming to terms with the fact that there was actually something wrong with Jack was very hard. Jack didn't want to, or couldn't cope with, wearing socks and shoes, jumpers or jackets. Trying to get him ready to go out was a continuous struggle. Having thought we were ready to go, I would turn round to find Jack had stripped off again. This was not a good way to start the day for Hugh: his mother stressed out due to the pressure of having to get both to school on time.

I was lucky in having a car and could pop the boys into it, but at that time, between the ages of two and six years, Jack was expert in his Houdini act. We tried every type of car seat and whichever one we chose I had constantly to watch him to prevent him getting out, jumping freely about in the car and trying to climb into the front. As a result we often had to make do with a large buggy, not because he couldn't walk but in order to try and contain him.

We hadn't explained to Hugh's teacher about our 'situation,' partly because we didn't feel able to do so, partly because we felt it was no one else's business and partly because we hoped that the situation would eventually improve, but Jack's lack of sleep was having an effect on all of us. Even with medication from the GP, I had to spend two to three hours each night trying to get him to sleep. As Jack was at risk of hurting himself, we had to have one ear open both day and night. Often he would sleep for only a couple of hours and then would be awake and wanting to get going again. We asked friends and family not to phone after 9.00 pm as the slightest noise — doors shutting or a toilet flushing — would waken him. Even the noise of the hoover was too much for him. When things became too stressful for Jack he would bite holes in the sleeves of his clothes or bite himself on the arm.

Once Hugh had been at school for a few months his teacher contacted me and asked if it would be possible for him to get to bed earlier as he was often very tired in class. I had to see her and explain how things were for us during day and night. She was very understanding and supportive. One day Hugh came home from school saying he had had a fight because other pupils were calling Jack a 'spaz.' Doing homework was particularly difficult because of Jack's demands on our attention. Hugh frequently had to wait and then any time that we did have with him was often disjointed and short-tempered. As he got older he managed to do more of his work on his own, but trying to protect his work or give him the peace to concentrate was a challenge. He spent an increasing amount of his time in his room in order to get away from it all.

Then we met a mum through the Autistic Society who told us how well her son had done at the Camphill Rudolf Steiner School. After a long and deep talk with her, we visited Camphill. On arriving in the School's grounds it immediately felt like a safe haven. There was a special calmness there, which it was clear that Jack also felt.

We turned up for Jack's interview with Dr Stefan with Jack wearing his grandma's high-heeled shoes! Jack spent his time switching lights on and off and opening and closing doors. The reaction, or rather lack of reaction, to this behaviour was typical. Jack was accepted for the person he was. We didn't feel we had to constantly apologize or make excuses for his behaviour. We were told that same day that he would be a suitable pupil. At last there was light at the end of what had been for us a very long and dark tunnel.

We can now proudly say that Jack is IN the loving and devoted CARE of our extended family at Camphill. He is now a happy and loving boy living a meaningful life, being with other young people and engaged in activities which have a purpose. Social interaction is part of the daily life routine and that suits his needs. Jack now speaks! Almost non stop!

Jack is now fourteen years old and has been at Camphill for seven years as a weekly boarder — home Friday to Monday and for holidays. I visit weekly and all the family regularly visit for special celebrations. Jack has grown and developed way beyond our expectations and dreams. At all times we have been fully involved in his individual educational plans and have had the opportunity to discuss the merits of different therapies and any possible problems. We have always had a very good relationship with Jack's house parents, which was essential. Letting go was very difficult, as it meant entrusting someone else with our vulnerable child. We have been open and honest with each other and have worked closely together with his teacher and co-workers so that Jack can reach his full potential at his own pace and in a truly holistic way.

Jack has only developed due to the input of certain individuals. As he has been calm and at peace with himself, he has begun to learn things that do not come naturally to him. One evening we had a phone call from his very excited co-worker to tell us that Jack had spontaneously drawn a mini-bus — his first drawing! We have shared the many special milestones that Jack has passed and have learned so much from some very special people who have devoted their lives to curative education and their very special way of life.

It is significant that the co-workers often speak of what they learn from the children there. On one occasion a co-worker told me she now knew for the first time the meaning of unconditional love.

Jack will always be autistic, so that just as we feel we have handled one set of problems, something else will come along! With the help, support and advice of Jack's housemother and co-workers and our extended family at Camphill, we now have a happy life again, no longer feeling that we just have to survive day by day.

Thanks to Jack, we have met many wonderful people. We feel that Camphill has brought Jack out of himself. He has developed and integrated at his own pace and has constantly surprised us with his achievements. This could not have happened with the kind of support arrangements that had been put in place when Jack was at home all the time. These interventions, though well-intended, seemed to lack purpose or were mere diversions failing to address the key needs of the family. The people who came to help had a number of things in common: they did not communicate with one another; they always knew better than us what we should be doing; and, those needing the respite often ended up spending their time making the arrangements to ensure continuity of care

Jack's life at Camphill has purpose. His daily routine builds into a complete year and through this his character is developing. The steadiness and purpose shown by those working in Camphill have allowed a unique relationship to develop between our family and Camphill. It is a relationship that goes beyond that of 'service provider' and 'client.' It is more that of an extended family in which all are working to the same purpose, which is supporting our son to achieve his full potential. Through Camphill — we can hope and dream again.

Scott

IVAN AND SHEILA BOUSFIELD

Our son Scott was a residential pupil at the Camphill School from August 1996 until May 2003, when he left at the age of eighteen to take up a full-time job with a local meat wholesaler, which he obtained by responding on his own initiative to a press advertisement. He stayed there for over a year-and-half, working more than forty hours a week, before leaving for a job with another meat wholesaler. A few years ago it would have seemed inconceivable that he could have even coped with a normal working environment, let alone hold down a job for any length of time. Now that he has been away from school and in steady employment for over a year, we are able to reflect on what we think have been the effects of the 'Camphill Experience.' Was it better for Scott to be at Camphill rather than in a mainstream environment, despite the contemporary trend towards so-called 'inclusion'? What was the impact of Camphill on us as Scott's parents, particularly in sharing his upbringing over the years with various houseparents? Has society in general benefited, given the financial input needed from public funds? And finally, was the 'Scott Experience' beneficial to Camphill itself? Clearly we cannot give definitive, or even objective answers to these questions, but here are our views anyway.

Scott was $2\frac{1}{2}$ and described as 'lively and mischievous' when we adopted him and his older brother in 1988. He suffered from foetal alcohol syndrome which, we were told, would leave him with significant learning difficulties and possible emotional and behavioural problems.

By the time he started primary school, Scott was chirpy, cute and charismatic, if something of a handful. At ten years old, he had become a pariah. Unable to cope with schoolwork, he was foul-mouthed, destructive and uncontrollable in his little primary school, loathed by most of his classmates and the despair of his teachers. Inevitably he was excluded and spent the following academic year as a day patient/pupil in the Assessment Unit at Aberdeen Children's Hospital. He hated this and his behaviour at home became impossible, vindictive, abusive, aggressive, physically violent towards his mother, and subject to inexplicable and uncontrollable rages. As his parents, we attended countless reviews with many professionals, but it was clear that none of the various strategies and action plans they were pursuing were working and we felt utterly defeated. Then Camphill was suggested as a last resort. How many times since then have we heard of children coming to Camphill as a last resort. And how much better might things have been for so many children if it had been a first resort instead!

As soon as we saw Camphill, we knew it was different. It didn't look like a school or a special unit or an institution of any kind. Although we were by now well-used to being talked *at* by child professionals of one sort and another, when we were interviewed by Camphill co-workers we felt the stirrings of an optimism we had not known for a long time. Two things in particular struck us as being unusual. First, there was no vaunting of 'well-tried and proven strategies' or assertions that 'we have dealt successfully with many children like Scott,' but simply a modest suggestion that 'we think we might be able to help your son.' Second, the co-workers actually seemed interested in hearing our views and gave the impression — which remained with us throughout Scott's time at Camphill — that what we had to say might be worth knowing. With one or two notable exceptions, this was something we had rarely come across previously. Five minutes into our conducted tour of Murtle Estate, we knew this was where Scott should be and, after assurances that he could bring his bike and his toys, Scott said he thought so too.

Despite our conviction that we had found the place for Scott, we were rather distressed when we were advised that he should be a full-time residential pupil if he was to gain the maximum benefit from what Camphill called 'curative education.' We had assumed, perhaps naively, that he would be a day pupil or at most a weekly boarder. However, it was explained gently that community life in the Camphill environment would be the bedrock of his therapy and would play a major part in helping him to come to terms with his problems. We asked about visiting him and were told that, while there were no hard and fast rules, it would help him to settle in if he didn't see too much of us for the first few weeks. This was when we might have felt that, having been recognized as a dead loss at parenting, we were being asked to hand our son over full-time to people who would be so much better at it than we were, but somehow we didn't. Certainly, there was much anguish and soul-searching, but we were realistic enough to see that this was effectively Scott's last chance, and that his needs had to come before our feelings. Also, we realized what perhaps, deep down, we had known all along — that Scott's problems were not going to be solved just by his attending a *suitable* school. His demons were intertwined with his whole being and would never be exorcised just by an alternative teaching regime. With the wisdom of hindsight, we know now that special needs don't come in discrete, administratively convenient bundles labelled 'educational,' 'social' 'medical' etc. For a child like Scott they are complex and all-consuming, and need an all-embracing approach if they are to be addressed with any hope of success. This is what Camphill was offering him and us — a new way of life for our troubled and lost little boy.

A few days before Scott was due to start at Camphill, he and we were invited to see where he would be living and to meet his houseparents (one of whom was to be his teacher for the next seven years). Any misgivings we may have had evaporated when they welcomed us as though they had known us for years and we realized that, far from giving Scott up to the 'professionals,' we were entering into a partnership with deeply committed and caring people, and so it proved over the next seven years.

There were no instant miracles, no overnight transformations for Scott at Camphill. He still exhibited extremes of behaviour, could be abusive towards those who were caring for him, and if he detected the slightest vulnerability in young co-workers assigned to him, he would bully them mercilessly. However, most of them could rise above it and continued to encourage and care for him. Over the years we have met some truly remarkable young people working at Camphill and their effect on Scott was immeasurable as they talked to him, played with him, took him out and, above all, befriended him. This was reinforced by the attitudes of the various houseparents who cared for Scott during his time at Camphill. Unexpected circumstances meant that Scott had to move house more often than had been intended and, knowing how change had always unsettled him, we worried at times that he might not be experiencing the stability that Camphill had said he needed. However, as one of the more able and loudly articulate children, and given his strong, attention-seeking personality, it was possible for Scott to dominate a household, but the changes and skill of his houseparents made it difficult for him to do this. Moreover, he came into contact with more people, both children and co-workers, and was able to learn the importance of adaptability. Scott had five sets of houseparents in all and each gave him slightly different, but complementary, sets of values for day-to-day living.

In school, Scott was lucky to have a gifted and intuitive class teacher who caught his imagination from the start and also came to be his (and our) close friend. To start with, Scott was prevented from disrupting the class by an astonishingly simple yet brilliantly effective device. He sat in the front row inside a 'sentry box' so that he could see his teacher but nobody else, and no one else could see him. So, at a stroke, the class clown was neutralized; *he* was hidden from his audience and *they* were invisible to him. He was thus encouraged to participate in lessons in a meaningful way and soon the sentry box was dispensed with as he progressed with his schoolwork in a way we had never believed possible. This was not just our subjective opinion, but was echoed by his educational psychologist. In time, he actually became — incredibly to us — a role model to some of his less able classmates!

Although Scott was weaned away from trying to be the centre of attention in class, his propensity for showing off was channelled into participation in a succession of school plays; *Hannibal, Magellan, A Christmas Carol, Noises Off.* But for us, the high point came in Scott's penultimate year at Camphill, when his entire class and their helpers staged an unforgettable performance of Shakespeare's *Henry V.* Not a simplified or abridged version, but the whole thing. As we watched this group of teenagers — with Down's syndrome, autism, cerebral palsy, foetal alcohol syndrome — perform their hearts out in this most challenging of dramas, we wondered just how many of them would have had starring roles in a mainstream school production of such a play. To us, this was truly 'inclusion.' Here were children in an environment shaped as much by them as their carers, and where they were clearly at ease, interacting enthusiastically with each other and displaying their many talents to their parents and friends. We should say that although this was a particular class play, exactly the same atmosphere has been generated at every end-of-term School festival we have attended over the years. Maybe we are unduly cynical, but it does seem to us that many of the ardent integrationists miss the point and equate 'inclusion' simply with 'being there in school hours.' Yet it is much more than that.

As Scott thrived in the calm, non-judgmental atmosphere of Camphill, what we had always believed to be his true personality gradually blossomed. The caring side of his nature flourished as he came to realize that he wasn't worthless, as he had always thought, but that he was an integral part of a community that had great faith in him. Children less able than he was looked up to him and wanted him to be their friend, and he saw that he had something to offer them. He discovered that if he showed people respect, they in turn would respect him. Certainly there were still times when his behaviour was poor, but they became less frequent and he was able to acknowledge when he fell short of what was expected of him, and to accept whatever sanctions might be imposed. During his last two years at Camphill, Scott spent much of his time working on the Murtle farm. He has written about that himself and all we shall say here is that being treated as a working colleague doing a real job rather than as a special needs child enabled him to make the transition to the world of full-time work more easily.

As we finish this article on this Saturday evening, Scott has gone off to meet his friends on the motor scooter he bought with his wages. He is an ordinary teenager, working all week and going out to enjoy himself at the weekend. In the words of his long-time teacher, he has finally got to where he always wanted to be. Without Camphill, he wouldn't have stood a chance.

Jennifer

AGNES GRAY

The hardest fact I have ever had to face in my life was that I couldn't give my beautiful daughter Jennifer the help that she desperately needed. I was acutely aware that, although I could give her all the love she would ever need or want, I couldn't provide the stimulation and teaching that she required, if she was to ever have any quality in her life. In fact, I had to face the fact that I was actually holding her back. To understand what I mean, let me start at the very beginning ...

Jennifer was born in March 1992 and took her own sweet time to enter this world. This particular trait, of taking her own time to do anything, remains with Jennifer to this day!

The pregnancy was 'normal' with a single exception, which at the time seemed unimportant. I had gone for a scan at thirty-four weeks and the baby wasn't moving about as much as it should have been. The nurse didn't seem unusually perturbed but asked me if the baby usually moved about a lot? I gave what I believed to be an honest answer and said 'Yes.' It was quite a difficult question for me to answer because I had never had a baby before and consequently had nothing to compare against. I remember the first seeds of doubt entering my head, that maybe something was wrong, and I asked if everything was okay. I had been very careful during the pregnancy and up to that point everything had been fine. What *could* possibly be wrong? The nurse replied that there was probably nothing to worry about and that the baby may simply be having a sleep. She asked me to come back the next day and she would check again.

I recall feeling worried when I left the hospital but trying to keep calm. On that particular day Jennifer's father was working in England and staying away overnight but phoned me in the evening to check how I was and how my hospital visit had gone. I got upset as I recounted the events of the day to him and he tried to allay my fears and said that everything would be all right. He asked me to stop crying. Little did I know then that these were the first of many tears that would flow. The next day, I returned to the hospital. I had my scan and everything seemed fine. Thank God. I said a silent prayer.

My due date came and went, and as the baby didn't appear to be making any plans on making an entrance, the birth had to be induced. It was a long, difficult labour but it was all worth it and instantly forgotten the moment Jennifer arrived. She was the most beautiful baby I had ever seen and I was so proud that she was mine! I recall my own father telling me that children change one's life forever and that was certainly true. The moment Jennifer was born, I knew that this was what life was all about. She immediately brought us so much happiness and made our lives suddenly complete. Her father and I couldn't wait to take our baby home from the hospital and begin our new life together. We had planned and hoped that Jennifer was to be the first of many children. It was only eight months before our dreams were shattered.

At first, everything was wonderful. We all settled into our new family life well and were very happy. Jennifer was a good baby; she didn't cry a lot and slept very well. I had always planned to return to work, finances dictated that, and had arranged a place for Jennifer at a new crèche facility that had recently opened on the industrial estate where I worked. Jennifer started at the crèche when she was two months old. This was really handy for me because I could drop Jennifer off on my way to work and go up to see her at lunchtimes. I was literally two minutes away from her by car and this was very reassuring, as I didn't really like leaving my precious baby with anyone, regardless of how qualified or caring they were.

The health visitor checked Jennifer on a regular basis and everything seemed normal. Family and friends admired our beautiful daughter and no one suspected anything was wrong, least of all us. Then came the day that was to change our lives forever. One of the nurses at the crèche recommended that we should take Jennifer to a paediatrician because she wasn't developing in the same way as the other babies. At eight month's Jennifer still couldn't sit up unsupported, didn't really have any interest in any of the toys around her and wasn't making any attempt to move about on her own. We were both horrified. I didn't want to admit to myself that the nurse was right even though I could see for myself that compared to the other babies in the crèche, Jennifer was certainly 'different.'

And so began the painful process of trying to establish what exactly was wrong with Jennifer. This seemed like an endless process — hospital visit upon hospital visit, test after test (including an evoked response hearing test, an EEG and an MRI), disappointment after disappointment as each test came back 'normal' but obviously there was something very wrong. We were desperate to be able to name Jennifer's condition — if we knew what was wrong then we would have some idea of what the future would hold. Would further children be similarly affected? We had so many questions but weren't getting any answers.

Eventually, the consultant in charge told us that although he couldn't diagnose Jennifer's condition precisely, she displayed symptoms similar to both autism and cerebral palsy but not classic of either. If we wanted to put a name to it we could call it the 'Jennifer Gray Syndrome.' The consultant also advised us that if we were considering having any further children, no pre-natal test would be able to pick up the condition that had so badly affected our daughter. Our plans for a large family were shattered that day. The pain of this realization was almost unbearable and I'm not sure, even now, if we have fully come to terms with this cruel fate. Her father and I resigned ourselves to take each day as it came. We had to live with the sadness that intensified year upon year as we witnessed for ourselves Jennifer's severely stunted progress. The years passed slowly and the burden of care was enormous.

Family and friends tried to support us as much as they could but the strain on us as a family was becoming unbearable. We struggled on but life was getting harder and harder. When Jennifer was four years old her Dad took a career change and started a new job that involved shift work. The consequence of this meant that I was with Jennifer on my own for longer periods and there were many times when I felt that it wasn't just Jennifer who couldn't cope, it was me too.

Jennifer started at a local 'special' school but, despite the best efforts of the teaching staff in the school, Jennifer never settled and wasn't making any visible progress. There were many times I was called to the school because Jennifer wasn't coping and the staff simply didn't know what to do for the best. I would take Jennifer home and go through a process of elimination to try to establish what was wrong. Was she unwell, was she hungry, thirsty, tired? Did she need to go the toilet? Sometimes I could work it out, sometimes I couldn't. When I couldn't, I felt inadequate, a failure, helpless but most importantly, hopeless. Everything was becoming harder and harder. This situation continued for three painful, sad years. Often, I look back to those black days and wonder how on earth I survived. If it hadn't been for the support and friendship of the lady who started out as Jennifer's childminder, but quickly became 'my rock,' I'm sure I would have broken down.

At seven years of age Jennifer couldn't do anything for herself and was totally dependent. She could hardly walk, couldn't communicate her needs in any way other than by crying or flapping her arms (a sign Jennifer used to display excitement, distress or panic) and simply couldn't cope with most situations 'normal' children thrive on. Nothing really seemed to make her happy but lots of things upset her. Jennifer demanded a lot of attention and the older she got the harder it got. What made the whole situation worse was the fact that we weren't even sure if Jennifer knew who we were. She didn't (couldn't?) show her emotions.

I remember very clearly the particular event that made me realize something had to change. I was called to school (again) because Jennifer was crying and they could not placate her. There was obviously something wrong, but what? She just cried and cried and cried. Again I took her home, went through 'the process' without success and eventually resorted to calling our doctor. I am not a person who panics easily but I was really worried. Unfortunately, even the GP was at a loss as he turned to me and said he didn't know what was wrong, but if things got worse I should call him immediately.

Jennifer lay on our sofa for five long days unable to eat anything. I nursed her as best I could but as the days went on and I became more and more tired, I knew I couldn't go on like this. Jennifer slept for short periods but it was during the nights that she cried the most. She looked like a limp rag doll and I felt totally helpless. That was the moment I knew that our lives couldn't continue as they were. I loved Jennifer with all my heart, and still do, but increasingly I found I was asking myself, 'What will happen to Jennifer if something happens to me?'

In July 1999, I phoned the Social Services Department. This was the first time I had ever approached them for any help and they were flabbergasted by my request. I asked them how to go about getting Jennifer into a residential home, as I couldn't cope any more. I genuinely believe that they thought I couldn't be serious — how could I be? I had managed up until now without their help and what an initial request!

They sent a social worker to visit us at home, who was an absolute gem! I have since heard many derogatory tales of social workers but for once, our luck was in and we had hit the jackpot! He listened carefully, had genuine empathy for our situation but most importantly of all was very honest. He told us it would be hard to get a placement for Jennifer but that he would support us all the way, and he did.

It took eight months of tears, soul-searching, letters, meetings and, what I consider to be, shameful treatment by many staff at our local authority to get the result we needed. However, in the end, both the Education and Social Services Departments agreed to jointly sanction and fund our request and for that I am grateful. Although those eight months were tortuous they were worth every minute, and they resulted in a placement for Jennifer at Camphill!

From the very first moment we turned off the main carriageway onto the winding road that leads up the hill to Camphill Estate, I knew instinctively that this was the place for Jennifer. I can't really explain how or why, it was just a feeling of utter calmness and tranquillity that was almost tangible.

On our first visit we were shown around some of the houses, one of which was to become Jennifer's 'home' (although we didn't know that at the time). The staff were so warm and welcoming and it was immediately obvious that this wasn't a 'show' that they put on for visiting parents, who were contemplating Camphill as the place for their child, this was what they were like all of the time. There were many children of varying ability in each house and it was almost a shock to have a first glimpse at the holistic approach to care and education provided at Camphill. It was certainly my first exposure to 'community living' in the true sense of the words and it is this very special way of life that makes Camphill so effective.

Each child is treated as an individual, they all have their own 'learning programme' tailored to their specific needs, but what struck me most on that first visit, was that all of the children were treated with respect. Here, at last, was an environment where the adults truly saw the child first, and then acknowledged the child's particular disability. Here, at last, was a place where Jennifer could learn and develop in her own time, being cared for by people who would genuinely care about her. Here, at last, was hope. We left Camphill knowing that this was the place for Jennifer.

A few months passed while arrangements were finalized, and in June 2000 everything was in place for Jennifer to start at Camphill. I decided that I would go and stay with her for as long as it took to help her settle in. Although I knew Camphill was going to be a real chance for Jennifer, I freely admit that I was very anxious about letting my little girl go. I had many telephone calls with the housemother whilst we prepared for Camphill and when I think about a particular telephone call now, it brings a smile to my face. For me, it is now one of the many benchmarks that evidence, for the world to see, just how much Jennifer has progressed. This is what the call was about.

The housemother advised me that Jennifer's start date coincided with their annual camping trip. Every year, usually in June and regardless of the weather, Witiko (Jennifer's house at Camphill) effectively packs up and goes camping! This includes all of the children (regardless of ability), co-workers, dog, tents, canoes, swimsuits, wellies, food and even special beds if necessary. I simply couldn't envisage *then,* how they could manage to co-ordinate such a massive operation and certainly couldn't begin to comprehend that Jennifer would be able to cope. Despite the housemother's best efforts to reassure me that Jennifer would be all right, I said that I thought it best if Jennifer didn't go along, and that we would come to Camphill after the camping trip. The housemother respected my opinion, said okay and that she looked forward to meeting us upon their return from the banks of the River Dee. That particular camping expedition was the only one Jennifer has *not* been on since her life began at Camphill!

Jennifer is now in her fifth year at Camphill and although I hoped Camphill would be able to help her in some way, her progress has surpassed my wildest dreams. The transformation between Jennifer when she started at eight years of age and today is almost unbelievable. I think that the best way to describe just how much Camphill has helped Jennifer, is to indicate the main areas where Jennifer has progressed.

1. Walking

Prior to Camphill Jennifer could barely walk. She could not walk at all without support and even then only for very short distances. She wasn't aware of any hazards in her way, couldn't co-ordinate her body so as to be able to turn independently, manoeuvre around objects or deal with an uneven surface. The maximum distance Jennifer could walk was approximately 200 yards and if we ever went out we had to take her 'buggy.' Jennifer also has very small feet that point outwards at 'ten to two' when she walks and they don't provide much of a base upon which she can balance.

Using their years of experience and as a direct consequence of their therapies, patience and encouragement, the staff at Camphill have managed to get Jennifer walking independently. In fact, sometimes she is almost running! Walking is a huge part of life at Camphill — being out in the fresh air, experiencing nature, allowing the children a chance to explore and grow strong. Jennifer's feet remain very small and we all still hope that they will grow sufficiently enough to allow her to 'stay on her feet,' but for the time being she has progressed in the walking department more than we ever thought possible. She no longer needs a buggy!

2. Feeding

Before Camphill we had to feed Jennifer as though she were a baby. She couldn't hold a spoon, couldn't even hold on to a biscuit and she hardly drank anything (I think this was the main contributory factor to why Jennifer was troubled with constipation and had to have Lactulose on a daily basis). Although there weren't any specific foods that Jennifer didn't like, most of her food had to be 'sloppy,' as she didn't really chew.

Meal times at Camphill provide a dual purpose — an opportunity for the whole house to get together and an opportunity to learn by example. Again, through patience and encouragement, Jennifer can now almost feed herself. Admittedly, she still requires someone to load her fork or spoon but she can now pick a utensil up, put it to her mouth and eat independently. The only problem now is loading the spoon or fork quickly enough! Jennifer has a healthy appetite. She also drinks from a special cup (sealed at the top with a straw) and can reach for her cup independently. I am delighted to say that Jennifer now drinks copious amounts of water or herb tea and doesn't have to be encouraged any longer to do so! This, combined with a high fibre, organic diet, means that Jennifer no longer requires medication to move her bowels.

3. Awareness

As I mentioned earlier, prior to Camphill, Jennifer didn't seem to be aware of herself, others around her or of her surroundings. We weren't even sure if she knew who we were. She showed little interest in anything and became very distressed in many normal situations. The transition between home and Camphill seemed easy for Jennifer and didn't upset her in any way. I used to phone her nearly every night, which may sound strange as Jennifer can't talk, but I needed to 'talk' to her and find out, from the caring co-workers, how she was. At first Jennifer made little or no noises on the phone — sometimes she would just breathe heavily (she hyperventilates a lot) and at other times she would make no noise at all.

What can I say except state the simple truth — Jennifer has woken up! She is now very aware of everything around her and the world isn't the terrifying place it once was for her. For about the first year after Jennifer went to Camphill, although she showed signs of recognition whenever we went to visit or brought her home for the weekend, the transition between home and Camphill didn't bother her. She was quite happy to go back and as soon as we were there, she seemed to forget about us. How things have changed! When I visit now, Jennifer becomes very upset when it is time for me to leave but settles quickly after a few hugs and some appropriate distraction from the co-workers. When she comes home, and I even talk about her going back to school, she shows her emotions by becoming very quiet or by crying. I find this open demonstration of emotion both distressing and rewarding. I feel sad leaving Jennifer but very happy about her significant emotional development. It is absolutely wonderful that Jennifer is now able to demonstrate how she feels. Before Camphill, whether she felt the emotion or not, she had been unable to show it. This is yet another clear sign of progress.

4. Behaviour

Jennifer used to be very withdrawn in the company of others and her behaviour was becoming difficult. When excited she would become very noisy and had an ear-piercing squeal that could be heard from the end of the street! If she was upset or agitated, she would become very 'slappy' and throw herself about. Her slaps could range from a playful slap to a hefty whack. The older, and consequently bigger and heavier she got, the harder this was to deal with. Also, there were no open signs of affection.

I am very pleased to say that Jennifer is now (for most of the time) a delightful child to be with. The most appropriate word I can use to describe Jennifer now is calm. She can cope with others around her, doesn't squeal as she used to and although she does sometimes still slap, it is quite infrequent. She also gives lots and lots of hugs — and somehow she seems to know just exactly when someone needs one! She is even able to 'cuddle in' when she requires to be comforted and often initiates this herself — she couldn't do this previously and, as her mother, I find this particular aspect of her development so rewarding. She is a loving child and, since she has been at Camphill, I have yet to meet anyone who doesn't enjoy her company.

5. Communication

Jennifer used not to be able to communicate her needs in any way other than by crying, flapping her arms if distressed or by squealing loudly when excited. She didn't seem to understand what was being said to her and had a very short attention span. However, it is very true when people say that you can tell how someone is feeling by looking into their eyes and this was certainly true with Jennifer. Because we knew Jennifer well, we learned to read her needs (most of the time) from her eyes, but even this 'communication' was difficult if she refused to make eye contact with you.

Although Jennifer cannot talk and is not yet responding to sign language she has developed her own way of communicating with those around her. She now smiles when happy, understands a lot of what you are saying (I mentioned earlier about her response when I talk about school) and now makes lots of noises, at the appropriate time during our nightly telephone calls. She has also developed a mind of her own and, when out walking, for instance, if she decides that she wants to go somewhere then she will go! She is no longer content to be merely led by the hand. Her hugs now show clear affection and the look on her face if someone passes by in the street without stopping to say hello speaks for itself! We remain hopeful that one day she will at least be able to sign and her housemother reckons that speech is not yet out of the question. Who knows? We will keep our fingers crossed!

6. Friends

Before Camphill Jennifer led an almost insular life. Most of her time was spent in the company of adults and she had no peer group from which to learn. Although this very different girl interested other children, they couldn't relate to her and she couldn't interact with them. Obviously this wasn't any fault of the children — Jennifer was very different and most children had never ever seen anyone so 'strange.' I often hear the term 'Inclusion' used when referring to special needs children but, in my opinion, inclusion only works when society is educated enough to accept. Jennifer now has many friends, both young and old at Camphill, who accept her as she is. She now has an opportunity to play with other children and decides for herself upon particular favourites. Although she can't keep up with many of the children whilst they run around, Jennifer is never excluded from any activity — indeed the staff at Camphill go out of their way to include everyone. This is true inclusion.

7. Fun

As I mentioned earlier, Jennifer never seemed to really enjoy any activity and, although we tried to find things she might like, for example, swimming, horse-riding, visits to the park she didn't appear to get much out of anything. The only thing Jennifer really enjoyed was watching videos, but I knew there had to be more in Jennifer's life than videos. Today — where shall I start? Fun is a huge part of the curriculum at Camphill and I have listed below just *some* of the activities that Jennifer clearly enjoys:

— swimming
— folk dancing
— birthday parties (with so many children and adults at Camphill this is almost a weekly event!)
— rounders
— camping (yes, Jennifer loves it and it was an awe-inspiring experience for me when I joined them all for part of last year's camping trip. Where the staff get their energy from I don't know but all of the children have a whale of a time!)
— stories
— music
— walking!
— painting
— baking
— outings (there are many of these to the beach or local beauty spots or even out to restaurants!)

I could go on and on but what I am trying to demonstrate is that, because of the support, help and organization of the staff at Camphill, Jennifer now has the opportunity to do things most other children take for granted. I freely admit that I never thought she would be able to do most of the activities listed above, let alone be able to show that she enjoys them. She would never have had these opportunities had she remained at home. I am also relieved to say that television and videos are not on Camphill's agenda and that the only time the children ever get to watch television is as a special treat, *some* weekends.

The above is a completely candid account of how much Camphill has helped Jennifer. I shall never be able to thank everyone at Camphill sufficiently for what they have done for my daughter. Years of knowledge and experience, warmth and genuine caring coupled with the seemingly endless energy of the co-workers all combine to provide an environment where children and young people, much less fortunate than ourselves, have a chance to grow and live with dignity. The selfless approach of all of the staff is truly humbling to see.

I would like to offer some final words of advice to others who may be considering Camphill for their child. If you know in your heart that your child could benefit from the holistic approach adopted by Camphill then don't give up. Don't accept 'No' as an answer from any local authority.

Be persistent and never lose sight of the fact that *you* know what is best for your child regardless of what any 'professional' may say. Keep going until you succeed! Be prepared to be astonished by the developments in your child. Watch and be thankful to those very special people who make Camphill what it is.

19. Inclusion

ROBIN JACKSON

This chapter differs from others in this book inasmuch as the content has already been published in the *Scottish Journal of Residential Child Care,* and has been reprinted here as a contribution to the current debate not only on the purpose and value of special schools but also on the meaning of inclusion, which are issues of critical concern for all who live and work in the Camphill Schools.* It is surprising that there has been little serious questioning of the philosophy underpinning the adoption and pursuit of the policy and practice of inclusion in the UK. There has also been virtually no informed discussion of the merits of residential special schooling in the professional literature. This chapter seeks not only to highlight the growing recognition of the relevance of the curative education/social pedagogic model in childcare, but also to place the discussion on the future role of the Schools in a broader professional context.

Introduction: normalization and inclusion

Culham and Nind (2003) have argued that normalization and inclusion are guiding philosophies, which have a common end but radically different approaches to attaining that end. Whilst there is a shared desire to see people with special needs as valued members of the community, there is a fundamental difference. In normalization, community presence and value are earned through minimizing difference, whereas in inclusion the person's difference is welcomed and valued. One way of eradicating that difference is through the process of assimilation (Allan 1999). Assimilation, however, is at odds with the kind of empowerment strategies adopted by most other devalued groups (for example: ethnic minorities; women; people with physical and sensory disabilities) who celebrate their differences, and welcome congregative identity and activity.

---

* Jackson, R. 2004. 'Residential special schooling: the inclusive option!' *Scottish Journal of Residential Child Care,* 3(2), 17–32.

The philosophy of normalization has left a legacy of negative attitudes with respect to the notion of 'normality.' Not only has normality tended to be viewed from a moral standpoint and equated with something good and desirable, but it has also been seen as something that can and should be prescribed.

Inclusion is primarily concerned with overcoming the traditional boundaries between those with and without a disability, by focusing on the actions and responsibilities of everyone, not just those who are disadvantaged, disabled or otherwise marginalized. Disagreement usually revolves around the operationalization of the concept and on what is realistically achievable and desirable (Hornby 1999; Low 1997).

The starting point for inclusionists is the recognition that inclusion is a right. This places a responsibility on all of us not to allow this human right to be ignored or transgressed. The response to those critics questioning the efficacy of inclusion (Hornby 1999) has been that because inclusion is a human right — a self-evident good — there is no point in seeking empirical proof of its value (Mittler 2000).

Wolfensberger (2003) has cautioned against the tendency to divorce rights from their attendant obligations, and has expressed particular concern at the increasing radicalization of the inclusionist movement — its confrontational stance and strident language — which threatens to antagonize and alienate those whose support is vital if appropriate services for people with special needs are to be developed.

What inclusionists have yet to resolve philosophically is what to do about those who want to exercise a right to stay outside of mainstream provision. There is still an assumption that a community of people who share a learning disability is in some way inferior to a mixed community in which people with a learning disability can be among more able peers. This chapter seeks to challenge that assumption.

Inclusive vision

The circular, *Guidance on the Presumption of Mainstream Education,* issued by the Pupil Support and Inclusion Division of the Scottish Executive (2002), is clearly permeated by an inclusive vision. Such a vision is traditionally linked with a commitment to the enforcement of civil rights for all disabled people. All too often, however, this inclusive vision can be seen as part of a mission or moral crusade. The propagation of the inclusion principle within a crusade is both dangerous and counterproductive, for it can foster professional intolerance, division and disaffection (Hansen 1976); lead to the application of powerful and insidious pressure on professional staff to conform (Boucherat 1987); devalue the worth of those who, for valid professional reasons, find ground for criticism (Mesibov 1990); promote the growth of a propaganda industry, which places a low value on objectivity and truth (Jackson 1989); prompt the use of strategies and techniques, which indoctrinate rather than teach (Renshaw 1986); encourage poorly-trained professional staff to believe that the application of a simple formula will resolve the complex problem of delivering effective and humane services (Tadd 1992); and result in the creation of an inflexible service that is unresponsive and insensitive to children's needs (Rhoades & Browning 1977).

A further problem with presenting the case for inclusion in civil rights terms is that people with a disability do not constitute a homogeneous population. They do not share a single defining feature that sets them apart. Discussion on the topic of inclusion is not assisted where it is represented in civil rights terms, and where the emotive language and rhetoric is drawn from the debate on racial and ethnic issues.

In the USA there has been increasing criticism of the inclusion movement, where the drive to full inclusion is seen as leading unhelpfully to an emphasis on:

— the process of education rather than educational outcomes;
— mainstream curricula rather than functional curricula;
— advocacy for programmes rather than advocacy for children;
— rhetoric rather than research evidence (Hornby *et al.* 1997)

The crucial point that advocates of the inclusion principle miss, but which earlier writers took pains to stress, is that inclusion is a philosophy and not a technology (Tizard 1964; Nirje 1969; Jackson 1996). It is a system of values and beliefs, which should help guide, not dictate, thought and action. This necessitates a sensitive and pragmatic approach, not an inflexible and dogmatic one. Thus, empirical examination should replace polemics; not to do so is to engage in a massive programme of social engineering (Zigler *et al.* 1986).

Inclusion through semantic sleight of hand

One way in which inclusion can be introduced is through a semantic sleight of hand. For example, over a decade ago the former Strathclyde Region published a policy paper on special education entitled *Every Child is Special* (1993). The key principles, underpinning Strathclyde's policy, were that:

— each child has individual learning needs;
— positive discrimination should be exercised in favour of those who are disadvantaged;
— children with special needs should not be segregated.

The document argued that it was necessary to take a broad view of what constituted special educational needs. It made reference to the 1978 HMI report which estimated that fifty percent of children experienced learning difficulties (Her Majesty's Inspectorate 1978); much more than the twenty percent estimated by the Warnock Committee (Department of Education and Science 1978). It was then asserted that any individual could experience difficulties in some contexts. Thus, there was a progressive widening (or dilution) of the definition of special educational needs, to the point where it became virtually meaningless.

The logic underpinning the first principle took the following form: all children have learning difficulties; special educational needs derive from learning difficulties; therefore, all children have special educational needs. Notwithstanding the suspect nature of the above propositions, the conclusion drawn is that every child is special, the snappy but empty title of Strathclyde's document. The logical *coup de grâce* is that if *every* child is special then there must be a sense in which *no* child is special.

One possible consequence of the proclamation and acceptance of this slogan was that the case for retaining and supporting existing specialist services in Strathclyde Region (i.e. special schools) for what might be termed the Warnock twenty percent was seriously weakened. One is left to speculate whether the logical shortcomings and the semantic confusion resulted from careful, or careless, deliberation on the part of the policy-makers.

The second principle was that a policy of positive discrimination must be more than a general recognition that some people have greater needs than others — it should constitute a commitment to deploy resources to meet their needs. Precisely how Strathclyde reconciled its notion that every child was special with a policy of positive discrimination is unclear.

The third principle advanced was that children should be placed in 'the least restrictive environment' compatible with meeting their needs. This principle has been borrowed directly from the least restrictive alternative principle, which has guided judicial and legislative thinking and decision-making in the USA. The right to the least restrictive alternative is nothing more than a requirement that common sense and respect for the humanity and individuality of every person be the touchstone of the law.

What Strathclyde Regional Council succeeded in doing was rendering meaningless the term 'special educational needs.' Mackay (2002) has recently expressed his concern at the tendency for policy-shapers and policy-makers to argue that disability does not exist and has asserted that:

> our job is not to make disability go away, nor pretend that it is not there. Instead, it is to respect its complexity, to respond to it with honesty, vision and intelligence. (Mackay 2002, 162)

A similar sentiment is expressed in the papal message addressed to participants of the 2004 International Symposium on the Dignity and Rights of the Mentally Disabled Person:

> A subtle form of discrimination is also present in politics and educational projects that seeks to conceal or deny the deficiencies of disabled people by proposing lifestyles and objectives that do not correspond to their reality and turn out to be unjust and frustrating. (Vatican 2004, 1)

Inclusion in practice

What evidence is there that the policy of inclusion is working? The Audit Commission (2002) in a recent survey of inclusion practice in England, found a tension between the standards agenda and the policy of inclusion. Almost every headteacher interviewed by the Commission raised the issue of 'league tables' of school performance, which were seen as having a damaging impact on staff morale and leading to a reluctance by some schools to admit children with special educational needs. It was the Commission's view that the Government should create new systems whereby schools could celebrate their work with children with special educational needs — such as raising its profile in school inspection and flagship initiatives, or introducing awards for inclusive practice. The Commission noted that some children with special educational needs were regularly excluded from certain lessons and extra curricular activities, and that most children who were permanently excluded from school had special educational needs: almost nine out of ten from primary schools and six out of ten from secondary schools. The Commission concluded that in contrast to the national focus on standards of attainment, little was known about how well children with special educational needs did in school. It was found that barely half of Local Education Authorities (LEAs) surveyed by the Commission systematically monitored the school performance of children with special educational needs, whilst monitoring by governors was found to be very variable.

In a recent review of the literature on inclusion, Dockrell *et al.* (2002) noted that there has been little research, which has succeeded in identifying those features of schools, which might be termed 'effective' or 'inclusive.' This is in part due to the difficulty of defining 'effectiveness' and 'inclusiveness' and partly due to the separate traditions of research and evaluation in these two areas. The authors acknowledge it is difficult to evaluate the outcome of inclusive education and that the studies which have attempted to do so have been largely inconclusive. In fact, there is no evidence of any serious attempt to evaluate outcomes of *any* form of provision for pupils with special educational needs (Hegarty 1993; Farrell 2000).

On the basis of the evidence available, Dockrell *et al.* (2002) found that children with special educational needs were routinely excluded. The authors noted that many everyday decisions about inclusion in the curriculum were complex, and placed considerable demands on teachers' moral and professional capacity. The review highlighted a number of significant gaps in the current knowledge about, and provision for, children with special educational needs.

A recent study examined the experiences of a group of physically-disabled students who moved from mainstream schools into a special needs further education college (Pitt & Curtin 2004). While acknowledging the small scale of the research, the findings are worth noting. The reasons identified by the students for moving were:

— problems with physical access;
— the lack of resources and additional classroom support;
— the limited access to therapy; and
— the negative attitudes of staff and other students.

Of those interviewed, the overwhelming experience of mainstream school had been one of social isolation, loneliness, overt and covert bullying and non-acceptance by non-disabled peers.

In the specialist college, the participants enjoyed positive relationships with staff, a greater flexibility in time-tabling, which permitted their therapy and course requirements to be better accommodated. Since attending the specialist college participants had also changed how they viewed their disability and felt more optimistic and confident about themselves. These changes in self-image were attributed to the encouraging attitudes of staff and fellow students. The participants were agreed that disabled students should have the opportunity to attend either mainstream or special school with the decision resting upon the students' individual strengths and weaknesses. The key factor singled out here was the opportunity for choice.

Cummins and Lau (2003), in a further review of the relevant literature, have indicated that the simple belief that mainstreaming is a positive experience for all children cannot be sustained by reference to the empirical literature. Just as it cannot be assumed that all children with a disability will make better developmental and scholastic progress in an integrated environment, so it cannot be assumed that all children with a disability will be embraced by their non-disabled peers. A further factor to which Cummins and Lau (2003) draw attention is the attitude of teachers to the inclusion of pupils with a disability in their classroom. Few teachers have a choice in the matter and may resent the children's inclusion for a variety of reasons. These may include feelings of personal and professional inadequacy to manage a mixed ability class, concerns about time distribution between class members, or even philosophical opposition to inclusive education. And there is no doubt that teacher attitudes to children with a disability can impact on the children's self-respect (Jordan & Stanovich 2001).

At the 2004 annual conference of the National Association of Schoolmasters/Union of Women Teachers (NASUWT) increasing concern about the effects of the inclusion policy was voiced. Delegates found difficulty in reconciling the policy of inclusion with the government's enthusiastic support for the development of specialist provision for able pupils, and the maintenance of a small but influential independent school sector. Delegates were also unable to reconcile the policy of inclusion with the strong internal and external competitive pressures brought about by the adoption of a 'target culture,' and the introduction of league tables. These were seen as seriously disadvantaging pupils with special needs. It was predicted that the pursuit of the policy of inclusion would result in increased pupil disruption and disaffection which, in turn, would accelerate the exodus of teachers from the profession thus making an already difficult situation worse. The NASUWT urged the government to retain the traditional system of special schools and units, which permitted those who needed it access to an appropriate education delivered by teachers with the relevant experience and expertise within a specially designed and supportive environment. At the conclusion of their debate, delegates overwhelmingly backed the call for more special schools to be built so that children with severe disabilities and serious behavioural problems received the education best suited to their needs.

However, the challenge to the policy of inclusion has broadened beyond the concerns of members of the teaching profession. In its submission to the 2004 General Assembly of the Church of Scotland, the Kirk's Education Committee questioned whether the presumption of mainstreaming could be maintained any longer. This follows upon a study commissioned by the Committee from the Scottish Council for Research in Education, in which inclusive practice in two primary and two secondary schools was examined. The Committee stated that the evidence suggested that all the schools visited were working to the limits of their capacity in respect of including children with special needs. The Committee indicated that questions needed to be asked about the limits to which schools can adapt to special circumstances, without jeopardizing their capacity to respond effectively to the needs of all children. The fact that three of the four schools involved in the study had units and resource bases where children spent most of their time prompted questions about the meaning of mainstreaming (Henderson 2004).

The case 'against' the residential special school

Cole (1986) has identified some of the objections to residential special schooling which are commonly raised:

— it separates the child from his family and interferes with the natural pattern of a child's growing up with his parents, brothers and sisters;
— it isolates a child from his local community;
— it denies a pupil a normal childhood, mixing and growing up with local children in an ordinary day school;
— it cannot provide the width and variety of the ordinary secondary school curriculum, and therefore limits the educational opportunities and achievements of their pupils;
— it can be uncaring, institutionalized, with the result that children's emotional and social needs are neglected;
— it can cocoon a child in an overprotected community divorced from the harsh reality of the outside world;
— by mixing with children with even greater difficulties, the child's problems can be exacerbated;
— it can lessen a young person's employment prospects;
— it is too expensive.

However, given the absence of hard empirical evidence, there is no means of judging whether any of these objections has any validity.

In a rather different critique, Morris (2002) has made the point that the placement of disabled children in residential special schools calls into question the implementation of the United Nations Convention on the Rights of the Child. The UN Convention upholds the rights of children:

— to live with their families, unless this is not in their best interests (Article 9);
— to be consulted and listened to (Article 12);
— to have 'special protection' if they are deprived temporarily or permanently of their family environment (Article 20);
— to have regular reviews of placements if they live away from home (Article 25).

Morris points to recent research, which discovered that it was rare for disabled children to be consulted when decisions were being made about sending them to residential schools. There was no monitoring of care standards in the majority of such placements, and rarely any consideration of disabled children's rights to 'active participation in the community.' In addition, parents generally received no help in maintaining contact with their children (Abbott *et al.* 2001).

According to Morris (2001) the research showed that for the overwhelming majority of parents, residential special school was not the preferred option, which was contrary to the common perception of many professionals that parents of disabled children were eager for their children to go to residential schools. However, in a later article Morris (2002) presents a slightly different slant on this finding. She indicates that whilst education and social work departments were reluctant to consider residential school placements, parents frequently decided such a placement was the only way in which their children's needs were going to be met. The parents also highlighted the difficult, protracted and often acrimonious nature of the decision-making process right up to the point at which the local authority eventually agreed to a residential school placement. By this time the parents had often reached breaking-point. One of the most striking conclusions of the research was that parents rarely experienced any sense that the local authorities wished to work in partnership with them to best meet the needs of their child.

Morris draws attention to the fact that the White Paper, *Valuing People,* highlighted the lack of information about disabled children in residential schools and residential homes (Department of Health 2001). She indicates that one of the major barriers to meeting the needs of disabled children, who are living away from their families, is the hidden nature of their experience:

> ... we don't know enough about who they are, where they are, what their life feels like for them, or what they think would improve the quality of their lives. If we knew more about their experience as they see it, policy and practice might be more motivated by a profound sense of the injustice inflicted on these children. We should all feel outraged that so many children have gone missing from our society, that they are denied the things we all take for granted and

that, as they reach adulthood, so many of them disappear
into long-term residential provision. (Morris 2000, 31)

The findings reported by Morris do not constitute of themselves
a convincing case against residential special schools, given the fact,
conceded by Morris, that we know so very little about the quality
of life for children in residential special schools. Whilst Morris is
wholly justified in lamenting the absence of such research, she is
not entitled to assume — in the absence of evidence to the contrary
— that the experience for children in residential special schools is a
wholly negative one.

The case 'for' the residential special school

Cole (1986) has argued that whatever the moral and egalitarian argu-
ments, it is unwise to disrupt an established special school network,
whatever its faults, for an alternative whose superiority is not established on a firm empirical base. Evidence produced by the Fish Report
(Inner London Education Authority 1982) indicated that the majority
of parents were satisfied with their children's placement in special
schools. In Cole's opinion, maintaining a choice of integrated and
segregated provision is important. For the vast majority of children
with special educational needs, day provision, possibly as part of their
local comprehensive system is likely to be preferable, but families
should not be denied the option of a segregated alternative, sometimes
residential, which might, in their particular circumstances, better meet
their *family* needs.

The needs of the family

In the debate on the merits of residential special schooling, a fact frequently ignored is that some families are forced to withdraw into a state
of self-imposed isolation, either through fear that their special needs
child will be bullied and tormented by other children, or verbally abused
by neighbours. Parents experience this kind of isolation as a form of
'imprisonment,' both for their child and themselves. In using the term
'imprisonment' parents are not simply seeking a convenient metaphor

to describe their existence. They are selecting a word that precisely mirrors reality, for prejudice, rejection and hostility can combine to create a barrier as real and enduring as a prison wall (Jackson 1996b; Taylor 1999).

Critics have overlooked the important fact that the value of a residential special school does not rest simply on the advantages it confers upon the child. It serves two purposes of equal importance — it seeks to meet the individual needs of the child *and the collective needs of the family*. It provides time for parents and siblings to re-establish links with the world outside the home and to return to a more 'normal' family regime. What critics ignore is that the unquestioning pursuit of the principle of inclusion can lead to significant casualties — not just children but whole families (Saunders 1994; Jackson 1996b).

The study undertaken by Abbott *et al.* (2001), which was cited by Morris as providing support for her argument against residential special schooling, merits closer examination. The study found that whilst the majority of the children and young people interviewed would not have chosen to go away to school, most appeared satisfied with their residential school experience. One of the principal benefits was the opportunity to be part of a friendship network. Most children interviewed were also positive about their relationships with the most important adult in the residential setting — their key worker. The study noted that once the child had been admitted to the residential special school most parents were very happy with the relationship they had with their child's school. The study, however, fails to give a clear and authoritative picture of children's experiences of residential special school life. In short, it does not provide an answer to the basic question posed in the report's title: *The best place to be?*

The findings of small-scale studies, the opinion of groups or individuals, or the case histories of pupils and their families should not be overlooked (Campling 1981; Jackson 1996b; Jones 1983; Taylor 1999). Whilst findings from these sources cannot be accorded the same weight as findings derived from large scale studies, the generally positive picture that does emerge cannot be discounted. A further useful source of general information about the efficacy of residential special schooling can be found in the content of inspection reports issued by the Care Commission and Her Majesty's Inspectorate of Education.

A *new approach to residential childcare*

A particular weakness in Morris' attack on residential special schools is its anglocentric emphasis, for no reference is made to residential child care practice in other countries. For example, if Morris had looked at practice in Denmark, Germany and the Netherlands, she would have found that the main requirement for people working in residential child care is a qualification in social pedagogy (Petrie *et al.* 2002). Social pedagogy is not narrowly concerned with just a child's schooling but relates to the whole child: body, mind, feelings, spirit, creativity and, crucially, the relationship of the individual to others (Hart & Monteux 2004). It has much more in common with parenting than with social work or social care, as social pedagogues working in residential settings share *all aspects of the children's everyday lives.* Petrie *et al.* (2002) expressed the view that:

> Framing children's work in terms of pedagogy has the potential for an inclusive, normalizing approach, with the main focus on children as children, while recognizing that some children have special and additional needs. (Petrie *et al.* 2002, 34)

According to Petrie *et al.* (2002), the emphasis on relationships and living alongside children, expanding their world through creative activities and providing positive role models, has much to commend it in the UK. What is noteworthy here is Petrie's contention that those residential special schools, which adopt a social pedagogic model provide a more inclusive and normal setting; one in which the individual needs of the children and young people are likely to be better met. Particularly important is the transformation in the nature of the relationship between care worker and child from clientship to friendship (Petrie *et al.* 2002).

It should be made clear that friendship should not be equated with friendliness. As John Macmurray has noted, whilst friendliness should not be despised, it is only the imitation of friendship and a poor substitute for the real thing (Costello 2002). Friendship is the social cement that binds individuals and communities together. The most important feature of that relationship is its reciprocity, which dispenses with all notions of those giving and those receiving care. Furthermore, a relationship which is based on mutuality is a relationship of equals in which each learns from the other. Acceptance of this model presents a clear challenge to the purpose and value of conventional professional relationships.

As Wolfensberger (2003) has observed, even if a child is fortunate enough to have a care worker who is a friend, that worker will be constrained by all manner of rules, regulations and restrictions from acting in true friendship. In addition, whilst childcare agencies may assume some parental roles, they cannot offer the love that goes with the parental role, and Wolfensberger argues that, where love is absent, weak and devalued people will continue to be at risk of exposure to abuse and violence.

The Social Education Trust (2001) has acknowledged that whilst the adoption of social pedagogy in the UK would not offer a panacea, it could offer a number of significant strengths:

— services would be provided, which better fitted the needs of individual children, rather than the current situation where too often children have to fit the needs of the services;

— by taking a holistic overview of the child and the way in which all parts of the child's life come together, there would not be the narrow negative focus on client pathology;

— those working directly with children and young people under the banner of social pedagogy would be provided with a professional image and identity, which would give them a sense of pride, self-worth and confidence;

— the debate associated with the establishment of a new profession could have an impact on the wider community's thinking about children, parenting and work with children and young people.

The wider acceptance of a social pedagogic approach would not only result in radical changes in the character of residential childcare in Scotland but would necessitate fundamental changes in the nature and purpose of professional training for those working in childcare services. Whilst detailed discussion of the merits or otherwise of establishing a new profession goes beyond the bounds of this chapter, nevertheless the outcome of that debate will directly affect the role and future of residential special schools.

Conclusion

If the debate on the future of residential special schools is to be well informed and constructive then there is an urgent need for research to examine:

— the nature of decision-making processes as they relate to the placement of pupils with special educational needs;
— the nature and extent of parental involvement in these processes;
— the quality of life experienced by pupils in residential special schools;
— the quality of life experienced by pupils with special educational needs in mainstream settings;
— the transition of young people from residential special schools to the adult world.

An interesting question remains. What happens if the research undertaken demonstrates unambiguously that placement in residential special schools is not only beneficial for most pupils but also advantageous to their families? Will national governments, local authorities, professional workers and academics so firmly wedded to the policy of inclusion be prepared to abandon their view of the residential special school as an option of last resort?

20. The Future

SAM SINCLAIR

The content of this chapter is influenced strongly by my belief that no challenge experienced by Camphill communities in Scotland in recent times, or likely to be faced by them in the foreseeable future, can exceed the magnitude of the challenge faced by Karl König and his colleagues both before they made their way to Scotland and as they founded Camphill in the middle of last century (Bock 2004). On the face of it, the challenges appear to be different now — but are they? Now, as then, the task is to provide a safe, stimulating environment in which to meet the needs of the people whose care and education are entrusted to Camphill communities. Now, as then, one of the main challenges is to satisfy others that Camphill communities are up to the task, use approaches to meeting people's needs that are beneficial to the whole person, and that the communities can be trusted to deliver.

The shape and future development of all organizations are influenced by external and internal factors. This is also true of Camphill communities. The vagaries of public scrutiny and funding mean that review and change are inevitable. No less influential are the dynamics within communities as they strive to preserve 'traditional values' and maintain a sense of community and family in changing times.

Around the turn of the century, the newly reborn Scottish Parliament launched an ambitious care agenda. The main thrust of this legislation involved the regulation of organizations that deliver care services and of the people who work in them. National Care Standards were introduced; the Scottish Commission for the Regulation of Care (Care Commission) was established to ensure these standards were met, and the Scottish Social Services Council (SSSC) was set up to ensure that the workforce was appropriately qualified. If Camphill communities are to survive then non-compliance with regulations is not an option as all communities are reliant upon the public purse.

The Camphill co-worker

In the not-too-distant past, a distinction used to be drawn between 'co-workers' and 'employees.' 'Co-worker' was the term adopted to identify live-in co-workers who had their needs met by the community in a way that did not involve payment of a salary: 'employee' on the other hand was the label for those whose needs were met by the community through payment of salaries. Whilst it may have been useful in the past to indicate whether an individual worker received a salary or not, it is not helpful in assisting the workforce to bond. This distinction is seen as anachronistic and the term 'co-worker' is now used to describe all who work together.

Receiving a salary can be a motivating factor but is essentially an external factor and such motivational factors are now recognized as having only short-term value. The factors that keep people motivated long-term are the intrinsic ones: a love of what they do, a sense of being valued and a sense of personal fulfilment. When this analysis of motivation is considered in the Camphill setting, it leads one to believe that co-workers, whether volunteers or employees, whether making a short or long-term contribution to the care of pupils, do so through intrinsic rather than extrinsic motivation.

Education

Politicians in the UK have taken the view that, wherever practicable, children with special needs should be integrated into mainstream schools. At first sight this is a noble aim, which deserves to succeed, but it is not that simple. One of my greatest fears is that a 'one-size-fits-all' approach will be imposed with the result that the individuality of children's needs will be lost and that the children placed in 'integrated' settings will not cope. However, there is cause for hope. Mary Warnock, who is regarded as the architect of special education in Britain, has argued recently that while the policy of inclusion, which has prevailed over the last two decades, may work for some children with special needs, it has proved disastrous for others, (Warnock 2005). Mary Warnock's conclusion in a recently published pamphlet reviewing the impact of the inclusion policy is of interest here:

> Of particular concern are children in care, who often need an environment within which they can be known and supported by their teachers so that relationships of trust may develop. It is my strong conviction that these must be small schools. (Warnock 2005, 55)

Spirituality

The human spirit is at the core of our existence. Most people speak readily and comfortably about the state of well-being of our spirits — being in good spirits, bad spirits, poor spirits, and so on — but most people tend to be uncomfortable and shy away from discussion when the words 'spiritual' and 'spirituality' are used. This shyness may have something to do with the link these words have with religion. What is not appreciated is that religious beliefs and spirituality are not indistinguishable. Religious adherence is one way of expressing one's spiritual beliefs and nurturing one's spirit, but there are those with no religious adherence who are equally concerned with addressing spiritual needs (Crompton & Jackson 2004).

In the early days of Camphill, Christianity was the spiritual vehicle chosen to move the community forward. Karl König, in his first memorandum to the School community in 1945, spoke of co-workers as being people who desire to do their work in devotion to Christ (König 1945). Whilst Christianity is still an important influence in Camphill communities, there is now a greater flexibility in how the human spirit may be nurtured. This reflects an increasing preparedness in the wider society to accept spirituality as a valid, discrete concept by those who may have reservations about the credibility and relevance of 'the churches' and their dogma and rituals. Interpreting the spiritual in this way makes it easier to comprehend and accept that we all have spiritual needs (Jackson & Monteux 2003).

The strong emphasis on working in a way that promotes the well-being of the human spirit has always been central to Camphill's beliefs and practices. This sets Camphill apart from most other forms of educational provision. König asserted that co-workers are people who do their work out of love for the children, the sick, the suffering, out of love of the soil, the gardens, fields, woods and everything that is embraced by the Community (König 1945).

Quality assurance

Reference has been made in this chapter to Camphill's evolution in response to changes in society. Some changes have resulted from recent legislation;.others have surfaced in the terms and conditions of contracts, and yet more have been occasioned by an increasing interest in relationships with, and the well-being of, our fellows. Most legislation and contracts stipulate what has to be done — or more accurately, what has to be measured. However, they do not prescribe the precise ways of measurement. Nowadays, decisions about such matters tend to be left to the provider of a service.

Camphill communities in Scotland have invested much time and effort in finding a form of quality assurance that will ensure consistency and effectiveness in performance in their daily work. Attempts to transplant systems from the commercial and public sectors have failed because of difficulties in adapting them to a Camphill setting. However, an approach has now been found that appears to be appropriate and most Camphill communities in Scotland have had co-workers trained in its principles. The programme which originated in Switzerland is called 'Ways to Quality' and is founded on the basic idea of people pulling together in a community setting.

The School has begun a programme of implementing 'Ways to Quality' practices and, in common with other communities, it is anticipated that these practices will be central to the School's provision of service for the future. Whilst the School has received very positive reports on the care and education provided for the children, co-workers are not content to rest on past achievements. The 'Ways to Quality' initiative involves robust methods of reaching decisions, developing organizations and the people who work within them. The implementation of this programme throughout the School will further strengthen the School's ability to deliver curative education.

Finally ...

In moving forward, we must each examine our own agenda and our own motivation. We must be very clear why we pursue what we pursue, promote what we promote and resist what we resist. Personal agendas must be pushed down the list of our priorities. If we live a lie about what is important to the people entrusted to our care and education, then what Camphill stands for is threatened. There is every sign at the time of writing that Camphill communities are working together towards identifying, defining, clarifying, developing and preserving those things that are essential to the core of 'Camphillness.'

It would run counter to the entrepreneurial spirit of Camphill's founders simply to transpose into the future everything that has been important in the past. Our founders' spirit of adventure and their level of commitment are required as much in the twenty-first century as they were in the mid-twentieth. There is currently a thirst to re-connect with the Movement's roots, which suggests the continuing presence of that original spirit and commitment. This augurs well for the future of the Camphill Movement and those whose well-being, education and development are nurtured within Camphill settings.

What needs to be done is simple enough to express but it will take time, effort and a willingness to compromise. This preparedness to compromise is especially important in our dealings with the regulatory authorities. In any situation where both the workers and decision makers are committed and principled people, it is not always easy to arrive at satisfactory compromises. The dilemma facing Camphill co-workers at a personal, community and Movement level is where, when and how to compromise. It is perhaps somewhat facile, but nonetheless true, to suggest that what is needed in taking forward 'Camphillness' is the ability to distinguish the essential from the desirable.

For the foreseeable future compromise is likely to take place only at the edges because it is clear that the regulatory changes which have been introduced do not constitute an overwhelming threat to the Camphill approach to caring for and educating people with special needs. Further regulation in Scotland will not be so much about changing the essence of what we do as about accounting for what we do. Through that process we are able to demonstrate the value of our work. It is acknowledged that the transition has been a painful one and has necessitated putting in place a battery of written policies and procedures, which has been burdensome for communities.

Whilst there are different views as to the best way forward, the future for curative education looks secure. The prevalent atmosphere in Camphill communities is one of keen anticipation for the opportunities and challenges that lie ahead. Within the Camphill Movement, there are stirrings of renewed interest in its founding principles and beliefs. There is every reason for believing that this will continue and that the high standards of holistic care for which Camphill is renowned will continue to be provided.

Bibliography

Abbott, D., Morris, J. and Ward, L. (2001) *The Best Place to Be? Policy, Practice and the Experiences of Residential School Placements for Disabled Children,* Joseph Rowntree Foundation/York Publishing Services

Albert, T. (1981) *The equus factor,* World Medicine (August 22)

Allan, J. (1999) *Actively Seeking Inclusion: pupils with special needs in mainstream schools,* Falmer Press, London

Angelo, T.A. (1999) *Doing assessment as if learning matters most,* American Association for Higher Education

Audit Commission (2002) *Special Educational Needs: a mainstream issue,* Audit Commission, London

Ayres, A.J. (1979) *Sensory Integration and the Child,* Western Psychological Services, USA

Bergstrom, M. in D. Mitchell and P. Livingston (1999) *Handwork and Practical Arts in the Waldorf School — Elementary through High School,* Anthroposophic Press, Herndon, VA

Bertoti, D.D. (1988) 'Effect of therapeutic horseback riding on posture in children with cerebral palsy,' *Physical Therapy,* 68, 1505–15

Bettermann, H, von Bonin, D., Frühwirth, M., Cysarz, D. and Moser, M. (2002) 'Effects of speech therapy with poetry on heart rate rhythmicity and cardiorespiratory coordination,' *International Journal of Cardiology,* 84: 77–88

Bock, F. (Ed) (2004) *The Builders of Camphill — Lives and Destinies of the Founders,* Floris Books, Edinburgh

Boucherat, A. (1987) 'Normalization in mental handicap — acceptance without questions?' *Bulletin of the Royal College of Psychiatrists,* 11, 423–25

Brock, B.J. (1988) 'Effect of therapeutic horseback riding on physically disabled adults,' *Therapeutic Recreation Journal,* 22, 34–42

Burnes, B. (2000) *Managing Change: a Strategic Approach to Organizational Dynamics,* Prentice Hall, London

Campling, J. (1981) *Images of Ourselves,* Routledge and Kegan Paul, London

Capra, F. (2001) *The Hidden Connections,* Harper Collins, London

Clarke, J. (2000) 'Daylit coloured shadow display therapy buildings,' *Journal of Curative Education and Social Therapy* (Easter)

Cole, T. (1986) *Residential Special Education: living and learning in a special school*, Open University Press, Milton Keynes

Comenius, J.A. (1639) *Pansophiae Prodromus* In V.J. Dietrich (1991) *Johann Amos Comenius*, Rohwolt, Reinbek

Cooper, A.P. (2003) *How to Play the Lyre: Celtic Lyre Project*, Camphill Community Mourne Grange, Northern Ireland

Copeland-Fitzpatrick, J. (1997) 'Hippotherapy and therapeutic riding: an international review,' In North American Riding for the Handicapped Association (ed.) *Proceedings of the Ninth International Therapeutic Riding Congress* (pp.10–12), CO, Denver

Costello, J.E. (2002) *John Macmurray: a biography*, Floris Books, Edinburgh

Crompton, M. and Jackson, R. (2004) *Spiritual Well-being of Adults with Down Syndrome*, Down Syndrome Educational Trust, Southsea

Culham, A. and Nind, M. (2003) 'Deconstructing normalization: clearing the way for inclusion,' *Journal of Intellectual and Developmental Disability*, 28(1), 65–78

Cummins, R.A. and Lau, A.L. (2003) 'Community integration or community exposure? A review and discussion in relation to people with an intellectual disability,' *Journal of Applied Research in Intellectual Disabilities*, 16(2), 145–157

Cysarz, D, von Bonin, D., Lackner, H. Heusser, P., Moser, M. and Bettermann, H. (2004) 'Oscillations of heart rate and respiration synchronize during poetry recitation,' *American Journal of Physiology, Heart Circulation Physiology*, 287, 579–87

Denjean-von Stryk, B and von Bonin, D. (2003) *Anthroposophical Therapeutic Speech*, Floris Books, Edinburgh

Dennison, P.E. and Dennison, G.E. (1994) *Brain Gym© Teacher's Edition Revised*, Edu-Kinesthetics, Inc, Ventura, California

Department of Education and Science (1978) *Special Educational Needs* (The Warnock Report), HMSO, London

Department of Health (2001) *Valuing People: A New Strategy for Learning Disability for the 21st Century*, Department of Health, London

Dockrell, J., Peacey, N. and Lunt, I. (2002) *Literature Review: meeting the needs of children with special educational needs*, Institute of Education, University of London

Douch, G. (2004) *Medicine for the Whole Person*, Floris Books, Edinburgh

Down, J.L. (1887) *On Some of the Mental Affections of Childhood and Youth*, Churchill, London

Farrell, P. (2000) 'The impact of research on developments in inclusive education,' *International Journal for Inclusive Education*, 4(2), 153–62

Friesen, M. (2000) *Spiritual Care for Children Living in Specialized Settings: Breathing Underwater*, The Haworth Press, New York

Hannaford, C. (1995) *Smart Moves — Why Learning Is Not All In Your Head*, Great Ocean Publishers, Alexander NC

Hansen, D.G. (1976) 'Slogans versus realities — more data needed,' *Journal of Autism and Childhood Schizophrenia*, 6, 366f

Harris, J.C. (1995) *Developmental Neuropsychiatry*, v 2, Oxford University Press, London

Hart, N. and Monteux, A. (2004) 'An introduction to Camphill communities and the BA in Curative Education,' *Scottish Journal of Residential Child Care*, 3(1), 67–74

Hauschka, M. (1978) *Fundamentals of Artistic Therapy*, Rudolf Steiner Press, London

Hegarty, S. (1993) 'Reviewing the literature on integration,' *European Journal of Special Needs Education*, 8(3), 194–200

Heipertz-Hengst, C. (1994) 'Evaluation of outcome of hippotherapy,' In P.A. Eaton (ed.) *Eighth International Therapeutic Riding Congress: the complete papers* (pp.217–21), National Training Resource Centre, Levin, New Zealand

Heitmann, R., Asbjornsen, A., and Helland, T. (2004) 'Attentional functions in speech fluency disorders,' *Logopedics Phoniatrics Vocology*, 29, 119–27

Henderson, D. (2004) 'Don't push inclusion too hard, warns Kirk,' *The Times Educational Supplement Scotland* (2 April)

Her Majesty's Inspectorate (1978) *Pupils with Learning Difficulties in Primary and Secondary Schools in Scotland*, HMSO, Edinburgh

Hewett, D. and Nind, M. (2000) *Access to Communication*, David Fulton Publishers, London

Hogenboom, M. (1999) *Living with Genetic Syndromes Associated with Intellectual Disability*, Jessica Kingsley Publishers, London

Hornby, G. (1999) 'Inclusion or delusion: can one size fit all? Educating students with disabilities,' *Support for Learning*, 14, 152–157

—, Atkinson, M. and Howard, J. (1997) *Controversial Issues in Special Education*, David Fulton Publishers, London

Husemann, A. (1989) *The Harmony of the Human Body*, Floris Books, Edinburgh

Inner London Education Authority (1982) *Educational Opportunities for All* (The Fish Report) ILEA, London

Jackson, R. (2003) 'The spiritual dimension in child and youth care work,' *The International Child and Youth Care Network*, Issue 57, (October 2003)

— (1989) 'The road to enlightenment,' *Social Work Today*, 21, 24

— (1996) 'The British roots of the normalisation principle: a study in neglect,' *Clinical Psychology Forum*, 93, 34–40

— (1996) *Bound to Care: an anthology*, Northern College, Aberdeen

— (2005) 'The origins of Camphill: The Haughtons of Williamston Part 1: Theodore Haughton,' *Camphill Correspondence*, 10–13 (Nov/Dec)

— (2006) 'The origins of Camphill: The Haughtons of Williamston Part 2: Emily Haughton,' *Camphill Correspondence*, 4–7 (Jan/Feb)

— (2004) 'Camphill pioneers: friendly enemy aliens!' *Camphill Correspondence*, 6–9 (November/December)

— and Monteux, A. (2003) 'Promoting the spiritual well-being of children and young people with special needs,' *Scottish Journal of Residential Child Care*, 2(1), 52–54

Jones, M. (1983) *Behaviour Problems in Handicapped Children*, Souvenir Press, London

Jordan, A. and Stanovich, P. (2001) 'Patterns of teacher-student interaction in inclusive elementary classrooms and correlates with student self-concept,' *International Journal of Disabilities, Development and Education*, 48, 33–52

Kirchner-Bockholt, M. (2004) *Foundations of Curative Eurythmy*, Floris Books, Edinburgh

König, K. (1952) *Superintendent's Report*, Camphill Rudolf Steiner Schools, Aberdeen

— (1960/1993) *The Camphill Movement* (2nd ed.) Camphill Press, Danby

— (1945) *The First Memorandum*, Camphill-Rudolf Steiner-Schools, Aberdeen

Lave, J. and Wenger, E. (1991) *Situated Learning: Legitimate Peripheral Participation*, Cambridge University Press, New York

Lorenz-Poschmann, A. (1982) *Breath, Speech and Therapy*, Mercury Press, Spring Valley, N.Y.

Low, C. (1997) 'Is inclusivism possible?' *European Journal of Special Needs Education*, 12, 71–79

Luxford, M. (1994) *Children with Special Needs*, Floris Books, Edinburgh

Macauley, B.L. (2002) 'More research in the field?' *NARHA Strides*, 8, 35

Mackay, G. (2002) 'The disappearance of disability? Thoughts on a changing culture,' *British Journal of Special Education*, 29(4), 159–62

Maier, H.W. (2004) 'Rhythmicity: a powerful force for experiencing unity and personal connections,' *The International Child and Youth Care Network*, Issue 66 (July 2004)

McGibbon, N.H. (1997) 'The need for research,' *NARHA Strides*, 3, 32

Mees-Christeller, E. (1985) *The Practice of Artistic Therapy*, Mercury Press, Spring Valley, NY

Mesibov, G. (1990) 'Normalization and its relevance today,' *Journal of Autism and Developmental Disorders*, 20, 379–90

Mittler, P. (2000) *Working towards Inclusive Education: social contexts*, David Fulton, London

Morris, J. (2000) 'At arm's length,' *Community Care* (12 June)

— (2001) 'Is boarding the only option?' *Community Care* (13 December)

— (2002) 'Schools morass,' *Community Care* (11 April)

Nelkin, D. and Linde, S. (1995) *The DNA Mystique: the gene as a cultural icon*, W.F. Freeman, New York

Nirje, B. (1969) 'The normalization principle and its human management implications,' In R. Kugel and W. Wolfensberger (eds) *Changing Patterns in Residential Services for the Mentally Retarded* (pp.181–94). President's Committee on Mental Retardation, Washington, D.C.

Norfolk, D. (2001) *The Therapeutic Garden*, Bantam Books, London

O'Brien, G. and Yule, W. (1995) *Behavioural Phenotypes*, Cambridge University Press, London

O'Reilly, P.O. and Handforth, J.R. (1955) 'Occupational therapy with 'refractory' patients,' *American Journal of Psychiatry*, 111, 763–66

Palmer, P. J. (1997) *The Courage to Teach: Exploring the Inner Landscape of a Teacher's Life*, Jossey Bass, San Francisco

Petrie, P. (2002) 'All-round friends,' *Community Care* (12 December)

Phillips, D. (2001) 'Therapeutic speech in relation to the individual with Down's Syndrome,' *Journal of Curative Education and Social Therapy*, Easter 2001: 15–19

Pietzner, C. (ed.) (1990) *A Candle on the Hill: Images of Camphill Life*, Floris Books, Edinburgh

Pitt, V. and Curtin, M. (2004) 'Integration versus segregation: the experiences of a group of disabled students moving from mainstream school into special needs further education,' *Disability & Society*, 19, 387–401

Poplawski, Thomas (1998) *Eurythmy — Rhythm, Dance and Soul*, Floris Books, Ediburgh

Probst, G. and Buchel, B. (1997) *Organizational Learning*, Prentice Hall, London

Ralph, J. (2005) *Eurythmy: Frequently Asked Questions*, available online at: www.eurythmy.org.uk/faq

Renshaw, J. (1986) 'Passing understanding,' *Community Care*, 17, 19–21

Rhoades, C. and Browning, P. (1977) 'Normalization at what price?' *Mental Retardation*, 15, 24

Rogers, C. (1994) *Client Centred Therapy*, Constable, London

Rolandelli, P.S. and Dunst, C.J. (2003) 'Influences of hippotherapy on the motor and socio-emotional behaviour of young children with disabilities,' *Bridges: practice-based research syntheses*, 2(1), 1–14

Rubin, J.A. (ed.) (2001) *Approaches to Art Therapy: theory and technique*, Brunner-Routledge, New York

Ruland, H. (1992) *Expanding Tonal Awareness*, Rudolf Steiner Press, London

Salter, J. and Wehrle, P. (2005) *Colour: Twelve Lectures by Rudolf Steiner between 1914 and 1924*, Rudolf Steiner Press, London

Sattler, F. and Wistinghausen, E. (1992) *Bio-dynamic Farming Practice*, Cambridge University Press, Cambridge

Saunders, S. (1994) 'The residential school: a valid choice,' *British Journal of Special Education*, 21(2), 64–66

Scottish Executive (2002) 'Standards in Scotland's Schools Etc Act 2000: Guidance on Presumption of Mainstream Education,' *Scottish Executive Circular* 3/2002

Sempik, J., Aldridge, J. and Becker, S. (2003) 'Social and Therapeutic Horticulture: Evidence and Messages from Research,' Thrive in Association with the Centre for Child and Family Research Loughborough University, Loughborough

Senge, P. (1990) *The Fifth Discipline: The Art and Practice of the Learning Organization*, Doubleday, New York

— (1994) *The Fifth Discipline Fieldbook: Strategies and Tools for Building a Learning Organization*, Doubleday, New York

Simson, S.P. and Strauss, M.C. (eds.) (2003) *Horticulture as Therapy: Principles and Practice*, The Haworth Press, New York

Social Education Trust (2001) *Social Pedagogy and Social Education: a report of two workshops held on 11–12 July 2000 and 14–15 January 2001*, at Radisson Hotel, Manchester Airport

Steiner, R and Steiner-von Sivers, M. (1981) *Poetry and the Art of Speech,* Published in agreement with the Rudolf Steiner Nachlassverwaltung, Dornach, Switzerland

— (1999) *Creative Speech,* Rudolf Steiner Press, London

Steiner, R. (1898) *Hochschulpädagogik und öffentliches Leben,* Dornach/ Schweiz: Sektion für redende und musische Künste

— (1919) *The Inner Aspect of the Social Question,* Rudolf Steiner Press, London

— (1920) *Verses and Meditations,* Rudolf Steiner Publications, London

— (1923) 'A Lecture on Eurythmy: 26th August,' 1923 (GA0279). Available online at: wn.rsarchive.org/Eurhythmy/19230826p01.html

— (1924/1995) *Manifestations of Karma,* 4th ed, Rudolf Steiner Press, London

— (1959) *Speech and Drama,* Anthroposophic Publishing Co, Spring Valley, N.Y.

— (1983) *Curative Eurythmy,* Rudolf Steiner Press, London

— (1988) *The Child's Changing Consciousness and Waldorf Education,* Anthroposophic Press, Hudson, N.Y.

— (1993) *The Inner Nature of Music and the Experience of Tone: Seven Selected Lectures 1906 through 1923,* Anthroposophic Press, Herndon, VA

— (1998) *Education for Special Needs,* Rudolf Steiner Press, London

Strathclyde Regional Council (1993) *Every Child is Special,* Strathclyde Regional Council, Glasgow

Swinton, J. (2001) *A Space to Listen: Meeting the spiritual needs of people with learning disabilities,* The Foundation for People with Learning Difficulties, London

Tadd, V. (1992) 'Dogma or needs?' *Special Children,* 59, 20–21

Taylor, M.J. (1999) *My Brother. My Sister: a study of the long term impact of sibling disability on the brothers and sisters within families,* Northern College, Aberdeen

Thun, M. and M. (2005) *The Biodynamic Sowing and Planting Calendar,* Floris Books, Edinburgh

Tight, M. (1996) *Key Concepts in Adult Education and Training,* Routledge, London

Tizard, J. (1964) *Community Services for the Mentally Handicapped,* Oxford University Press, London

Ulrich, R.S. (1984) 'View through a window may influence recovery from surgery,' *Science,* 224, 420–21

UN Charter (1999) *Convention on the Rights of the Child* (Second Report to the UN Committee)

Vatican (2004) *Message of John Paul II on the Occasion of the International Symposium on the Dignity and Rights of the Mentally Disabled Person,* Vatican: 5 January 2004

Warnock, M. (2005) 'Special Educational Needs: a new look,' *Impact* 11, Philosophy of Education Society of Great Britain

Wenger, E. (1999) *Communities of Practice: Learning, Meaning and Identity,* Cambridge University Press, London

—, McDermott, R. and Snyder, W. (2002) *Cultivating Communities of Practice,* Harvard Business School, Boston

Weihs, A. (1975) *Fragments from the Story of Camphill,* Internal Camphill Paper

Weihs, T. (1962) *The Camphill Rudolf Steiner Schools for Children in Need of Special Care Report 1955–1962; Aberdeen,* Greyfriars Press, Aberdeen

— (1972) *The Camphill Rudolf Steiner Schools for Children in Need of Special Care Report 1962–1972; Aberdeen,* Greyfriars Press, Aberdeen

— (1983) *Annual Report 1982–1983; Aberdeen: Camphill Rudolf Steiner Schools,* Greyfriars Press, Aberdeen

West, J. (1996) *Child Centred Play Therapy,* Arnold Publishers, London

Wigram, T., Pederson, I.N. and Bonde, L.O. (2002) *A Comprehensive Guide to Music Therapy,* Jessica Kingsley, London

Wolfensberger, W. (2003) *The Future of Children with Significant Impairments: what parents fear and want, and what they and others may be able to do about it,* Training Institute for Human Service Planning, Leadership and Change Agentry (Syracuse University), New York

Woodward, B. and Hogenboom, M. (2002) *Autism: a Holistic Approach,* Floris Books, Edinburgh

Zigler, E., Balla, D. and Kossan, N. (1986) 'Effects of types of institutionalization on responsiveness to social reinforcement, wariness and outerdirectedness among low MA residents,' *American Journal of Mental Deficiency,* 91, 10–17

Index